INFLATION AND THE STRUCTURE OF AGGREGATE OUTPUT

Theoretical, Empirical & Policy Issues

Adonis & Abbey Publishers Ltd

St James House
13 Kensington Square,
London, W8 5HD
United Kingdom

Website: http://www.adonis-abbey.com
E-mail Address: editor@adonis-abbey.com

Nigeria:
Suites C4 & C5 J-Plus Plaza
Asokoro, Abuja, Nigeria
Tel: +234 (0) 7058078841/08052035034

British Library Cataloguing-in-Publication Data
A catalogue record for this book is available from the British Library

ISBN: 978-1-909112-75-9

INFLATION AND THE STRUCTURE OF AGGREGATE OUTPUT

Theoretical, Empirical & Policy Issues

Abraham E. Nwankwo

TABLE OF CONTENTS

PART I: EMPIRICAL INVESTIGATION OF THE OUTPUT-INFLATION RELATIONSHIP

CHAPTER ONE

CHAPTER TWO

CHAPTER THREE

CHAPTER EIGHT
Bank of England and Monetary Policy

CHAPTER NINE
The U.S.A. Federal Reserve System and Monetary Policy

CHAPTER TEN
The European Central Bank and Euro Area Monetary Policy

List of Tables

List of Figures

x

PREFACE

This book provides readings for diverse areas of economics in a developmentally integrated form and in two parts. Part I is mainly a case study of inflation in a developing economy and an exposition of the problems of sectoral interaction and output composition in the process of economic growth, including the sensitive problem of "balanced growth". It also queries the approach to the study of the relationship between output and the price level and attempts to provide answers to some outstanding problems in applied econometrics. Apart from propounding extensions to issues of macroeconomic theory (e.g., the Phillips Curve) it also provides, at least implicitly, an inflation-based dimension to policy programming of stable growth. In Part II, the book surveys monetary policy and central banking in seven selected economies and provides further insights on major issues analysed in Part I.

Economists and students of economics at all levels of study, as well as policy makers will, therefore, find the book useful since areas covered range from monetary economics, through economic growth and planning to applied econometrics.

I am very grateful to my friends Mike Mba and Moses Oduh who helped with running the econometric experiments; I admire their patience and dedication. This book has been developed around a seminal idea in the author's Ph.D. thesis presented to the University of Nigeria in 1985. Accordingly, I remain grateful to my professors, particularly, R.N. Ghosh, A.E. Okorafor, M.N. Ogbonna and R. N. Ogbudinkpa. My wife, Dr. Stella Obioma Nwankwo continued to inspire me, not minding that the spirit of the book often diverted my attention from her: I owe her boundlessly.

PART I

EMPIRICAL INVESTIGATION OF THE OUTPUT-INFLATION RELATIONSHIP

Part I of this book focuses on a methodological and quantitative study of inflation in six chapters. It investigates how the relationship between inflation and output varies with the composition of the output. Chapter 1 defines the purpose of the book, which is a structure-of-the-economy approach to understanding the challenge of inflation. Chapter 2 discusses some characteristics of the Nigerian economy and their implications for the behaviour of the general price level. The characteristics discussed are: the agricultural-non-agricultural sector interaction, the composition of money supply and the nature of the financial system, public expenditure and development plans, and foreign trade. A critical survey of the literature on inflation is taken up in Chapter 3. In Chapter 4, the theoretical framework is developed and the methodology outlined. The results of the econometric estimation are presented in Chapter 5 and the working hypotheses are evaluated. In Chapter 6, the results are discussed in such a way that their policy, empirical and theoretical implications are revealed.

CHAPTER ONE

Introduction

Inflation, simply defined as persistent rise in the general price level, remains a persistently complex economic and social problem of all economies. This assertion remains valid notwithstanding the concerns with deflation in a number of economic regions since the early decades of the 2000s. However, the rate and nature of inflation differ from economy to economy depending on, among other factors, the level of economic development, the structure of production, and the efficiency of resource utilization. Naturally, the reactions of most scholars to the problem have been to consult economic theory for possible explanations. However, as Weintraub (1977) has succinctly noted: "Our knowledge of macro-economics is not so secure that prejudgment can be attempted lightly. Economics is not theology, where the articles of faith must be supported to the end of time" (p.2).

In view of this, there is a compelling need for more empirical studies on inflation in diverse directions, conditioned by striking observations and intellectual insight. Such studies would unravel new facts on the causes, nature and consequences of inflation and would be useful for control policy formulation.

1.1 The Problem: Basic Observations on Inflation in Nigeria

Since 1960, Nigeria has witnessed continuously rising prices of goods and services. For example, with 2005 as base year, Nigeria's consumer price index (C.P.I.) which was less than 0.2% in the 1960s and up to 1977, rose to 0.53% by 1978, 0.85% by 1982 and 1.05% by 1983. By 2000, the price index had risen to 48%, by 2005 to 100% and by 2011 to 178.93%, as shown in Appendix A. The implication is that the internal purchasing power of the naira had fallen considerably.

Spectacular upward price movements could be associated with identifiable pressure factors. For example, there was the 'Udoji Salary Awards' of 1974 by which general salary increases and arrears were granted to public servants. There resulted excess liquidity which found outlet in increased demand for consumer durables and non-durables and led to the development of new tastes by Nigerians, particularly for imported goods. Similarly, uncautious monetization of oil foreign exchange revenues, particularly during prolonged periods of oil boom, is one of the peculiar pressure factors on inflation in Nigeria. Accordingly, it is not surprising that significant and persistent rises in the C.P.I. echoed the huge oil revenue inflows from 1971 to 1977.

Inflation brings with it many economic and social difficulties some of which are summarized hereunder.

1.1.1 Aggravation Of Inequitable Income Distribution

A long-standing cause of concern about for inflation is that it aggravates the already existing problem of inequitable distribution of income. It redistributes income from poor wage earners, pensioners and others with relatively fixed money incomes, to rich profit earners (Bronfenbrenner and Holzman, 1963). This situation arises from the fact that costs of factors of production tend to lag behind prices of final products. This problem has also been lucidly described by Bulir (2001). According to him, lower inflation rates tend to improve income equality and their impact tends to be uniform for all levels of GDP per capita. In addition, he states, in line with cost-of-inflation literature, the negative impact of inflation is more prominent during hyperinflation.

1.1.2 Destruction of The Basis for Allocation of Scare Goods

Reese (1977) is of the opinion that there is a more serious problem associated with inflation, than its income distributional effects. One of the basic premises of a market economy, he argues, is that incomes of people should be based on their productive contributions. But inflation renders this premise inoperative. This is because inflation encourages cost-plus pricing and when cost-plus pricing is the practice, there would be no reliable base for allocating scarce supply of goods and services.

1.1.3 Weakening of the Function of the Price System

Clark (1982) has pointed out another possible negative consequence of inflation. Inflation, by increasing the variance of relative prices, may reduce the ability of the price system to transmit information effectively. As a result, the optimality of economic decisions in a market economy

14

will be jeopardized. Tobin (1972) has discussed specific ways by which such distortions of the market-signalling system caused by inflation can lead to misallocation of resources. First, they can lead to misallocation of time by workers who overestimate their real wages. Second, they can cause oversupply by sellers who contract for future deliveries without taking correct account of the increasing prices of the inputs necessary to fulfil such contracts.

The adverse consequences of inflation notwithstanding, there is a growing trend of thought that it cannot be suppressed and that the best thing to do when it occurs is ``to learn to live with it" (Curwen, 1976:134). In addition, more recent concerns about the debilitating impact of deflation and the need for a minimum level of inflation in such economic regions as the Euro zone and Japan, constitute a new dimension of some sort in the argument for cohabiting with inflation. But even if it is accepted that people should live with inflation, it still remains necessary to understand it. One can only live comfortably with what one understands. A diagnosis of inflation, therefore, remains useful whether for the purpose of eliminating it or for the purpose of accommodating it. Such diagnosis should be carried out for individual countries because the causes and nature of inflation often reflect the peculiar characteristics of the given economy.

One major strand of explanations for inflation causality in Nigeria and other countries is that it is due to excess of demand over the supply of goods and services. (See for example, Okurounmu, 1976). Implicit in such explanations is the view that increases in output of goods and services will, ceteris paribus, exert a downward pressure on the general price level. But this reasoning entails too much generalization. It is necessary to proceed further and analyze the structure of the economy in terms of the composition of output, as well as sectoral interaction before useful conclusions about the output-price relationship can be drawn. It would appear that it is of limited relevance to express price as a function of aggregate output and to argue that increases in the output variable will necessarily have a significantly depressing effect on the price level.

For example, a considerable proportion of Nigeria's GDP is exported; for 2011, the export-GDP ratio for Nigeria was about 24%. Though it may be possible to use export revenues to import goods and services, there is no guarantee that the items imported will be those that would satisfy current demands for consumer goods and services. Imports may be concentrated on capital goods that add to growth potential and which would support the output of final goods and services in the medium to long term but would not add to the supply of currently needed consumer goods. Moreover, there is reason to argue that imports, even if they are of final goods, could accentuate inflationary pressures if they are purchased from economies with relatively high inflation rates. This is the case of imported inflation.

Nigeria's crude oil which is mainly for exports could exacerbate inflation in two ways. First, oil exports diminish the capacity of rising real GDP to depress the price level, particularly during the relevant accounting period. Second, the monetization of oil export revenues is a major cause of increases in money supply which, ceteris paribus, has accentuating influence on the general price level. Thus Osagie (1982) pointed out that oil exports are "positively and significantly related to the index of domestic prices" in the Nigerian economy. Similarly, growth in output of construction industry which does not lead directly to increases in final consumer goods and services, while increasing money income, could accentuate inflation, in the short run at least.

1.2 New Thinking

Therefore, it is necessary to disaggregate the GDP so as to investigate how the different components relate to the general price level. The results from the use of aggregate output in an empirical study, therefore, would appear to be of limited relevance since they would obscure a lot of the underlying influences which are necessary for the understanding of the structure and dynamics of inflation. It is for this reason that a "structure-of-the economy" approach is used in this book. By the term "structure of the economy", we mean the make-up of economic activities as reflected in the composition of the GDP. The term also refers to the interrelationships and interactions between and among different sectors of the economy.

An emerging corollary is that while the price level may be inversely related to certain components of output, it may be positively related to other components. Deriving from this possibility is an important theoretical problem: the intertemporal stability of the parameters of an aggregated explanatory variable (regressor) composed of items, some of whose impact coefficients on the explained variable (regessand) are negative and others of whose impact coefficients are positive.

Furthermore, as has been noted by Thirwall (1974) and Kaldor (1980), the relative sizes of certain sectors usually impart inflationary pressures on the economy. This is generally considered to be true with a rapid expansion of the non-agricultural sector relative to the agricultural sector in a developing country like Nigeria. As real income in the non-agricultural sector expands, there is likely to be increased demand for products of agriculture such as food and raw materials. Where the growth of agriculture is lagging behind the growth of the non-agricultural industrial sector, and where because of weak export base and scarcity of foreign exchange, domestic raw materials and food deficits cannot be readily offset by imports, excess demand for food and raw materials would develop and the prices of these items would rise. Other prices may rise in sympathy.

The focus of this book, therefore, is to discuss the implications of the structure of the economy – both in terms of output composition and in terms of the relative sizes of the agricultural and non-agricultural sectors – for the behaviour of the general price level.

In the bid to achieve this objective, the relationship between the general price level and the following variables – aggregate output (GDP), agricultural output, non-agricultural output, non-agricultural output excluding oil output, manufacturing output, building and construction output, wholesale and retail trade, petroleum export, and, the ratio of non-agricultural output to agricultural output, will be explicitly examined.

Certain questions which arise from the last paragraph, which this book will try to answer, are: How reliable is it to use aggregate output as an explanatory variable for the price level? Are all components of the GDP homogeneous in terms of the direction of their impacts on the price level? If they are not, what are the implications for model specification and estimation? In particular, what are the conditions for inter-temporal stability of the parameter of an aggregated explanatory variable (regressor)? Is the size of non-agricultural output relative to agricultural output an important determinant of price behaviour? This book attempts to provide some answers to these questions, relying on data from the Nigerian economy spanning from 1960 to 2011.

1.3 Relevance of the Approach

The structure-of-the-economy approach is important for several reasons. The first is that it attempts to reveal to what extent inflations is an inevitable cost for desirable structural changes and to what extent it could be mitigated through deliberate adjustments in sectoral balance. It is also important because of the realization that the structure of economic activity is significantly influenced by public policy: from this point of view, it is hoped that the investigation will provide policy makers, with some indications of the inflationary repercussions of alternative structural patterns of growth. Anti-inflation policies can be better rationalized if they are based on empirical diagnosis of the problem. Specifically, the underlying research of the book will explore the connections between the concepts of 'balanced growth' and price stability and could contribute to the understanding of the problem of persistent disequilibrium which has characterized most developing economies in their process of growth.

In the context of the development of economic theory, it seeks to suggest a modified framework for the analysis of the role of output variations in price dynamics. It points out a special aspect of aggregation bias: that which arises from the non-homogeneity in the direction of the influences of components of an aggregated regressor, on a dependent variable. The sign heterogeneity referred to has implications for the inter-temporal stability of the estimate of the parameter of the aggregated regressor.

This theoretical issue has a far-reaching practical implication for as Gupta (1969:4) has observed:

> Use of macro structural coefficients for assessing the influence of a change in any macro variable/s will depend upon the continuation of the stability of these coefficients. Therefore, if this condition is not fulfilled their use as guidelines for policy formulation can lead to misleading results.

CHAPTER TWO

Some Characteristics of the Nigeria Economy Related to Inflation (1960 – 2011)

A discussion of the structure of the Nigerian economy is an overwhelming task given the large size and diversity of its economic geography. Be that as it may, some knowledge about that structure is a useful background to a study on inflation. This chapter is, therefore, limited only to a survey of the major and relevant characteristics of the economy.

2.1 Agricultural and Non-agricultural Sectors: Nature and Performance

It is common in a study of a developing economy to emphasize the relationship and the differences between the agricultural and non-agricultural sectors. This procedure owes much to the fact that after political independence, hitherto predominantly agricultural countries attempt to industrialize and modernize rapidly. Such an aspiration is developed against the background of their experience under colonialism, whereby the colonial administration shaped the colonies as sources of raw materials for the imperial countries, while paying little or no attention to the colonies' industrialization.

Although the Nigerian economy has, since independence in 1960 established many industries and is a dualistic one, it is still a predominantly traditional, rural, agricultural-based economy. The agricultural sector remains characteristically a subsistence one that relies largely on non-wage labour for its production, with almost completely non-commercialized, communally-owned land, often regarded as sacred. This picture remains largely valid even if we take into account that in the last two decades up to 2011, some investments in commercial-scale agriculture has been recorded. It is in this regard of a culturally-bound, modernization-constraining, land tenure system that one recalls the assertion by Ajayi (1978) that "it is impossible, perhaps... unrealistic, to write any economic survey of Africa without taking into account some noneconomic factors" (p.61). An important implication of the land tenure system and the world view on land in rural Nigeria is that commercial and entrepreneurial activities in this sector are rather limited. The complement to Nigeria's dualistic economic structure is the relatively modern, non-agricultural sector consisting of manufacturing, mining (mainly oil and gas), construction, and service industries. These are characterized by wage-type employment, commercially organized production, a relatively high degree of monetization and keen entrepreneurial activities.

In dualistic models, the relationship between the agricultural and non-agricultural sectors is provided by rural-urban migration, which links rural and urban labour markets. Workers migrate from rural to urban areas " in response to perceived differential in income" (Myint, 1965). This phenomenon is true of Nigeria. However, the Lewis (1954) and Fei-Ranis (1964) views on "surplus labour" – that part of the rural labour force, which can be absorbed by the urban sector without causing declines in the output of the rural sector – seems inapplicable to Nigeria. This is particularly because rural urban migration is one of the major causes of the secularly declining agricultural production in Nigeria, as rural people migrate to urban areas in pursuit of real or perceived more attractive opportunities in the cities. Therefore, it is hardly accurate for Nigeria's circumstances that the loss of rural workers to the urban sector does not hurt output in the rural sector. Moreover, the predominantly rain-fed status of farming and the inherent seasonality of farm activities and employment, make it extremely difficult to identify what constitutes surplus labour in the Lewis-Fei-Ranis sense.

Table 1 shows the real value of the GDP and the contributions of agriculture and non-agricultural over the period, 1960 to 2010. It can be observed that the GDP grew from a 1960 figure of N2,233 million to a 2010 figure of N54,204,800 million. Agricultural output's contribution declined almost consistently from 63.5% to 30%, between 1960 and 2010. On the other hand non-agricultural output's contribution grew almost consistently from 36.5% to 70%, over the period.

Although conventional economic thinking posits that as an economy modernizes, the contribution of agriculture compared to the industrial sector is expected to decline, without constituting any serious problems, that conclusion is based on a   number of assumptions, which were hardly applicable to Nigeria for much of the period under consideration. First, the conventional position assumes that the agricultural output would be growing sufficiently enough to take care of the population and that the relative loss in its contribution to total output reflects mainly the rapid rise of the non-agricultural output, rather than the former's lacklustre performance. The actual rate of growth of agricultural output in Nigeria did not comply with this logic: performance was largely unimpressive. Second, and more importantly, modernizing economies, it is assumed, are characterized by falling fertility and slowing population growth rates, reflecting rising literacy and urbanization. This important and indeed decisive demographic assumption does not hold true yet for Nigeria. Over the period, at a rate of above 3%, Nigeria has continued to rank among countries with the highest population growth rates in the world. Conceivably, therefore, the implicit tension between a high population growth rate and a lagging agricultural sector would manifest in inflationary pressure generated by food scarcity.

Table 2.1: Agriculture and Non-Agriculture Contributions to Nigeria's GDP (1960-2010)

GDP Components	Years					
	1960	1970	1980	1990	2000	2010
Amount (M) GDP (%)	₦2,233.0 100	₦5,281.1 100	₦49,632.3 100	₦267,549.9 100	₦4,582,127.3 100	₦54,204,800.0 100
Agric (%)	63.5	49	80	32	26	30
Non-Agric (%)	36.5	51	20	68	74	70

Source: Central Bank of Nigeria, Statistical Bulletin, Various Issues.

One can infer from these observations that poor agricultural performance is an important cause of the prevailing inflation: increasing income in the non-agricultural sector would lead to increased demand for goods, particularly food for the high growth rate population, from a sector that is sluggish. Another point worth nothing is that expanding industrial sector requires proportionately increasing amounts of raw materials from the agricultural sector. However, this demand is unlikely to be satisfied given the declining weight of agriculture in the GDP. Inevitably, therefore, this situation exacerbates inflationary pressure.

Weakened weight of agriculture in GDP has another adverse impact on the economy. It leads to increased reliance on imports for food and raw materials. This is a precarious reliance for Nigeria whose chief export, crude oil, alone accounted for over 90% of total foreign exchange earnings since the 1970s. Even if foreign exchange were available, importation may lead to higher domestic prices if the sources of major imports happen to be experiencing high inflation rates.

Even within the non-agricultural sector, manufacturing is highly dependent on imported raw materials, rather than on domestic agricultural produce. Adejugbe (1982a) estimates this dependence to be as high as 40% on the average: this again, exposing the country to the risk of imported inflation. Another intriguing issue is whether the growth of wholesale-and-retail reflects over-intermediation and, therefore, constitutes an important factor contributing to inflation. Figures in this regard could be revealing: in 1960, 1970, 1980, 1990, 2000 and 2010, wholesale- and-retail was 2.6 times, 1.77 times, 1.86 times, 2.43 times, 3.1 times and, 7.2 times, respectively, as large as manufacturing output. This, too, could have had the undesirable consequence of accentuating price increases because middlemen mark up prices successively. It should not be construed to mean that distributive trade is not important to the economy. Distributive trade creates place or location utility which is an important function in the complete production process. Wholesale-and-retail is necessary to link producers and consumers. But payments made for services done by distributors no doubt increase the final costs of commodities to consumers, thus contributing to inflation and raising concerns about whether there is over-intermediation.

2.2 Money Supply and the Financial Market

One could begin a discussion on the financial market with an examination of money supply because a clear understanding of the structure of the latter gives useful insights into the nature of that market. For the Nigerian case, basing our analysis on the narrow definition of money supply (M1), that is, currency in circulation plus demand deposits, time-series data on the composition of money supply between 1960 and 2011 are given in Table 2.2. A marked feature is the declining trend of the currency component of money supply from about 62% of the total in 1960 to about 19% in 2010 and 18% in 2011. In contrast to the behaviour of the currency component, the demand deposits component increased from about 38% in 1960 to about 81% and 82% in 2010 and 2011, respectively. If one accepts the view that high ratio of currency to money supply is an index of underdeveloped banking habit and the inadequacy of banking facilities, (Ajayi, 1978) then one can conclude that the declining trend of currency and increasing trend of demand deposits, are indicative of improvements in both banking habit and banking facilities over time. But Nigeria's financial market is still far from being organized compared with those of say Great Britain, U.S.A or Western Germany. It is due to the unorganized nature of the market that conventional tools of monetary policy have proved ineffective, in controlling inflation. And so it has been observed that in the 1970s and 1980s, the Central Bank of Nigeria discarded the traditional techniques of open market operation, variable liquidity ratios and bank rate and relied more on direct action to control the volume, direction and cost of money and credit in the economy (Nwankwo, 1984). For example, for several years commencing 1969, the Central Bank gave directives to deposit money banks, not only on the percentage allocation of credits to different sectors, but also on the interest chargeable on loans and advances to such sectors. Under such regimentation, there was no guarantee that financial resources were efficiently allocated to competing uses. Given the limited ability of Nigerian entrepreneurs to employ credit productively, the liberal credit terms in the 1970's must have added to the inflationary pressure.

Table 2.2: Composition of Nigeria's Money Supply (1960 – 2011)
(Amounts in Million Naira)

Year	Money Supply (M1)	Currency in Circulation		Demand Deposits	
		Amount	% of M1	Amount	% of M1
1960	217.6	135.3	62	82.3	38
1965	326.4	200.9	50	125.4	50
1970	641.5	342.4	53	299.1	47
1975	2,605.4	1,030.7	40	1,574.7	60
1980	9,650.7	3,185.9	33	6,464.8	67
1985	13,878.0	4,909.9	35	8,968.1	65
1990	39,156.2	14,951.1	38	24,205.1	62
1995	201,414.5	106,843.4	53	94,571.0	47
2000	637,731.1	274,010.6	43	363,720.6	57
2005	1,725,395.8	563,232.0	33	1,162,163.8	67
2010	5,571,300.0	1,082,300.0	19	4,489,000.0	81
2011	6,771,600.0	1,245,100.0	18	5,526,400.0	82

Source: Central Bank of Nigeria, Statistical Bulletin, Various Issues.

Table 2.3 illustrates the historical series on the five-yearly growth rates of money supply, which were rapid, overall. Among other factors, periods of oil boom must have contributed to rapid growth of money supply in view of the practice of automatic monetization of the foreign exchange derived from oil-export. The automatic monetization derives from the provision in the constitution of the federation, which requires that all revenues from oil be remitted to the federation distributable pool and shared out to all the governments in the three tiers – the federal government, the state governments and the local governments. Accordingly, the oil booms of 1973 -1974, 1978 – mid 1982, the short-lived one in 1990, and, the one that commenced in 2011 before bursting by mid 2014, must have all generated substantial growths in money supply in their wakes. Such monetary expansion would be associated with inflationary pressure.

Another factor that influenced the behaviour of money supply over the period was the role of the central bank in the financing of government budget deficits.

Table 2.3: Growth Rate of Nigeria's Money Supply (1960-2010)

Year	Money Supply (M1), M ₦	Periodic Growth Rate (%)
1960	217.6	-
1965	326.4	50.0
1970	641.5	96.5
1975	2,605.4	306.0
1980	9,650.7	270.0
1985	13,878.0	44.0
1990	39,156.2	182.0
1995	201,414.5	416.0
2000	637,731.1	217.0
2005	1,725,395.8	170.0
2010	5,571,300.0	223.0

Source: Central Bank of Nigeria Statistical Bulletin, Various Issues.

For about twenty-five years starting from 1978 to around 2003, most of which were during the era of military governments, the governments funded much of the fiscal deficits by issuing short-dated treasury bills, which were underwritten by, and subscribed to mainly by the Central Bank of Nigeria. Effectively, therefore, the government funded its economic and social development projects through short-tenured but cumulated borrowings from the central bank, rather than through issuing longer-tenured debt instruments in the capital market. Of course borrowing from the central bank meant growing the money supply. An important institutional characteristic of the time was the absence of a public debt management agency charged with the responsibility of borrowing and managing the public debt. Rather, in practice the central bank had its proper role of monetary authority distorted by playing some roles of the public debt manager as well. This defect was corrected with the establishment of the Debt Management Office (DMO) in 2000. The DMO commenced the process of resuscitating the domestic bond market and by 2003 it started the healthy practice of borrowing for government from the open market through the issuance of long dated bonds in monthly auctions, as well as through issuance of treasury bills. This effectively ended government recourse to money-supply financing of fiscal deficits.

Appendix B, which is the schedule of the holding structure of the Federal Government of Nigeria domestic debt outstanding from 1960 to 2011, illustrates this evolution. Between 1968 and 1977, the central bank was not a major holder of sovereign debts. Indeed, the non-bank public segment dominated the holdings until the military governments abandoned the practice of subjecting public domestic borrowing to the discipline imposed by the then healthily developing capital market and resorted to borrowing from the central bank, instead. And so, the holdings of the monetary authority started growing and ranged from 40% to 86% between 1981 and 2003.

But as a result of the DMO's resuscitation of the domestic debt market commencing in 2003, the ratio started dropping significantly and almost consistently from 2004 and was only about 6% by 2011. Indeed much of the paltry amounts held by the central bank were not subscriptions won at the primary auctions as the Bank did not actually participate in the auctions; they were rather amounts acquired from other holders, prominently deposit money banks, who discounted their bills at the central bank's discount window. On the other hand, the holding of the non-bank public began to regain its pre-military era dominance starting from 2002.

2.3 Public Expenditure, National Development Plans and Government Regulations

Governments in modern societies play the role of providing social and economic infrastructure and regulating the economy. For less developed economies (LDCs) such governments have an additional *raison de entrée*: to accelerate growth and development. These governments wish to close the development and welfare gaps between their countries and the advanced countries. Leaving the task to private entrepreneurs would make the attainment of the goal uncertain. On the other hand, active government participation would guarantee rapid economic growth, so goes the argument.

Table 2.4 shows the enormous rise in the size of the public sector in Nigeria over the period: total expenditure of the federal and state governments rose from about N5.305 billion in 1960 to about N35.915 trillion in 2010. The major source of this growth was the export of crude oil. As documented in Central bank of Nigeria Statistical Bulletins, up till 1964, oil exports were an insignificant contributor of total export and had reached the annual value of only N64 million or 15% of the total by 1964. However, staring from 1965, oil export began to grow rapidly, accounting for dominant contributions to total export earnings as follows: 1965, N136.2 million or 25%; 1970, N509.6 million or 57%; 1980, N13, 632.3 or 96%; and, 2010, N10, 639,417.4 million or 96%. Correspondingly, oil export's contribution to government revenues rose from less than 2% in 1960 to above 70% from the 1970s onwards. One could rightly rationalize that with larger revenue at its disposal, the Federal Government was able to undertake several capital projects.

Table 2.4: Size of Nigeria Government Expenditure

Expenditure & GDP (Amounts in ₦ Million)	10 Years Cumulative Up to:				
	1970	1980	1990	2000	2010
Total Government Expenditure (TGE)	5,305	92,697	326,756	4,756,018	35,915,265
GDP	31,333	247,090	1,075,130	20,350,963	191,000,634
TGE: GDP (%)	17	38	30	23	19

Source: Central Bank of Nigeria, Statistical Bulletin, Various Issues.

One may say that much of government expenditure is directed at services like defence and general administration which do not add directly and significantly to the production of purchasable output. Spending on these service programmes means pumping a lot of money into the economy. Similarly, a sizeable proportion of government expenditure is channelled into physical infrastructural development in huge doses (Ukpong, 1979). One fact of spending on social goods is that they generate incomes to their producers without corresponding immediate increase in goods that such income earners would buy. This asymmetry leads to excess demand and hence, upward pressure on prices.

It is also relevant to review the place of development planning in shaping the structure of the economy. Governments of less developed countries depend on development planning for achieving their goals of social and economic development. A development plan can be regarded as a programme of action for bringing about growth and development in a more predictable manner. It has a special appeal to LDCs who are anxious to develop. Over the period 1962-1985, Nigeria had four development plans, each characterized by distortions that emanated from over fulfilment of planned expenditure on administrative machinery and under-fulfilment of planned expenditure on the more productive economic sectors (Tomori & Fajana, 1979). This bias, one would expect, is favourable to inflation.

2.4 Foreign Trade

The impressive growth of the Nigerian economy from 1960 to 2011 owed much to the rapid expansion of foreign trade. The country needed imports of capital equipment and machinery to achieve rapid industrialization. It also needed considerable exports in order to earn foreign exchange with which to import. Table2. 5 shows that import and export trades grew considerably between 1960 and 2010 and that the economy is substantially an open one as evidenced by the Trade:GDP ratios. Another important development in foreign trade is that over the period, the percentage contribution of agriculture to export earnings declined from the region of 90% to the region of 5%, while that of crude oil rose from the region of 3% to the region of 90%.

What are the possible consequences of these features for the stability of the Nigerian economy? One is that any adverse development in the export market, which results in foreign exchange scarcity, would lead to shortage of both consumer and producer goods in the Nigerian economy. Such shortages would add to inflation. Another is that with the rising import dependence, the susceptibility of Nigeria to imported inflation increased. Moreover, the structural shift in the composition of Nigeria's export from dominance by agricultural produce to crude oil has a spectacular consequence. Revenues from the later type of exports accrue mainly to the government. As Adeyeye and Fakiyesi (1980) have noted, the expansion of petroleum exports meant that the government could undertake development projects without increasing taxes and levies, meaning that there would be no offsetting reduction in aggregate expenditure as the private sector purchasing power would remain intact. Thus the period was marked by rapid expansion of aggregate liquidity with the consequent excess demand and inflation effects.

Table 2.5: Nigeria's External Trade & Openness (Amounts in ₦ million)

Year	Imports	Export	Total Trade	GDP	Total Trade: GDP (%)
1960	431.8	339.4	771.2	2,233.0	34.5
1970	756.4	885.7	1,642.1	5,281.1	31.0
1980	9,095.6	14,186.7	23,282.3	49,632.3	47.0
1990	45,717.9	109,886.1	155,604.0	267,549.9	58.1
2000	985,022.4	1,945,723.3	2,930,745.7	4,582,127.3	64.0
2010	8,005,374.2	11,035,794.5	19,041,168.8	54,204,800.0	35.1

Source: Central Bank of Nigeria, Statistical Bulletin, Various Issues

One would appear justified to conclude from the analysis in this chapter that a lot of inflationary impulses are embedded in the Nigerian economy.

28

CHAPTER THREE

Literature Review

The literature on inflation is copious. Not surprisingly, it is also variegated and has many strands, some of which seem to conflict, in line with the contesting schools of thought in economics. It is pertinent to note that even in the economic analyses of early times, the core issues which this book sets out to address were highlighted in various forms. Accordingly, contrary to the generalized practice of focusing on more recent literature and given that there is a tendency for the essentials of the argument to be lost as an economic postulation evolves into more sophisticated forms over time, the approach in this book is to pay adequate attention to both the older literatures and the more recent ones. In this way, by showing how older strands of thought evolve to later ones, the cumulative nature of the corpus of knowledge would be brought out. This approach is also in alignment with the pursuit of this book, which is to interrogate and upgrade the existing status of the established form of the relationship between inflation and aggregate output.

3.1 The Basic Theories

Forerunner economists, including David Hume, John Locke and Adam Smith, identified increases in money supply as the major cause of inflation. But it was Irving Fisher who formalized the "Quantity Theory of Money" – as this strand of thought came to be known – with the exchange equation. The Fisherine equation formulates a relationship between money supply (M), income velocity of circulation (V), the average price level (P), and real national income (Y), thus:

$$MV = PY \qquad\qquad (3.1)$$

Based on the assumptions that Y is fixed since the economy was taken to always operate at full-employment and that V remains relatively stable, proponents of the Quantity Theory concluded that a change in money supply produces a directly proportionate change in the price level.

If, therefore, money supply is increased period after period, there would be successive rises in the average price level: this phenomenon is inflation.

The Quantity Theory of Money evolved into one of the major contending schools of economic thought in the twentieth century – Monetarism – led by Milton Friedman. Monetarists argue that money supply is the dominant determinant of both output and prices in the short run, and of the price level in the long run when the effect of changes in money supply on the level of output becomes neutral. The claim of dominant impact for money supply rests largely on the assumptions which Monetarists made about the other variables in the Exchange Equation. They assumed long run stability or near constancy of the velocity of circulation; otherwise, it would have a non-zero rate of change which would impact on the price level independent of monetary growth (Humphrey, 1975). It also assumes exogeneity of the nominal stock of money supply, as well as the absence of reverse causality from income to money supply. These critical assumptions, however, hardly match with the realities of many economies.

Moreover, the Quantity Theory is deficient because it recognised only transactions demand for money and was based on the unrealistic assumption of full employment equilibrium and perfect flexibility of price. The assumption of perfect flexibility of prices is particularly unrealistic for an underdeveloped country like Nigeria characterized by institutional and behavioural inhibitions.

For example wages and interest rates are significantly regulated by government legislation so that those prices cannot be adequately flexible. The idea of full employment is also absurd. A developing country like Nigeria should be expected to have a lot of unemployed human and material resources and the real issue at stake is to fashion strategies for removing bottlenecks, so as to expand production and reduce involuntary unemployment.

In reaction to the flaws of the Quantity Theory, Keynes (1936) showed, among other things, that exogenously induced increases in aggregate demand could generate price rises even when money supply remains unchanged. According to him, moreover, there is an additional motive for holding money – the speculative motive. People will hold money if they expect interest rate to rise in the future so that they can make capital gains. On the other hand, when people expect a fall in interest rate, they will reduce their cash holdings. Thus total demand for money (M) is composed of two major parts: transactions demand (M_T) which is a positive function of income (Y) and speculative demand for money (M_{SP}) which is an inverse function of interest rate. Notationally,

$$M_D = M_T + M_{SP}$$
$$= M_T(Y) + M_{SP}(r)$$
$$= f(Y) + g(r); \text{ for } f' > 0, g' < 0 \qquad (3.2)$$

In this model, the precautionary demand for money, which is the motive to hold cash to meet unforeseen or unscheduled expenditures, is subsumed under the transactions demand. By implication, an increase in money supply may not produce a price rise if the excess money supply is absorbed into speculative balance. Thus, an increase in money supply is not a sufficient condition for a price rise, as the quantity theorists had reasoned.

Keynes provided the neo-Keynesians the basis on which they argued that fiscal rather than monetary policy should be relied upon to stabilize prices. According to the Keynesians, fluctuations in employment and output arise largely from fluctuations in nominal aggregate demand. And, changes in aggregate demand have real effects because nominal wages and prices are rigid. But as Ball, Mankiv and Romer (1988) have noted, earlier Keynesians simply assumed nominal rigidities but failed to explain them. This situation left the Keynesian position vulnerable for a long time until more recent research which has provided evidence that optimizing economic agents can and do indeed, create nominal rigidities, because the price of price rigidity to the firm is small even though the macroeconomic effects are large.

As has been noted earlier in this section, contrary to the Keynesians, the Monetarists, notably Friedman (1956), insist that monetary policy should be relied upon for economic stabilization because money supply is the major variable influencing, not only price level, but also the money national income. Even though both Monetarists and Fiscalists saw excess demand as a cause of inflation, their analyses are inadequate for an economy with undeveloped financial system like Nigeria's where the economy is not sufficiently monetized. Moreover, they considered only the demand side of the problem while neglecting the supply side. Relative to the Monetarist-Keynesian debate, a more realistic position is one canvassed by such scholars as Totonchi (2011) to the effect that inflation is a net effect of a number of macroeconomic and institutional phenomena which include money supply and aggregate demand factors.

'Cost Push' theorists such as Hines (1964) argue that inflation is caused by rising factor cost, particularly, wage rises. When trade unions successfully raise wages, for example, producers will mark up prices in order to maintain existing profit margins. The contribution of the cost-push school notwithstanding, the problem is that once inflation is in process, it is not practicable to separate demand pull from cost-push inflation because they become mutually reinforcing.

Further, regarding the relevance of the wage rate in the inflation dynamics, Phillips (1958) provided statistical evidence of an inverse functional relationship between the rate of change of money wage rates and the rate of unemployment, implying that there is a conflict between the policies of full employment and price stability. Samuelson and Solow (1960) have argued that changes in money wage rate have a direct causal relationship to the inflation rate and have, therefore, modified Phillips curve by replacing the rate of change of money wage rates with the rate of inflation. The Phillips-Samuelson-Solow unemployment-inflation trade-off theory has not tallied with the experience of many economies where inflation gets worse as unemployment rises. This situation known as stagflation, suggests the existence of rigidities in economies. In a related study, Andres and Hernando (1997) reasoned that an explanation why rapid growth is associated with higher inflation could be that there is a movement along a negatively sloped Phillips curve, as prices respond after a period of rapid expansion in demand.

Schultze (1969) in his "intersectoral demand shift" theory gives a picture of such rigidities. He argues that prices rise in expanding industries but do not fall in declining ones, the result being an upward bias in the average price level. But Schultz did not concern himself with how the operation of transnational corporations could be a possible source of market rigidity. The "Profit push" theory of Levison (1971) helps to fill this gap. Levinson traces inflation to the activities of multinational corporations who fix prices on an international basis to maximize global profits. While the recognition of the importance of multinationals in influencing local market outcomes is praiseworthy, it is questionable whether such multinationals can afford to neglect to a reasonable extent and for a reasonable period, the demand situations in individual countries when they fix prices. Other non-conventional sources of rigidities have been identified by more contemporary studies.

For example, as demonstrated by Ball, Mankiv and Romer (1988), "nominal rigidities" could even be created by the explicit, optimizing choice of economic agents.

3.2 Some Extensions of the Basic Theories

An interesting development is the explanation of inflation in terms of "expectations" of which there are two major versions. The "adaptive" expectations model (Cagan, 1956) proceeds from the assumption that economic agents correct their errors step by step. The process is represented by the expression:

$$\pi^*_{t+1} = \pi^*_t + \lambda (\pi_t - \pi^*_t) \qquad (3.3)$$

where π_t is the actual rate of inflation in the present period, π^*_t is the rate of inflation expected for the present period and π^*_{t+1} is the expected rate of inflation in the next period. The adaption coefficient, λ, is subject to the constraint:

$$0 < \lambda < 1$$

If the observed rate, π_t is greater than the expected rate π^*_t, the inflation rate is raised in proportion to the error, $(\pi_t - \pi^*_t)$. Similarly, if the error is negative, the expectation is corrected downwards.

This version has been criticized by proponents of rational expectation on the ground that it neglects the ability of economic agents to utilize information provided by economic theory. According to Muth (1961), for example, there exists a relevant economic theory into which all available information enters and whose predictions are the best possible. Therefore, expectations are rational when they occur within the predictions of the relevant economic theory. Put in another language, rational expectations of inflation, π^*_t are unbiased estimators of the actual rate, π_t, given all information at the beginning of the period, Z_{t-1} thus:

$$\pi^*_t = E(\pi_t / Z_{t-1}) \qquad (3.4)$$

The expectations models are very idealistic; it is unlikely that in practice, economic units will have the knowledge and convenience to undertake the complicated calculations entailed in theories before taking decision. While corporate organisation with their specialized personnel, information systems and research facilities may, to some extent, exhibit the type of rational behaviour postulated by the expectation models, one doubts very much whether the models apply to individual economic agents acting as factor sellers and consumers. Further, in less developed countries characterized by unorganized and less sophisticated markets with consequent dearth of both price discovery and transparency, rational decision-making based on market information are much more improbable both at the corporate and individual economic agent levels. However, the theories have provided the base for further scholarly contributions

Friedman (1968) and Phelps (1972) have applied the adaptive expectation model in critiquing the Phillips curve. They argue that different values of the expected rate of inflation will generate different Phillips curves at a given unemployment rate. Thus, the Phillips curve cannot be located with certainty. However, like the Phillips-Samuel-Solow model, the Friedman-Phelps model neglected the role of labour productivity in the wage inflation problem.

The wage-inflation relationship has been extended by Turnovsky (1977) to incorporate the rate of change of labour productivity. The rate of change of price, p, he argues, is equal to the rate of change of money wage rate, w, minus the rate of change of labour productivity, θ, thus:

$$p = w - \theta \qquad (3.5)$$

Practical application of Turnovsky's principle faces a serious difficulty because the measurement of labour productivity is not a settled issue. Rather, it is confounding to know labours contribution to the total product because labour is often combined intimately with other factors, notably technology whose quality is continually changing.

On the other hand, commenting on general productivity growth rather than on labour productivity, Dew-Beeker and Gordon (2005) take a more confident stance that an acceleration or deceleration of productivity growth trend affects the inflation rate proportionately and inversely. On the related issue of whether inflation harms growth,

Andres and Hernando (1997) argue that since evidence from the theoretical literature suggests bi-directional causation, it would not be reasonable to ascertain the real cost of inflation, simply by observing the correlation between growth and inflation.

In relation to the interaction between labour and capital in the production process, Brecher and Heady (1979) have propounded that for a given wage rate, the higher the ratio of labour-intensiveness to capital intensiveness in production the less severe is the inflation-unemployment trade-off and vice versa. This view is relevant to Nigeria's experience with inflation and unemployment because the oil industry which has dominated the economy since the 1970s is capital intensive and employs little labour, while at the same time the rapid monetization of oil export revenue is inflationary. A stagflationary tendency is, there, inherent in the economy dominated by such a capital-intensive, low-job but high-liquidity sector.

Bronfenbrenner and Holzman (1963) have reviewed another aspect of the inflation-unemployment problem: in their view, inflation is the cost of the movement from a lower full-employment to a higher full-employment position. That is, there is no unique full-employment position. Okun (1970) agrees with this position and established that a reasonably stable relationship exists between output and the rate of employment. A one percent increase in the unemployment rate was associated with about a three percent decrease in real output. Okun's law is thus a justification for the drive to higher full-employment with its inflation cost.

Tobin (1972) argues that in any labour market, the rate of increase of money wages is the sum of two components – the equilibrium component and the disequilibrium component. "The disequilibrium components are relevant only if the disequilibria persist" and the disequilibria persist because of an underlying "never-ending flux" caused by new products and processes, new tastes and fashions, new developments of land and natural resources, etc, Based on this, Tobin concludes that a "substantial amount of unemployment compatible with zero inflation is "involuntary and non-optimal." This analysis is relevant to an economy like Nigeria's where rapid structural changes are bound to take place as the economy drives to modernization. The moves to re-orientate production and consumption practices, from outward-looking to inward-looking, are likely sources of disequilibria. In his own view, Hicks (1974) is of the view that due to specialization of labour, scarcities are bound to be revealed while there is still considerable unemployment, causing wages to start rising before the attainment of full employment.

Whether and to what extent inflation affects growth has been one of the major issues in the literature. For example, Gregorio (1996) concludes from his study that inflation limits growth by reducing the efficiency of investment rather than its level. He further posited that there are strong indications that central bank independence produces lower inflation at no real cost. In their own study, Khan and Senhadji (2001) examined the issue of the existence of threshold effects in the relationship between inflation and growth, using data for 140 developing and industrialized countries for 1960 to 1998. They concluded that empirical results strongly suggest the existence of a threshold beyond which inflation exerts negative effect on economic growth. They found out that for industrialized economies, the threshold of inflation above which inflation significantly slows growth is estimated at 1 – 3 percent; and, for developing economies, 11 – 12 percent.

The monetarist model of inflation has been extended along the acceleration and temporariness theories. (Frisch,1977). The acceleration theorem implies that only a change in the rate of growth of money supply induces real effects – employment and output effects. In contrast, every constant rate of growth of money supply is consistent with equilibrium in the real sector although at different rates of inflation. The temporariness theorem states that a monetary impulse influences the unemployment rate for only a short period; over the long period, money wages and market interest rate will adjust to the higher inflation rate and the real effect will disappear.

The acceleration and temporariness theorems are aspects of the "monetary neutrality" hypothesis which posits that real output and employment respond only to that part of inflation that is unanticipated. However, some empirical findings are not in agreement with this hypothesis. For example, Garner (1982) tested the hypothesis for the United Kingdom and found out that the "anticipated money growth significantly affects real variables" and that "monetary surprises are at best, marginally significant."

It could be commented that the limitation of all monetarist models is that they are based on the assumptions of efficient market signalling process and rationality of economic agents. In less developed economies, the limitations are certainly serious because of cultural and institutional bottlenecks. In either case, rational behaviour by economic agents is greatly constrained. Much of the literature so far surveyed reflects the reactions of scholars to inflation in the already industrialized countries. In more recent times attempts have been made to explain inflation in LDC against the background of their peculiar characteristics. In this regard, the structuralist school in Latin America is outstanding.

3.3 Structuralism: The Latin American Experience and Other LDCs

The "Structuralist" school of thought emerged in Latin America in the 1950s and questioned the applicability of orthodox monetarist theories of inflation to the LDCs. As portrayed in the work of their leader, Osvaldo Sunkel (1960), the structuralists contend that inflation in LDCs is caused by certain structural bottlenecks like inelastic food supply, foreign exchange constraint, imported high prices, etc., associated with a developing economy. It is these structural inhibitions that are the root causes of inflation. Money supply only plays a permissive role, allowing the inflationary impulse to manifest itself; so the structuralists argue.

Lioi (1974) has observed that the main difference between monetarists and structuralists is in their conceptions of how the economy really works. In the pure monetarist view, the real structure of the economy can generate stability and growth. Inflation and stagnation are the products, not of inadequate structure, but of erroneous policies. In the extreme structuralist view, on the other hand, the structure cannot generate stability and growth: therefore, to stop inflation and to increase growth, the structure should be changed.

The monetarist-structuralist controversy has led to a number of empirical studies. One such work was by Harberger (1963). Using the ordinary least squares regression method, he found out that money supply and real income influence the price level positively and negatively, respectively. Vogel's (1974) study for sixteen Latin American countries confirmed Haberger's findings. Vogel concluded that difference in rates of inflation in Latin American countries cannot be attributed to structural differences but rather to differing behaviour of money supply in these countries.

Diaz-Alajandro (1965) had used a synthesis of the monetarist and structuralist models to study Argentina's inflation. The results showed that both monetary and structural variables were significant explanatory variables for inflation although structural variables had less proportionate impact on the rate of inflation than monetary variables. In a similar study of twenty LDCs, Argy (1970) found out that money supply influences the rate of inflation significantly, while structural variables do not. Adolfo Diz's (1970) study produced results similar to Argy's.

It can be deduced from the empirical studies reported that there is a tendency for monetary variables to be consistently significant in explaining inflation, while structural variables yield mixed results. However, on the basis of available evidence, neither the extreme monetarist nor the extreme structuralist view can be exclusively accepted. Each approach contributes to the understanding of some aspects of the inflation dynamics. To that extent one would agree with Olivera Campos (1967) that the controversy between the monetarists and structuralist is a spurious one. For according to him, the structuralists if in power would have to adopt monetarist policies as a short-term measure and the monetarists would in the long run, accept the need for structural change. He, therefore, describes the monetarist is "a structuralist in a hurry" and the structuralist as "a monetarist without policy-making responsibility".

While debate and research on inflation in Latin America has been outstanding, there has also been research in other LDCs. For example, Aboagye (1982) studied the role of imported inflation for the Ghanaian economy during the period 1952 – 1977. He found out that imported inflation was not a serious problem but that excess demand and expectations-induced inflations were serious.

Like other studies, Aboagye's own no doubt throws some light on certain aspects of inflation in LDCs. But it could be observed preliminarily that the use of such omnibus explanatory variables like "excess demand" limits the usefulness of the findings. Could excess demand be a reflection of structural composition of output and sectoral interactions in the economy? Would it then not be advisable to introduce these later factors as explicit explanatory variables in the study of inflation in LDCs?

3.4 The State of the Art in Nigeria

Recorded accounts of inflation in Nigeria date back to as far as the 1920s. For example, Hopkins (1973) has described how consumers, especially urban wage earners, suffered declines in their standards of living during the Second World War, as a result of rising prices of imports and food, and rising urban house rents. In 1978, Akinnifesi and

Phillips concluded from their study that a "way to curb the inflationary trend effectively is through a rational supply of money process ......" These researchers, however, did not say how money supply can be rationalized in an economy with numerous structural constraints. In another empirical study based on ordinary least squares regressions, Adeyeye and Fakiyesi (1980) concluded that money supply and government expenditure are important determinants of rate of inflation; they, however, failed to discuss government expenditure behaviour within the context of the structure of the economy.

Obinna (1981) reasoned that fiscal drag, which operates through progressive marginal tax rates produce implicit surplus for the government while retarding production in the private sector. As one solution to inflation, therefore, he recommends that part of the public sector surplus should be recycled into the private sector through subsidies and lower tax rates. Obinna's observation is in consonance with the view of Bacon and Eltis (1975) that greater control of economic resources by the government produces a shift from a low to a high non-marketed output with the possibility that growth declines and inflationary pressure heightens.

In a study which investigated the impact on inflation on economic growth in Nigeria, Chimobi (2010) concluded that inflation has an impact on growth but he did not confirm whether the impact was positive or negative. In their own study, Awogbemi and Taiwo examined the causes and effects of inflation in Nigeria between 1969 and 2009 and concluded that inflation growth in Nigeria is adequately explained by money supply growth rates, GDP growth rates and expenditure-revenue ratio. Further, they concluded that the negative coefficient of GDP is an indication that expenditure backed by real productive activity may be counter-inflationary. It is interesting to note that latter conclusion is predicated on the negative sign of aggregate output variable in the study, whereas the major hypothesis of the analysis in this book is that the result from the use of aggregate output, rather that its disaggregated components, is of limited value.

Doguwa (2013) studied the issue of the existence and level of inflation threshold in the relationship between inflation and growth in Nigeria. Based on the results from the use of different techniques, he concluded that the threshold level of inflation above which it is detrimental to growth in Nigeria, would lie between 10.5 and 12.0 percent.

3.5 Need for an Improved Perspective

Although some empirical studies have investigated the relationship between output and the price level, such studies have relied on aggragate output. These studies include those by Adejugbe (1982b), Falegan and Ogundare, (1982) and Owosekun and Odama (1982). The notable exception was a study by Osagie (1982) which considered the structure of the Nigerian economy, and from which he concluded that both import prices and crude oil exports are positively and significantly related to the index of domestic prices. Credit goes to Osagie for recognising the importance of the concept of the "structure of the economy" for explain the inflation dynamics. Although he did not develop the idea within the theoretical and empirical contexts of the questionable use of aggregate output as a regressor in an empirical study of inflation, his study has a closer bearing to the perspective and argument of this book.

As was indicated in Chapter 1, it is the thematic contention of this book that different components of output relate to the price level differently: some positively, others inversely. These underlying variations are lost sight of when aggregate output is used as a regressor in a price equation. But such details are of practical importance for anti-inflation policy formulation. Accordingly, the econometric analysis underlying this book will employ disaggregated output variables as explanatory variables.

Derived from the first issue is the second, which is that there is need to analyze the problem of inter-temporal stability of the parameter estimate of the aggregated output regressor. Since, as this book attempts to articulate, aggregate output components can be dichotomised in terms of whether they are inversely of directly related to the average price level, the sign of an aggregate output regressor is likely to be unstable. The present study attempts an exposure of this special case of the aggregation problem.

A third issue of focus is the need to investigate, empirically, the sectoral interaction between agricultural and non-agrictural sectors as a factor in inflation, within the context of the structural problems of a growing economy.

3.6 Implied Hypotheses

From the discussions so far, two interrelated working hypotheses could be derived. The first is that in Nigeria, growth of certain components of real GDP will put upward pressure on the price level. This hypothesis which we would term, *Disaggregation Dissonance Hypothesis* is based on the contention that some components of Nigeria's output affect the price level positively, while others affect the price level inversely - in contradistinction from the traditional position in economic literature, based on the Equation of Exchange, that output is inversely related to the general price level. The second hypothesis is that in Nigeria, the price level is positively related to the ratio of non-agricultural to agricultural output. This is justified by the argument that, in a developing economy like Nigeria's, where agriculture is underperforming, the growth of real income in non-agricultural will lead to excess demand for agricultural products with inflationary consequences (Kaldor, 1980). This type of inflationary potential materializes because domestic food and raw materials deficits cannot be readily offset by imports because of shortage and instability of foreign exchange earnings, for such a developing economy.

CHAPTER FOUR

Conceptual Framework

The empirical analysis in this book takes the Equation of Exchange (Quantity Theory of Money) as outlined in Chapter 3, Section 1, and one of its variants, the Harberger Model of Inflation, as its foundation, and relies on the conceptualization of the essentials of output and how they relate to the price level. In so doing, the study extends the Quantity Theory, more or less radically, by using disaggregated output variables in the equation linking money supply, the income velocity of circulation, the price level and real national income or output. This departure from the conventional approach is based on the argument that, in contrast to the claim of the Quantity Theory, some components of output impact the price level positively rather than inversely. In addition, it extends the Harberger Model of Inflation, which has as one of its major thrusts, the exploration of the relevance of structural factors in an extended form of the Quantity Theory. First, the book does this by highlighting the impact of the composition of output through disaggregation. Second, it does so by investigating the impact of the relative size of non-agriculture output to agriculture output, as two broad components of aggregate output; that ratio is a variant of the measure of low agriculture output, which the Harberger Model considered as one of the structural constraints which put upward pressure on the price level.

4.1 Basic Observations

Nigeria is a developing, fossil oil-export dependent economy. Broadly, the economy can be divided into a largely traditional agricultural sector and a relatively more modern and more monetized, non-agricultural sector. Also, the GDP could be divided into the export and non-export components, with crude oil exports being an important distinctive part of the export component.

In terms of its role in the inflationary process, aggregate output may be partitioned into two groups:

(i) Those components whose growth exert a downward pressure on price and,

(ii) Those components whose growth accentuates price rises.

Elements in the first group would include agricultural output, while those in the second group would include petroleum exports. The comparative sizes of the components of output may also be a factor in price level behaviour; for instance, the rapid expansion of non-agriculture and the lagging of agriculture are likely to lead to rising food price and subsequently to a possible rise in the general price level.

4.2 Notations

The operational variables (including ratios) resulting from this conceptual framework, can be summarized as follows:

Y = GDP,
Y_A = agricultural component of GDP,
Y_{NA} = non-agricultural component of GDP,
Y_E = exported GDP,
Y_{NE} = non-exported GDP,
Y_{CE} = crude petroleum export,
Y_{NCE} = non-crude petroleum export,
Y_D = sum of components of GDP, that influence the price level, positively or directly,
Y_V = sum of components of GDP that influence the price level, inversely,
Z = ratio of non-agricultural output to agricultural output,
P = the average price level.

4.3 Identities

From the above notations, some definitional equations or identities of the national income can be formulated as follows.

$$Y \equiv Y_A + Y_{NA} \qquad (4.1)$$
$$Y \equiv Y_E + Y_{NE} \qquad (4.2)$$
but,
$$Y_E \equiv Y_{CE} + Y_{NCE} \qquad (4.3)$$

So that Equation 4.2 becomes:

$$Y \equiv Y_{CE} + Y_{NCE} + Y_{NE} \tag{4.4}$$

Finally, $Y \equiv Y_V + Y_D \tag{4.5}$

4.4 Functional Relationships

Based on the foregoing reasoning, the following price behavioural equation can be formulated:

$$P = P(Y) = P(Y_D, Y_V) \tag{4.6;}$$

$$\frac{dP}{dY_D} > 0$$

$$\frac{dP}{dY_V} < 0$$

$$\text{and,} \quad \frac{dP}{dY} \begin{array}{c} > \\ < \end{array} 0$$

Equation 4.6 together with the accompanying constraint signs of the parameters $\dfrac{dP}{dY_D}, \dfrac{dP}{dY_V}$ and $\dfrac{dP}{dY}$, reflect the problem of the inter-temporal instability of the marginal effect of the aggregate output variable, Y, on the average price level, P: as the relative sizes of Y_D and Y_V in Y vary over time, so would their net effect in terms of direction of impact on the price level also vary . This problem had been stated in Section 2 of Chapter 1.

Similarly, a second behavioural equation using the ratio of non-agricultural output to agricultural output could be formulated, thus:

$$P = P\left(\frac{Y_{NA}}{Y_A}\right) = P(Z) \tag{4.7}$$

The resultant direction of changes in aggregate output on the average price level, dP/dZ, will tend to be positive (accentuating), as the rate of growth of the non-agricultural component tends to be greater than the rate of growth of the agricultural component; and, tend to be negative (dampening), as the rate of growth of the agricultural component tends to be greater than the rate of growth of the non-agricultural component.

By logical extension, there could be a relative rate of growth of the two broad components of aggregate output for which the resultant impact is zero. This leads to the comprehensive possible outcomes, thus:

$$P \quad = \quad P(Z) \qquad\qquad (4.7) \text{ repeated;}$$

$$\frac{dP}{dZ} > 0, \quad \text{or} \quad \frac{dP}{dZ} < 0, \text{ or} \quad \frac{dP}{dZ} = 0.$$

There is another important implication: the result of the analysis of price behaviour with respect to the ratio variable as specified in Equation 4.7 will be period-sensitive. For a period of time under empirical investigation, the result would depend on which of the two broad output components is dominating the scene with data points of greater growth rate. The result based on such a characteristic will change as the set of time-series data used changes. Therefore, from a different but complementary perspective, the sign characteristic of the ratio variable emanating from Equation 4.7 reinforces the idea of inter-temporal instability of the relationship between aggregate output and the price level which was highlighted in Equation 4.6.

However, it would be recalled that one of the working hypotheses stated in Chapter 3 is that in Nigeria, the price level is positively related to the ratio of non-agricultural to agricultural output. Accordingly, having examined the inter-temporal possibilities, it is appropriate for the investigation to proceed with the assumed form:

$$P \quad = \quad P(Z) \qquad\qquad (4.7) \text{ repeated;}$$

$$\frac{dP}{dZ} > 0$$

Equations 4.6 and 4.7 can, therefore, be combined thus:

$$P \quad = \quad P(Y_D, Y_V, Z) \qquad (4.8);$$

$$\frac{dP}{dY_D} > 0$$

$$\frac{dP}{dY_V} < 0$$

$$\frac{dP}{dZ} > 0$$

Since $\qquad \{Y_D\} \;\rightarrow\; \{Y_{D1}, Y_{D2}, Y_{D3}, \ldots,\}$

and, $\qquad\quad \{Y_V\} \;\rightarrow\; \{Y_{V1}, Y_{V2}, Y_{V3}, \ldots,\},$

Equation 4.8 can be written as

$P = P\;(Y_{D1}, Y_{D2}, Y_{D3}, \ldots, Y_{V1}, Y_{V2}, Y_{V3}, \ldots, Z)$ (4.9);

$$\frac{dP}{dY_{Di}} > 0 \qquad (i = 1, 2, 3, \ldots);$$

$$\frac{dP}{dY_{Vi}} < 0 \qquad (i = 1, 2, 3, \ldots);$$

$$\frac{dP}{dZ} > 0$$

4.5 Comparison with an Alternative Framework

It may be useful to compare the framework which has been developed in the foregoing, with that most commonly used in investigating the impact of output changes on inflation, which is the Harberger Model of Inflation, in its various forms, which is derived from the exchange equation as follows.

$\qquad\quad$ MV $\quad=\quad$ PY $\qquad\qquad\qquad\qquad\qquad\qquad\qquad$ (4.10);

where, M = money supply,

$\qquad$ V $\quad=\quad$ income velocity of circulation

$\qquad$ P $\quad=\quad$ average price level

$\qquad$ Y $\quad=\quad$ real national income.

$\qquad$ The exchange equation can be rearranged to get,

$\qquad\quad$ P $\quad=\quad V\dfrac{M}{Y}$ $\qquad\qquad\qquad\qquad\qquad\qquad\qquad$ (4.11)

Which, when transformed logarithmically yields the linear form

$\qquad\quad \log P = \log V + \log M - \log Y$ $\qquad\qquad\qquad$ (4.12)

If the logged equation is differentiated with respect to time, it yields:

47

$$\frac{1}{p}\frac{dp}{dt} = \frac{1}{v}\frac{dv}{dt} + \frac{1}{m}\frac{dm}{dt} - \frac{1}{Y}\frac{dy}{dt} \qquad (4.13)$$

Some researchers who rely on this model use the logarithmic form, some use the rates of change form and others even use the ordinary linear form of the variables. However, the essence of the model is summarized by the general form:

$$P \quad = \quad P\,(M,\,Y) \qquad\qquad (4.14)$$

$\dfrac{dP}{dM} > 0$ (marginal effect of changes in money supply on the price level);

$\dfrac{dP}{dY} < 0$ (marginal effect of changes in output on the price level).

As can be observed, this model is based on aggregate real income and regards the marginal effect of changes in output on the price level as definitely negative in sign. On the other hand, the model which has been developed in this Chapter (Sections 4.1 - 4.4) partitions aggregate real income (GDP) into two categories each containing elements with a priori identically signed marginal effects on the price level. Based on this differentiation, the model also recognises the possibility of the marginal effect of aggregate output (that is, net effect of different components of output) on the price level being positively signed or negatively signed.

In concluding this section, we refer back to Equation 4.8 and note that the model developed for this empirical work incorporates two broad ways through which the structure of the economy can generate inflation. First, the growth of some components of output is directly a source of price rises. Second, the faster growth of the non-agricultural sector relative to the agricultural sector favours price rises.

CHAPTER FIVE

Estimation of the Price-Output Relationship

In order to establish the responsiveness of the price level to changes in the GDP and its components, the econometric technique of regression is applied. The focus is to examine the direction of the impact of the respective output components of GDP on the average price level.

5.1 Data Presentation

Annual time-series data spanning the fifty-two year period 1960-2011 were collected on the following variables:

a)   Consumer Price Index (CPI);
b)   Real Gross Domestic product (GDP);
      i. Agricultural Output (AGDP);
      ii. Non-agricultural Output (NAGDP);
      iii. Non-agricultural Output excluding oil output (NAGDPN);
      iv. Manufacturing Output (MGDP);
      v. Building & Construction (CGDP);
      vi. Wholesale & Retail Trade (WRGDP);
      vii. Value of Petroleum Export (PEXP);
c)   Non-agricultural-Agricultural GDP ratio (NAAGR);
d)   Import Price (IMPX); and,
e)   Nominal Money Supply (MS).

It could be observed that in addition to the CPI and output variables, two other variables, namely, import price index and money supply are included. The import price index caters for the possibility of inflation being imported from other countries. Given that a significant proportion of domestically traded goods are imported, rising prices in the countries of origin could be transmitted to the domestic economy through such imports. Indeed, imported inflation is in itself a reflection of the structure of the economy as it reflects how open the economy is, as well as the composition of its aggregate production relative to its expenditure.

In the case of money supply, it is important to include it in the analysis so as to remove the specification error which the omission would cause because economic theory strongly identifies it as influencing movements in the price level and it has, indeed, been found to be a strong explanatory variable for inflation in most empirical studies (Imimole & Enoma, 2011; Ahmed & Suliman, 2011; Ratnasiri, 2011; Gyebi & Boafo, 2013). With the exception of money supply which is retained in nominal value, all the other variables have been normalized at 2005 prices; hence, the output variables are in real terms. The comprehensive set of the data used is presented in Appendix A.

5.2 Functional Combinations

The combinations of the explanatory variables in each regression model with the dependent variable, CPI, have been designed mainly to reflect the search for the direction of the impact of the output variable at different levels of disaggregation. Money supply has also been included in each combination to avoid the bias which the omission of such an important explanatory variable would introduce in the estimates. The intendment of the design is that the results from the specified functions will make it possible to test the hypothesis that the direction of the impact of the growth of aggregate output on the price level could be either positive or negative but not always positive. The formulation will also allow for the testing of the hypothesis that the price level is directly related to the non-agricultural-agricultural output ratio.

Accordingly, the combinations of the variables for estimating the functional relationships, with the CPI as the Dependent Variable are as follows:

i)   **CPI** = f(GDP, MS)   (5.1)

ii)   **CPI** = f(AGDP, NAGDP, MS)   (5.2)

iii)   **CPI** = f(PEXP, AGDP, NAGDPN, MS)   (5.3)

iv)   **CPI** = f(MGDP, CGDP, WRGDP, PEXP, IMPX, NAGDP, MS)   (5.4)

v)   **CPI** = f(MGDP, CGDP, WRGDP, PEXP, IMPX, NAAGR, MS)   (5.5)

5.3 Stationarity Tests and Co-integration Analysis

In line with Granger and Newbold (1974), Davidson and Hendry (1978), Dickey and Fuller (1981), Granger (1981), and Engle and Granger (1987), regarding the appropriate handling of regression analysis using time-series data, it is important to understand the vital properties of the data that could affect the analysis. Brooks (2008) identified the stationarity property of the data as a key element that helps to avoid generating "spurious regressions" (p.319). The aims of the co-integration method and the associated error correction model of regression could be said to be essentially three-fold: (i) to avoid "nonsense" or "spurious" regression by ensuring that variables included in a regression model are at the same level of stationarity; (ii) to establish valid long-term relationship between the dependent variable and various independent variables; and, (iii) to extract the separate impacts of individual independent variables on the dependent variable by untying their joint impacts. Essentially, from the point of view of the central objective of this investigative book, the method will ensure that the resulting directions of the impacts of the various components of the GDP on the price level are credible.

To avoid using a non-mean-reverting data, all the variables were tested for stationarity (level of integration), using the Augmented Dickey-Fuller (ADF) method. All the variables have been used in their natural log form. Results of the unit root test or test of stationarity are in Table 5.1. The table shows that all the variables are stationary after first differencing, that is, they are integrated to order one, or, they are I(1).

51

Table 5.1: Summary of Augmented Dickey-Fuller Unit Root Statistics for variables used in the model

Variable	ADF test statistics	Probability	1% level	5% level	Max. Lag (based on SIC)	Level of integration	Constant	Trend
Consumer Price Index	-2.043873	0.0403	-2.612033	-1.947520	10	1	Yes	No
GDP at 2005 prices	-7.657916	0.0000	-3.568308	-2.921175	10	1	No	No
Agriculture GDP	-6.497589	0.0000	-2.612033	-1.947520	10	1	No	No
Non-Agriculture	-6.882068	0.0000	-2.612033	-1.947520	10	1	No	No
Non-Agriculture-Non-Oil	-7.202895	0.0000	-2.612033	-1.947520	10	1	No	No
Manufacturing Output	-8.268947	0.0000	-3.568308	-2.921175	10	1	No	No
Building & Construction	-5.734261	0.0000	-2.612033	-1.947520	10	1	No	No
Wholesale and Retail Trade	-7.008803	0.0000	-2.612033	-1.947520	10	1	No	No
Value of petroleum export	-9.019348	0.0000	-2.612033	-1.947520	10	1	No	No
Non-Agriculture/Non-Agricultural GDP%	-7.039131	0.0000	-2.612033	-1.947520	10	1	No	No
Import price index	-3.597076	0.0092	-3.565430	-2.919952	10	1	Yes	No
Money supply	-3.775484	0.0057	-3.56831	-2.92118	10	1	Yes	No

Note: Schwartz Information Criteria (SIC) Optimal lag length was automatically generated

As a result of the foregoing, the variables qualify to be tested for co-integration, using Engle-Granger two-step procedure (or what is called the residual approach to co-integration analysis), in order to verify if they have long run relationship, or it is a mere coincidence that they have the same I(1) process. Referring back to Section 5.2 and using Equation 5.1 to demonstrate, if we apply the Ordinary Least Square (OLS) method, the long run co-integrating regression equation is:

$$\text{LOG(CPI)} = r_1 + r_2 \text{LOG(GDP)} + r_3 \text{LOG(MS)} + e_t \qquad (5.6)$$

where e_t is the error term, which contains any other information about the independent variable that are not captured in the model. From (5.6), we can derive that:

$$e_t = \text{LOG(CPI)} - (r_1 {}_+ r_2 \text{LOG(GDP)} + r_3 \text{LOG(MS)}) \quad (5.7)$$

Equation (5.7) is what is known in analysis as the linear combination of the variables: CPI, GDP and Money Supply.

Having estimated the coefficients, the "r"s, from (5.6), the time series of the residual, e_t, is generated from (5.7). The above exercises constitute **Step 1**.

In **Step 2**, the residual series is tested for stationarity using the ADF procedure: if it is confirmed to be stationary at level, that is, e_t is $I(0)$, then GDP and MS are co-integrated with CPI, since their linear combination is stationary.

Table 5.2 contains the results of the co-integration tests and confirms that each of the five models specified in Section 5.2 is co-integrated. Accordingly, their error correction model (ECM) equations can be validly estimated.

For example, for Equation 5.1, the residual time series from (5.7) when lagged one period, (ecm(-1)), is added as an explanatory variable in the short-run dynamic version of (5.6) where all variables are differenced once thus:

$$\mathbf{D}\text{LOG(CPI)} = v_+ \mathbf{w}\,\mathbf{D}\text{LOG(CPI)}(-1) + x_0\,\mathbf{D}\text{LOG(GDP)} + x_1\,\mathbf{D}$$
$$\text{LOG(GDP)}(-1) + x_2\,\mathbf{D}\ \text{LOG(GDP}(-2)) + \ldots + x_n\,\mathbf{D}\text{LOG(GDP(-}$$
$$\text{n)}) + r_0\,\mathbf{D}\text{LOG(MS)} + r_1 \mathbf{D}\text{LOG(MS)}(-1) + r_2\,\mathbf{D}\text{LOG(MS)}(-$$
$$\text{2)} + \ldots + r_n\ \mathbf{D}\text{LOG(MS)}(-n) + becm(-1) + u_t \qquad (5.8)$$

where: *v, w, x_0....,x_n, r_0,....,r_n, b, are coefficients to be estimated and u_t is the new* error term.

Table 5.2: Summary of Two-step (Residual) test for Cointegrated Equations

Variable	ADF test statistics	Probability	1% level	5% level	Maximum Lag	Co-integration
Price, GDP, and Money supply	-2.625756	0.0096	-2.612033	-1.947520	10	Yes
Price, Agriculture, non-agriculture, and Money supply	-2.624634	0.0097	-2.612033	-1.947520	10	Yes
Price, petroleum export, Agriculture, Non-Agriculture-non-oil, and Money supply	-2.884705	0.0047	-2.612033	-1.947520	10	Yes
Price, Manufacturing, Construction, Wholesale & Retail trade, petroleum export, Import price, agriculture, and Money supply	-2.872670	0.0049	-2.612033	-1.947520	10	Yes
Price, Manufacturing, Construction, Wholesale & Retail trade, Petroleum, Import price, Non-Agriculture-Agriculture output ratio, and Money supply	-2.987876	0.0036	-2.612033	-1.947520	10	Yes

Note: Schwartz Information Criteria (SIC) Optimal lag length was automatically generated

Method used: Granger Residual or Two-step Co-integration test.

In equation (5.8), the specification is over-parameterized with long lags of GDP and money supply but in the automatic process of iteration based on Schwartz Information Criteria (SIC), insignificant variables are eliminated and the variables which are relevant in explaining the behaviour of the price level become obvious.

The specification of the error-correction mechanism equations of the other four functional combinations follows the same procedure as for the first.

5.4 Regression Results

The regression results of the five long-run equations (which generated the error correction variable used for the error correction estimations), and the corresponding five short-run dynamic equations are presented in Tables 5.3, 5.4, 5.5, 5.6 and 5.7, while their summaries are in Appendix C. Our comments will focus on the directions of the impact of the output variables on the price level in the short-run. However, comments will equally be made on the coefficients of the long-term regression equations although we are mindful of the fact that they cannot be the basis of conclusions given the widespread contention that static long-run ordinary-least-squares regression parameters are likely to be biased unless a correction procedure is undertaken (Banerjee, Dolado, Hendry, & Smith, 1986).

5.4.1 CPI, GDP, Money Supply

The coefficient of GDP is significant and negative, in both the long-run and short-run dynamic equations (Table 5.3), implying that rising aggregate output (GDP) puts downward pressure on the price level. This is consistent with the Harberger model of Inflation which itself is derived from the classical Quantity Theory of Money.

Table 5.3: Estimates for Equation (5.1)

5.1 LONGRUN	Dep. Var:	LOG(CPI)		
Variable	Coefficient	Std. Error	t-Statistic	Prob.
LOG(GDP)	-1.239	0.247	-5.023	0.000
LOG(MS)	0.982	0.047	20.976	0.000
C	4.410	2.283	1.932	0.059

5.1 SHORTRUN	Dep. Var:	D(LOG(CPI))		
Variable	Coefficient	Std. Error	t-Statistic	Prob.
ΔLOG(CPI(-1))	0.598	0.069	8.647	0.000
Δ(LOG(GDP))	-0.124	0.056	-2.229	0.031
Δ(LOG(MS))	0.491	0.076	6.495	0.000
MODEL_ONE_ECM(-1)	-0.107	0.034	-3.147	0.003
C	-0.038	0.020	-1.881	0.067

5.4.2   CPI, Agriculture, Non-Agriculture, Money Supply

The results are captured in Table 5.4. When broken into agriculture and non-agriculture, in the long-run equation, each of these major components of the GDP still exercises downward pressure on the price level as indicated by the negative signs of their coefficients. However, the agriculture GDP is not statistically significant in the long-run equation, even at 10% level of significance. Therefore, it is clear that in the long-run a sustained increase in agricultural production will dampen prices in Nigeria. In the short-run equation, the agriculture GDP is statistically significant with negative sign. But as indicated earlier, little weight should be attached to the coefficients of the long-run co-integrating equation. So it is sufficient to say that agriculture GDP's coefficient in the error correction equation is well-behaved in size and direction: indicating that, increases in the agriculture component of the GDP exerts downward pressure on the price level. The error correction component indicates that any disequilibrium observable in the short run adjusts by 13.6 percent yearly until such distortion disappears.

On the other hand, the one period lag of non-agriculture output GDP is statistically significant (at 1% level); particularly obvious is the delayed effect.   Therefore, the result is consistent with the 'a priori' theoretical expectation in the short-run. This results leads to the interesting outcome that increases in the non-agricultural component of the GDP could exert an upward pressure on the price level, thereby supporting the hypothesis, that some components of the GDP could impact the price level directly rather than inversely in the short-run.

Table 5.4: Estimates of Equation (5.2)

5.2):2) __LONGRUN__	Dep. Var:	LOG(CPI)		
Variable	Coefficient	Std. Error	t-Statistic	Prob.
LOG(AGDP)	-0.482	0.305	-1.578	0.121
LOG(NAGDP)	-0.837	0.155	-5.412	0.000
LOG(MS)	1.014	0.054	18.878	0.000
C	4.048	2.829	1.431	0.159
5.2 SHORTRUN	Dep. Var:	D(LOG(CPI))		
Variable	Coefficient	Std. Error	t-Statistic	Prob.
ΔLOG(CPI(-1))	0.608	0.089	8.848	0.000
Δ(LOG(AGDP))	-0.167	0.082	-2.030	0.048
ΔLOG(NAGDP(-1))	0.155	0.055	-2.801	0.008
Δ(LOG(MS)(-1))	0.297	0.073	4.052	0.000
MODEL_ONE_ECM(-1)	-0.136	0.042	-3.244	0.002

5.4.3   *CPI, petroleum export, agriculture, non-agriculture-non-oil, and money supply*

To obtain the non-agriculture-non-oil GDP, we removed petroleum GDP from the rest of non-agriculture, and added petroleum export as a variable to observe its impact on the price level. The result as shown in Table 5.5 is that the non-agriculture-non-oil GDP impacted the CPI inversely both in the long-run and in the short run. However, from the result, petroleum export is positive and significant both in the long-run equation and in the short-run dynamic equation, indicating that its influence could be the major reason why all non-agriculture taken together had a positively signed coefficient in the sort-run equation under Table 5.4. That is, the growth of petroleum export puts upward pressure on the price level. This result again lends credence to the validity of the working hypothesis which states that growth in some components of the GDP can contribute to fuelling inflation. As in Equation (5.2), the results in Equation (5.3) for agriculture GDP show that it is inversely related to the CPI. It can also be observed from the results of the short-run dynamic equation that the impact of petroleum export, non-agriculture-non-oil GDP and money supply occur with a lag of one period, two periods and one period, respectively.

Table 5.5: Estimates of Equation (5.3)

5.3 LONGRUN Variable	Dep. Var: Coefficient	LOG(CPI) Std. Error	t-Statistic	Prob.
LOG(PEXP)	0.154	0.011	13.649	0.000
LOG(AGDP)	-0.089	0.037	-2.392	0.021
LOG(NAGDPN)	-0.654	0.022	-29.388	0.000
LOG(MS)	0.794	0.007	110.276	0.000
C	-0.862	0.322	-2.673	0.010

5.3 SHORTRUN Variable	Dep. Var: Coefficient	D(LOG(CPI)) Std. Error	t-Statistic	Prob.
ΔLOG(CPI(-1))	0.430	0.056	7.657	0.000
Δ(LOG(PEXP(-1)))	0.035	0.011	3.115	0.003
Δ(LOG(AGDP))	-0.184	0.052	-3.554	0.001
ΔLOG(NAGDPN(-2))	-0.134	0.047	-2.856	0.007
Δ(LOG(MS(-1)))	0.405	0.067	6.006	0.000
EQ02_ECM(-1)	-0.153	0.034	-4.560	0.000
C	0.010	0.013	0.709	0.482

5.4.4 CPI, Manufacturing, Construction, Wholesale & Retail trade, Petroleum Export, Import price, Agriculture, and Money supply

When non-agriculture-non-oil GDP is further disaggregated into its major components, we observe that petroleum export continued to influence the price level positively in the long-run equation as well as in the short-run dynamic equation Table 5.6). Although its coefficient in the static long-run equation is weak, it is statistically significant with a lag of two periods in the short-run dynamic equation which is the more reliable model for assessing our hypothesis. Manufacturing and construction both have negatively signed coefficients in both the long-run and short-run regressions, ordinarily indicating that they are inversely related to the price level. However, both of them have statistically insignificant coefficients in the all-important short-run dynamic regression equation. In the case of wholesale-and-retail, in the long-run regression, it has a statistically significant but positively signed coefficient, while in the short-run model, it has a statistically significant and negatively signed

58

coefficient: one would be justified to conclude from the short-run dynamic equation results that the true relationship between wholesale-and-retail and the price level is an inverse one.

Table 5.6: Estimates of Equation (5.4)

5.4 LONGRUN Variable	Dep. Var: Coefficient	LOG(CPI) Std. Error	t-Statistic	Prob.
LOG(MGDP)	-0.513	0.052	-9.964	0.000
LOG(CGDP)	-0.449	0.041	-10.840	0.000
LOG(WRGDP)	0.410	0.076	5.403	0.000
LOG(PEXP)	0.010	0.021	0.490	0.627
LOG(IMPX)	0.426	0.092	4.644	0.000
LOG(AGDP)	-0.182	0.074	-2.461	0.018
LOG(MS)	0.727	0.019	38.580	0.000
C	-2.913	0.758	-3.844	0.000

5.4 SHORTRUN Variable	Dep. Var: Coefficient	D(LOG(CPI)) Std. Error	t-Statistic	Prob.
ΔLOG(CPI(-1))	0.547	0.055	9.952	0.000
Δ(LOG(MGDP))	-0.078	0.044	-1.773	0.084
Δ(LOG(CGDP))	-0.010	0.034	-0.299	0.766
Δ(LOG(WRGDP(-2)))	-0.149	0.037	-4.033	0.000
Δ(LOG(PEXP(-2)))	0.031	0.011	2.660	0.011
Δ(LOG(IMPX(-2)))	0.164	0.062	2.643	0.012
Δ(LOG(AGDP))	-0.209	0.061	-3.434	0.001
Δ(LOG(MS))	0.502	0.060	8.393	0.000
EQ01_ECM(-1)	-0.159	0.039	-4.039	0.000
C	-0.025	0.016	-1.573	0.124

5.4.5 Price, Manufacturing, Construction, Wholesale & Retail trade, Petroleum Export, Import price, Non-Agriculture-Agriculture output ratio, and Money supply

In the last set of regressions, the non-agriculture-agriculture output ratio, which is an indicator of the tension between the relative sizes of the agricultural sector and the non-agricultural sector, is introduced in place of the agriculture output variable. Its coefficient is positively signed and statistically significant in both the long-run cointegrating regression and the short-run dynamic regression (Table 7), indicating that the tension generated by the faster rate of growth of the non-agricultural sector (industrial sector) compared to the agricultural sector tends to put upward pressure on the general price level. The coefficient of petroleum export is significant and positively signed in both the long-run and in the short-run equations. Manufacturing has negatively signed and statistically significant coefficients in both models. Construction has a negatively signed coefficient in both equations, but the coefficient in the short-run dynamic model is statistically insignificant. However, wholesale-and-retail which has a positive but statistically insignificant coefficient in the long-run equation has a negatively signed and statistically significant coefficient in the short-run dynamic model.

Table 5.7: Estimates of Equation (5.5)

5.5 LONGRUN Variable	Dep. Var: Coefficient	LOG(CPI) Std. Error	t-Statistic	Prob.
LOG(MGDP)	-0.621	0.130	-4.781	0.000
LOG(CGDP)	-0.422	0.082	-5.127	0.000
LOG(WRGDP)	0.179	0.187	0.956	0.344
LOG(PEXP)	0.052	0.047	1.119	0.269
LOG(IMPX)	0.211	0.204	1.038	0.305
LOG(NAAGR)	0.289	0.123	2.353	0.023
LOG(MS)	0.719	0.032	22.803	0.000
C	-2.720	1.066	-2.551	0.014

5.5 SHORTRUN Variable	Dep. Var: Coefficient	D(LOG(CPI)) Std. Error	t-Statistic	Prob.
ΔLOG(CPI(-1))	0.540	0.055	9.831	0.000
Δ(LOG(MGDP))	-0.154	0.046	-3.320	0.002
Δ(LOG(CGDP))	-0.063	0.035	-1.792	0.081
Δ(LOG(WRGDP(-2)))	-0.134	0.036	-3.751	0.001
Δ(LOG(PEXP(-2)))	0.042	0.011	3.780	0.001
Δ(LOG(IMPX(-2)))	0.189	0.063	3.006	0.005
Δ(LOG(NAAGR))	0.149	0.038	3.948	0.000
Δ(LOG(MS))	0.487	0.058	8.399	0.000
MODEL_THREE_ECM(-1)	-0.175	0.039	-4.524	0.000
C	-0.029	0.016	-1.821	0.076

5.5 Other Results

We also note that, as expected from both theoretical and empirical evidence, the coefficient of money supply was positively signed in all the equations, long-run and short-run, attesting that growth of money supply fuels inflation. Import price index was included in the last two equations. In the long-run equations, the resulting coefficient was significant in one (Equation 5.4) but insignificant in the other (Equation 5.5). But in both of the short-run dynamic equations, its resulting coefficients were positively signed and statistically significant, indicating that imported inflation is an important factor contributing to inflation in Nigeria. Regarding the error correction term, the resulting coefficients in the five short run dynamic equations are all statistically significant with the expected negative signs. They confirm the adjustment response of the price level when there is a shock that knocks it off from its long run equilibrium level: the relationships will return to equilibrium in the long run even if there is a drift in the short run since the adjustment factor, ECM, is negatively signed.

5.6 Evaluating the Hypotheses

In summary, the results of the regressions confirm the *Disaggregation Dissonance Hypothesis* which states that the growth of some components of the GDP accentuate rather than dampen the general price level. In addition, the results corroborate the hypothesis that the tension between the agricultural and non-agricultural sectors in the process of economic growth is capable of fuelling inflation. In essence, the results confirm that in the exploration of the relationship between GDP and inflation, the structure of the economy, and specifically, the composition of GDP, as well as sectoral interaction and tension, ought to be explicitly taken into consideration.

CHAPTER SIX

Implications of the Results

A number of theoretical, empirical and policy implications can be derived from the results examined in the last chapter. An attempt to formalize those implications is the objective of this chapter.

6.1 Theoretical and Empirical Implications

6.1.1 The Inappropriateness of Using Aggregate Output as Regressor

The study has shown that it is inappropriate to use aggregate output as a regressor in the empirical study of inflation. This is because the average price level is inversely related to some components of output but directly related to other components. As a result, the impact of aggregate output is not definitely inverse or positive, but could be either.

Thus, the longstanding procedure whereby, the GDP is used as a regressor in the estimation of inflation functions is called to question on empirical grounds. This suggests that it is more rewarding, analysis-wise, to use the output of individual sectors rather than the GDP, in such studies. Such an approach reveals the varied effects which different types of production could have on the price behaviour and thus places policy-makers on a better footing to monitor and control inflation.

6.1.2 Condition for Inter-temporal Stability of Macro Parameters

The effect of aggregation bias on temporal stability of relationships has been a matter of serious concern for quantitative researchers. Thus, Gupta (1969) suggests as an item for research, the examination of "the temporal behaviour of the aggregation bias for a given model" (p.72). The findings of this study provide some useful insights in this regard: for the macro parameters to be temporally stable, the relative weights of the inflation-accentuating components and the inflation-dampening components of the GDP must remain constant over time. Suppose the weight of the inflation-accentuating component of the GDP is 'w' and that of the inflation-dampening component is 'v'. Then a condition for the stability of the macro parameter over time is that:

$$\Delta \left(\frac{W}{V}\right)_t = 0 \qquad (6.1),$$

for all the time periods, t= 1,2,3, ..., where Δ is the first difference operator. It is plausible to reason that, if all other factors that influence the value of the macro parameter are held constant, it is variations in $\frac{W}{V}$ that will determine the behaviour of the macro parameter. If the relative weight is not constant, not only the sign but also the magnitude of the macro parameter may change in response to the changing composition of aggregate output.

Based on this rule, a prediction can be made for the data of the present study: if over time, the relative share of the inflation-accentuating component in the GDP (Y_D) is increasing, while the relative share of inflation-dampening component (Y_V) is declining, the sign of the GDP parameter estimate in the price output function (Equation 5.1) will, eventually, turn from the observed negative to positive. Notationally expressed, the condition reads thus:

If for any time, t > 0

$$\Delta \left(\frac{Y_D}{Y}\right)_t > 0$$

and,

$$\Delta \left(\frac{Y_V}{Y}\right)_t < 0$$

then,

$$\left(\frac{dP}{dY}\right)_t \rightarrow \text{positive} \qquad \text{as } t \rightarrow \infty;$$

where, Y_D = inflation-accentuating component of GDP,
  Y_V = inflation-dampening component of GDP,
  Y = GDP,
  Δ = first difference operator.

6.1.3 *A View on Optimal Partitioning*

Partitioning of an aggregate into similar groups has been suggested by some scholars as one method of generating valid parameters in a macro-model of functional relationships. Amidst the controversy about the relative gains and losses in error through the use of aggregated economic variables (Theil, 1954; Grunfield and Griliches, 1960), Gupta argues that aggregation bias can be considerably reduced through partitioning. The partitioning is to be done in such a way that "(i) the independent variables in each partition move together and (ii) the micro coefficients in each partition are close to each other" (pp.22 – 23). Gupta's first rule means that for aggregation bias to be reduced, correlation among components in each partition should be high. The second rule requires the marginal effects of the components in each partition to be near as possible to each other (Gupta,1969).

The analysis in this book suggests another condition for optimal partitioning and reduction of aggregation bias. This new condition is that the micro coefficients of the elements in each partition should have the same direction of causation. This condition was not satisfied when the average price level was regressed on the GDP, instead of on its component. The removal of this aggregation error requires the partitioning of the GDP into:

a)   Those components that influence the price level inversely and
b)   Those components that influence the price level positively.

Economic theory will, in some cases provide information for the classification. But as the evidence from this study shows, the predictions of economic theory do not always hold. For this reason and because, there are cases in which economic theory does not have any explicit information, economic theory should be complemented with empiricism. Empiricism would involve experimenting with different components of the aggregated variables as regressors to find the directions of their various impacts on the relevant dependent variable.

Figure 6.1: Optimal Partitioning for Valid Causal Relational Specification

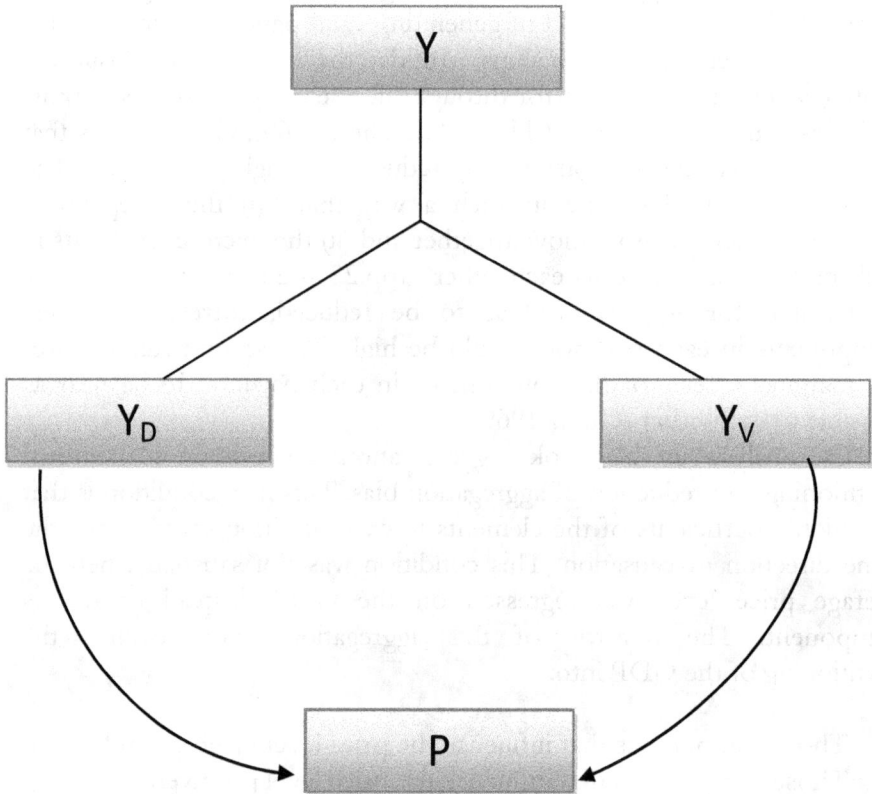

This new condition posited for optimal partitioning is shown diagrammatically in Figure 6.1 for the case of the effects of changes in output on the average price level. Y is the GDP in real terms. It is partitioned into two components: Y_D contains components of the GDP whose impact coefficients on the average piece level are positive, while Y_V contains components of the GDP whose impact coefficients on the average price level are negative. The partitioning is indicated by the bifurcation of the ray from the Y box, into Y_D and Y_V, which are then related to the average price level. The causal flows from Y_D and Y_V to the average price level, P, are indicated by the arrows that originate from the Y_D and Y_V boxes and feed into the P box. The positive and negative flows from Y_D and Y_V, respectively, to P, reflect the essence of the partitioning.

6.1.4 An Explanation for Statistically Significant but Wrongly Signed Coefficients

A common cause of worry in empirical research is the appearance of 'wrongly' signed coefficients in regression models. It is the view of Rao and Miller (1972) that "when the coefficient is significantly different from zero and has the wrong sign, then some aspect of the problem has not been unveiled" (p.46). Such a wrong sign, they note, may be "a warning, inter alia, of incorrect definitions, specification or interpretations" (p.46).

The results from the foregoing regression analysis enables one to suggest one possible source of the wrong sign, namely: the misconception of an explanatory macro variable as influencing a dependent variable in a particular direction, whereas, such an explanatory macro variable is actually made up of components which influence the dependent variable in opposing directions. For example, the common prediction of an inverse relationship between the GDP and the average price level, assumes that all components of the GDP influence the price level inversely. This is erroneous. The signs of the impact coefficients of output components on the price, as the results of the regressions in this study show, differ. Some are positive, others are negative; and, the sign of the overall or net impact of aggregate output on the price level could be positive or negative. In view of this, an important consideration about data used in econometric research should relate to the homogeneity or otherwise of the impact signs of the aggregated components of the explanatory variable.

6.1.5 Additional Reason for Instability of the Phillips Curve

It may be recalled that the Phillips-Samuelson-Solow model established an inverse functional relationship between the rate of inflation, $\dot{P}$, and rate of unemployment, $\dot{U}$. Friedman (1968) and Phelps (1972) have argued that the Phillips curve is not a steady state situation; they argue that for any specific unemployment rate, different expected rates of inflation, $\dot{P}^e$, will yield different actual inflation rates. Thus instead of a unique Phillips curve, there will be a family of Phillips curves.

In the present study it has been argued and confirmed by empirical findings that, a given level of real GDP can be made up of different mixtures of inflation-accentuating and inflation-dampening components. For any given level of aggregate output, Y, the higher the share of the inflation-accentuating component, Y_D, the greater will be the attendant inflationary pressure, *ceteris paribus*. Since the ratio,

$$\frac{Y_D}{Y} = \emptyset \qquad (6.2)$$

is a variable, there is an additional reason why a given unemployment rate may be associated with varying rates of inflation and why the Phillips curve may be, thus, unstable. At any unemployment rate and given the expected rate of inflation, the actual rate of inflation will depend on $\emptyset$.

The versions of the Phillips curve can be summarized as follows:

Original Phillips-Samuelson-Solow Model:

$$\dot{P} = f(\dot{U}) \qquad (6.3)$$

Friedman-Phelps Extension:

$$\dot{P} = f(\dot{U}/\dot{P}^e) \qquad (6.4)$$

The suggested new Extension:

$$\dot{P} = f(\dot{U}/\dot{P}^e/\emptyset) \qquad (6.5)$$

Equation 6.3 states that the rate of inflation is dependent functionally on the rate of unemployment. Equation 6.4 states that the rate of inflation is dependent on the rate of unemployment, given the expected rate of inflation. Equation 6.5 states that the rate of inflation is a function of the rate of unemployment, given the expected rate of inflation and, given the proportion of the GDP that is made up of inflation-accentuating components.

6.2 Policy Implications

The regression analysis indicates that Nigerian's inflation is, to a large extent, a cost of the attempt by the economy to achieve rapid growth without considering the mix of output. Since growth is desirable, the challenge is how to stop inflation without stopping growth of the economy. To that extent, the challenge should be to find ways of limiting inflation to less distorting proportions rather than of completely eliminating it.

Clearly, it is possible to choose between different growth rates and different degrees of inflationary stress; greater growth rates are associated with greater inflationary stress generally, and vice versa. Since a minimum level of price stability is itself necessary for an orderly economic and social development, one option to anti-inflationary policy is to choose a less explosive growth rate. Particularly, although the growth of social and physical infrastructure is desirable for greater future level of aggregate output, given their inflationary consequences, such infrastructure development must necessarily be limited.

The idea of 'balanced growth' has a peculiar meaning in this context. A given level of aggregate output can be more or less inflationary depending on its composition. The larger the inflation-accentuating components of aggregate output compared to the inflation-dampening components, the higher the inflationary pressure associated with a given level of aggregate output, and vice versa. Policy makers can, therefore, choose between different output mix points and their corresponding inflationary pressure points. The combination chosen will depend on whether or not, in the evaluation of policy makers, it is more beneficial for the society to increase production, for example, of investment goods that will enhance future growth, while worsening the inflationary pressure, in the short run, in the hope that in the medium-to-long run, the boost to output of final goods will offset the inflationary pressure.

The expansion of output that may accentuate inflation is often undertaken because it is a means to a goal desirable to society, for example, economic growth. A trade-off relation thus exists between growth and inflation. Therefore, one cannot recommend an optimal mix of the national product because this would depend on the subjective evaluation of policy makers regarding how much disutility from inflation is considered worth bearing for a given value of future growth.

The task of economic analysis in this regard is to point out the implications of alternative lines of policy choice and to emphasize that the usual broad recommendation for greater output is deficient. The composition of that greater output is important. But the choice of what is considered 'good' composition of output for the society is to be left to policy makers.

In relation to this issue, how efficiently resources are used in the process of growth is an important consideration. Even if inflation is growth-induced, a given level of growth and structural composition of output could be more or less inflationary depending on how efficiently resources are used and the resultant real output of goods and services for a given monetary outlay. This possibility is demonstrated in Figure 6.2, which shows two members of a family of transformation curves (growth-inflation efficiency curves), E_1 and E_2. If the economy is operating on E_1, a growth rate of G1 leads to an inflation rate of C_{1A} while a growth rate of G_2 leads to an inflation rate of C_{2A}. But if the economy is operating on E_2, the growth rate of G_1 and G_2 would produce inflation rate of C_{1B} and C_{2B}, respectively. Since $C_{1B}>C_{1A}$ and $C_{2B}>C_{2A}$, E_1 is a preferable growth-inflation efficiency curve. For any given growth rate, E_1 yields a lower cost (that is, inflation rate) than E_2.

Figure 6.2: Growth-Inflation Efficiency Curves

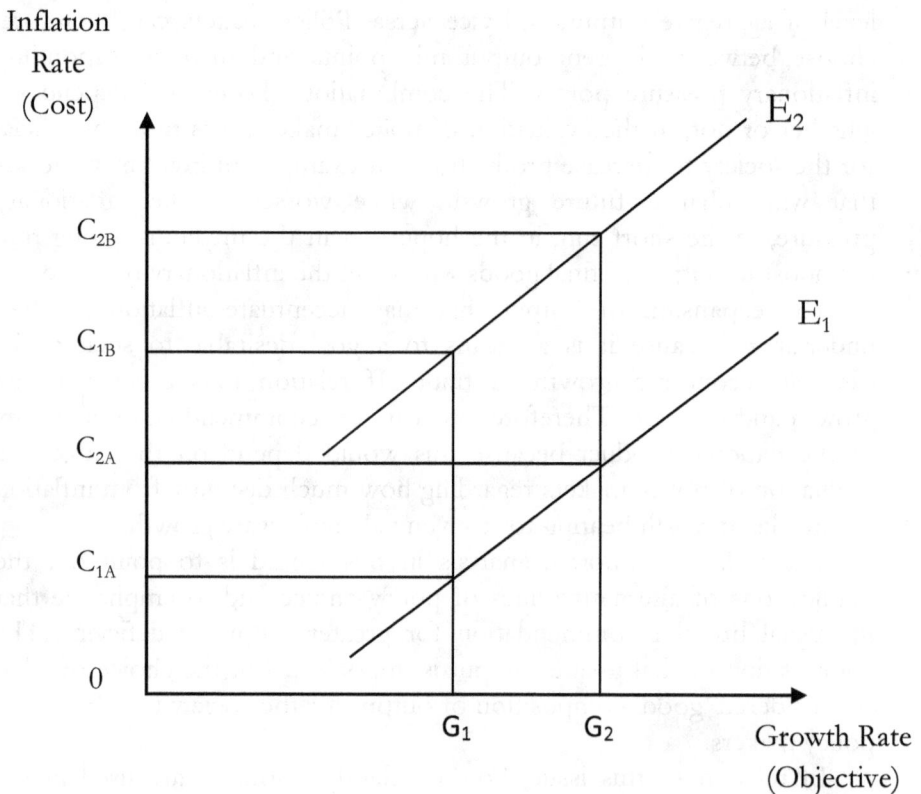

For an economy to operate along E_1 rather than E_2, policy makers should ensure that public expenditure is directed to the more production-stimulating infrastructure like railways, road networks, water supply and electric power supply, rather than to showplace and showpiece projects like football stadia, arts theatres, administrative secretariat and international fiestas. The emphasis on public expenditure should be functionalism at minimum cost.

Two critical questions are thus to be answered by policy-makers about public expenditure:

a) What will be the relative allocations between prestige programmes and economic programmes?
b) Within the allocation to economic programmes, what will be the allocations of expenditure between production of currently consumed goods and services on the one hand and capital expenditure, on the other?

For any given period, the more the allocation of resources to economic programmes, as well as to production goods and services for current consumption, the less the inflationary pressure associated with a given level of aggregate output, ceteris paribus.

The findings with respect to the non-agricultural-agricultural sector interaction suggest that a crucial anti-inflationary measure is that of improving agricultural production. While it is desirable that the industrial sector be expanding, the rate of expansion may be a source of concern because of the stress it places on the agricultural sector. Conceivably, there are two approaches to reducing such stress: either limit industrial expansion or improve agricultural production to keep pace with the demands of expanding industrial sector. Ceteris paribus, the second option is more desirable because it puts the economy on a higher production curve.

One obvious reason for the poor performance of agriculture in a less developed country like Nigeria is that it is largely based on manual labour and is largely rain-fed. The uneasy interaction between agriculture and non-agriculture is a result of the slow rate of modernization of the former. As can be learnt from the experience of such countries like England in the eighteenth century, the uneasy interaction can be minimized if fundamental transformations and innovations in the agricultural sector occur simultaneously with, or before industrial expansion. Hence in England of the eighteenth century, while the industrial revolution led to growth in real income and increased demand for agricultural products, the agricultural sector responded adequately because such innovations as the enclosure system and mechanization enabled large-scale commercial farming.

There is, therefore, need for technical as well as organisational changes in Nigeria's agriculture. To meet the challenge of the time, agricultural modernization entails that scientific farming by formally-trained agronomists, biologists, animal scientists, veterinary scientists, agricultural engineers and agricultural economists should replace subsistence farming by illiterate, mainly elderly, though hardworking, farmers. This analysis accepts Arthur Lewis' (1971) view that a country could achieve economic growth by getting the educated to do jobs formerly done by the illiterate. Such modern commercial-scale agriculture should be based on a complete value-chain strategy, supported by innovative organizational arrangements such as production clusters and cooperatives.

Anti-inflation policy should favour integrated rural development programme. Good roads, electric power and water supplies should be extended to rural areas. These measures will, among other desirable effects, encourage the educated to remain in rural areas and take up farming and agro-processing as a profession.

It is implied from the above considerations that for an effective check of Nigeria's inflation, agricultural modernization policies must be designed and effectively implemented. Otherwise, the expansion of non-agricultural sector will generate stresses that transmit into inflationary pressures. As has been demonstrated, different combinations of the two broad components of aggregate output will generate different levels of inflationary impulse.

Another salutary approach is to introduce measures that will make it possible for any given non-agricultural-agricultural output ratio, to produce a lower inflationary pressure than was the case previously. Such an improvement requires changing some underlying characteristics of the economy. One such measure is to increase efficiency in the use of agricultural products by the non-agricultural (particularly manufacturing) sector, so that there is greater industrial output per unit of agricultural input. If such efficiency is achieved through, for example, technological improvements that reduce wastage and enable intensive use of inputs by processing what was formerly considered disposable waste, into useful products, for a given desired industrial output level, there would be a lower requirement for agricultural inputs.

A second way is to make more efficient, agricultural sector's use of its own products, through, for examples, the reduction of food wastage and prevention of spoilage of agricultural products due to inadequate perseveration measures. If the intended efficiency is achieved, the surplus production of agriculture over its own needs will increase and the requirements of the non-agricultural sector can be satisfied with less friction. In summary, efficiency in the use of agricultural products by both the agricultural and non-agricultural sectors will reduce the inflationary stress at any given non-agricultural-to- agricultural output ratio.

Thirdly, the inflationary stress can be reduced by finding and making use of non-agricultural substitutes for the raw materials which non-agricultural requires from agriculture. For example, some cotton-, leather- and rubber-based products of industries, can be replaced with synthetic substitutes derived from Nigeria's rich crude petroleum deposits. With such substitution, the needs of non-agricultural sector from the agricultural sector will fall at any level of the non-agricultural-agricultural output ratio. As a result, there will be lower inflationary stress.

PART II

SURVEY OF CENTRAL BANKING AND MONETARY POLICY

The history and peculiar economic and social conditions of a country, or of an economic grouping, could significantly influence how the broad principles of central banking and monetary policy play out in practice for such an economic entity. In the next eight chapters, we present a survey of the general principles of central banking and monetary policy, as well as of the specific experiences of seven economies, namely: United States of America, The U.K, the Eurozone and Japan – which are advanced market economies; China and India – which are essentially emerging market economies; and Nigeria – which is a less developed economy. The reason for selecting this combination of countries is to see how the practice of central banking and monetary policy reflect the level of economic advancement. The survey sufficiently demonstrates the immense complexity of monetary management, in general, and inflation management, in particular. Chapter Seven discusses the essentials and frameworks of monetary policy, while the subsequent seven chapters survey the practice of central banking and monetary policy in the selected economies.

CHAPTER SEVEN

Monetary Policy Essentials and Frameworks

Central banks are the institutions charged with the statutory responsibility for controlling inflation in the economy; and, monetary policy, which is the preserve of central banks, is preoccupied with grappling with the problem of inflation. The nature and functioning of central banks and how they design and practice monetary policy should, therefore, be a useful accompaniment to the empirical investigation of the relationship between inflation and the structure of output, which was undertaken in Part I.

7.1   Monetary Policy: The Essentials

Monetary policy is the process by which the monetary authority of a country (generally called the central bank) controls the supply of money, often aimed at influencing inflation rate or interest rate to ensure price stability and sustain trust in the national currency. Other goals of monetary policy include economic growth and stability, lower unemployment and predictable exchange rate with other currencies. For definitional purposes, monetary policy is often contrasted with fiscal policy, which refers to taxation (government revenue), government spending, and associated borrowing.

Monetary policy could take either of two stances: expansionary stance or contractionary stance. It is expansionary when it increases money supply in the economy more rapidly than usual and contractionary when it expands money supply more slowly than usual or when it even shrinks it. The tradition in economy management is to use expansionary monetary policy to combat unemployment during a recession by lowering interest rate in the hope that cheaper credit will encourage business to expand and households to spend. On the other hand, contractionary monetary policy would intend to slow down inflation in other to avoid erosion of purchasing power, deterioration of asset values and distortions, all of which could lead to loss of trust in the currency and threaten the very foundation of the modern economic system.

It could be observed immediately that expansionary and contractionary monetary policies are not necessarily symmetrical: what one tends to promote is not necessarily and directly what the other aims to fight or suppress. When expansionary policy aims at combating unemployment in a recession, it is not necessarily aiming at encouraging inflation – even though this might be one of the results; whereas, contractionary policy is necessarily and directly aimed at slowing inflation. This type of asymmetry provides a peep into the complexity of monetary policy. Monetary policy could further be described as: accommodative, if the interest rate set by the monetary authority is intended to create economic growth; neutral, if it is intended to neither to create growth nor combat inflation; or, tight if it is intended to reduce inflation.

In the monetary system, interest rate is the price at which money can be borrowed. Monetary policy essentially rests on the relationship between interest rates and the supply of money. In modern times, the issuance of currency is either under a monopoly or under a regulated system where banks which are subject to a central bank could be used to issue currency; under such a system, the monetary authority can alter the money supply and thus influence the interest rate. Whether monetary policy is: (i) expansionary or contractionary; (ii) accommodative, neutral or tight, there are several monetary policy tools available to achieve the goals. To curtail money supply can be achieved by: increasing interest rate by fiat; reducing the monetary base; and, increasing the reserve requirement. To expand money supply can be achieved by reversing those actions. In particular, to change the monetary base, the primary tool of monetary policy is open market operations. This is the process of managing the quantity of money in circulation through the buying and selling of various financial instruments or products such as government debt instruments (treasury bills, treasury bonds etc), corporate bonds or foreign currencies. Such purchases or sales result in more or less base currency being injected or withdrawn from market circulation.

Ordinarily, the short-term goal of open market operations is to achieve a targeted short-term interest rate. This is the case with the USA where the Federal Reserve targets the federal funds rate, which is the rate at which member banks lends to one another overnight. When the Federal Reserve Bank buys government debts from the open market, usually mostly from financial institutions, its payments constitute increases in money supply which drives down inter-bank rates and makes bank lending cheaper. But in other cases such as with China, monetary policy might rather target a specific exchange rate relative to other foreign currencies; in this case, the target of the Bank of China is to focus on a desired exchange rate between the Chinese renminbi and a basket of foreign currencies. A similar strategy was adopted by Nigeria in July 2016 following the floating of the Nigerian Naira. In order to moderate the free fall in the external value of the Naira, the Central Bank of Nigeria, through the Monetary Policy Committee moved the policy rate (Monetary Policy Rate) which was already at a high level of 12 percent to 14 percent. Given that the actual cost of credit, particularly to manufactures was already considered very stiffening at a mark-up on the existing 12 percent policy rate, the decision of the central bank to raise the policy rate, which is the reference rate, by 200 basis points, was a clear indication that the Bank had chosen the stabilization of the exchange rate of the Naira relative to foreign currencies, as its priority objective, at least for the time being.

The monetary authority could also influence interest rate and, therefore, the availability of money supply, by changing the policy discount rate, that is, the rate at which eligible banks and other depository institutions can borrow from the central bank. This rate in turn directly influences the federal funds rate, the rate at which depository institutions lend their reserves at the central bank to one another. For example, in the U.S.A., the Federal Discount Rate is reviewed every 14 days in order to control money supply and stabilize the financial markets. Meanwhile, the Federal Open Market Committee (FOMC) sets the target for the Federal Funds rate which it signals in action through open market operations. The Federal Funds rate is so important because it is the base rate that determines the level of all other interest rates in the economy.

The third main tactical tool for maintaining monetary stability is the reserve requirement, under fractional-reserve banking system. By this practice, a bank accepts deposit, makes loans and investments to earn income and holds reserves equal to a fraction of its deposit liabilities, either as currency in its tills or as deposits with the central bank. By changing the reserve requirement, the monetary authority influences money supply because money lent out by banks increases the money supply. More particularly, in relation to inflation, too much money, whether lent or printed will lead to inflation - hence, the nexus, again, between monetary policy and inflation.

Indeed it could be concluded that overall, the preoccupation of the three standard approaches to monetary policy – money supply (open market operations), money demand (policy discount rate) and systemic risk management (fractional reserve requirement) – is to keep market interest rates and inflation at desirable target values by balancing the banking system's supply of money against the demands of the aggregate market.

It is interesting to note that the effectiveness of monetary policy has a lot to do with how much faith households and businesses place on the policy pronouncements of monetary authorities. As ably articulated by scholars such as Forder (2004), this is because depending on the level and direction of credibility they attach to announcements by policymakers, private agents will form expectations appropriate for the circumstances and behave accordingly. For example, if private agents believe that policymakers are committed to lowering inflation, they will anticipate future prices to be lower than otherwise. If an employee expects prices to be high in the future, they will draw up wage contract with a high wage rate to match the expected higher prices. On the other hand, the expectation of lower prices is reflected in wage-setting behaviour between employers and employees; since wages are in fact lower, there is no demand-pull inflation because employees are receiving smaller wages and there is no cost-push inflation, because employers are paying out less in wages. Therefore, to achieve this low level of inflation, private agents must have confidence that policymakers are committed to doing what they announce in respect of lower inflation.

In essence, for monetary policy to succeed, the policy announcements should be the credible. There are different ways to contribute to credibility. It could be by having an independent central bank, so that private economic agents know that political influences on the pursuit of the goals declared by monetary authorities will be minimal. Credibility could also be derived from reputation: if the central bank is associated with consistently good performance in conducting monetary policy, it will enjoy a favourable reputation for reliability and, therefore, enjoy credibility. Another subtle factor that contributes to faith in monetary policy is adequate shared knowledge about the issues and, in particular, common definition of what credibility means. Does it mean capability to serve the public interest? Does it mean the reliability with which the central bank keeps its promises? Clarity is critical; otherwise as cautioned by Adelina-Geanina (2011) "lack of definition can lead people to believe they are supporting one particular policy of credibility when they are really supporting another" (p. 4). From the foregoing, there is little doubt that beyond sincerity of stance, capacity to deliver is important for credibility of announcements. A central bank should, therefore be enamoured with high quality analytical, technical and technological resources, and backed with elaborate and robust database, which would enable it to understand: (i) the circumstances of the economy and (ii) the responsiveness of the economy.

7.2 From Gold Standard to Evolution of Central Banking and Monetary Policy

Monetary Policy as an issue came into being only with the introduction of interest rate and credit as part of the phenomena in the conduct of economic activities. Before the evolution of monetary policy as we know it today, monetary policy was concerned with the limited issues of: discussions about the production of coins or metals used as medium of exchange and, decisions to print money to create credit. At this early stage, interest rates were not yet linked to the other basic components of monetary policy. Those basic monetary policy decisions were exercised by the authority with the power to create coin money, that is, seigniorage. They were executive political decisions because there were no monetary authorities as we have them today.

As trade networks expanded across more geographies, the practice of setting the price between gold and silver (the two metals most commonly used to make coins), and the price of the local currency to foreign currency emerged. The origin of paper money has been traced to 7th century China where promissory notes called "jiaozi" were used alongside with metallic currency. Modern monetary policy could be said to have begun with the creation of the Bank of England in 1694, with the responsibility to print notes and back them with gold; hence the idea of monetary policy as independent of political executive action and of special institutions focused on monetary policy. These early special institutions – the Federal Reserve System in the United States, the Bank of England, the European Central Bank, the Peoples Bank of China, the Bank of Japan, the Reserve Bank of New Zealand and the Reserve Bank of India and the - handle the task of executing the monetary policy independent of the political authority. The goal of early monetary policy was to maintain the value of the coinage, print notes which would trade at par with their metallic counterparts (called specie), and prevent coins from leaving the circulation system. Therefore, monetary policy was used to maintain the gold standard and the establishment of central banks by industrializing nations, particularly in the 19th century was associated with the goal of maintaining the sovereigns peg to the gold standard, while trading in a narrow band with other gold-backed currencies. To achieve this objective or indeed, "target", central banks began to set interest rates they charged their own borrowers and other banks that required liquidity.

In its strictest form, the gold standard is a system under which the price of the national currency is measured in units of gold bars and is kept constant by the government's promise to buy or sell gold at a fixed price in terms of the base currency. It could be regarded as a special case of fixed exchange rate. It was widely used between the mid-19th centuries through 1971. Although it had the advantages of simplicity and transparency as a system of monetary policy, it was abandoned during the Great Depression because countries were pushed to stimulate and grow their economies by increasing their money supply (Einchengreen, 1992). Following the Bretton Woods Agreement in 1944, the Bretton Woods system which was a modified gold standard replaced the gold standard following the experiences of the World War II. Each country was to have a monetary policy which pegged its currency to the gold – within a fixed value of plus or minus 1%; in addition, the U.S. dollar was seen as a reference currency, linked to the price of Gold. But in 1971 faced by serious challenges, the United States decided not to allow the conversion of dollars to gold. By 1973, foreign countries let their currencies float, and that was the end of the Bretton Woods System.

The major problem with the Gold standard is that it induces deflation because the economy usually grows farther than the supply of money: when an economy grows, the same amount of money supply is used to execute a larger number of transactions. By implication, prices of goods and services would have to fall, so that the larger supply of goods and services would be bought off in a fewer number of transactions and with a smaller amount of money – a case of artificial fall in aggregate quantity demanded. During recession, a deep deflation would prolong the period before the inception of a turnaround, that is, it would constitute a drag. The same challenge would face recovery from financial crisis, if there is deflation.

The dangers of the gold standard and its deflationary bias are particularly manifest in a situation of liquidity trap. Under normal circumstances, management of money demand is one of the tactical approaches the central bank applies in the conduct of monetary policy. Interest rate is the price charged for money to borrowers. When the central bank raises the banking system lending rate, such as the central bank discount rate – the rate at which it lends to member banks – the demand to borrow money falls; on the other hand when, the central bank lowers the discount rate, money becomes cheaper, and the demand to borrow money rises. However, if the nominal interest rate is already at or very near zero - a condition of deflation - the central bank cannot lower it further with any effect. This is the situation of liquidity trap. When interest rates are that low, the prevailing belief is that interest rates will soon rise; as a result, consumers prefer to keep their funds, including additions, in saving accounts and other liquid forms while avoiding bonds and other income yielding assets. They know that soon interest rates will rise and the price of bonds, being inversely related to interest rates, will fall. And, they do not want to hold assets whose price will fall and cost them capital losses. And because, the improved liquidity in terms of more money supply caused by the lower discount rate of the central bank does not lead to more demand for bonds (and other assets), the asset prices do not rise; hence the interest rate cannot fall lower. Similarly, from the point of financial institutions, the banks will have a problem finding qualified borrowers because with interest rates already near zero, there is little scope for additional incentives to attract qualified borrowers. A dramatic way to look at the challenge of liquidity trap is that it is a condition under which initiatives are taken by the monetary authority to stimulate the economy through increased money supply; but rather than the additional money supply going into economic "activity", it goes into "liquidity".

As already noted, starting from the 19th century, many industrialized countries set up central banking systems, with the Federal Reserve set up in 1913 being among the last. By this time the role of the central bank as the "lender of last resort" had been established. Also, that interest rates significantly affected the whole economy had been understood because in the mainstream economics, marginal analysis showed how economic agents would change their decisions based on changes in the economic trade-offs, which were derived from changes in interest rates. Moreover, there was a growing excitement among economist about how money-supply growth could affect the macro economy. For example Milton Friedman (1948) advocated that during recessions, government budget deficits should be financed fully with money creation to stimulate aggregate economic activity. He moderated his prescription later, advising that the money supply increase should be at a low, constant rate, so as to maintain low inflation and stable output growth (Friedman, 1960).

In practice, it has been found that the relationship between monetary aggregates and other macroeconomic variables is highly unstable, meaning that direct money supply targeting might not be as successful as envisaged. For example, under the chairmanship of Paul Volcker, the United States Federal Reserve starting from October 1976 tried the direct money supply prescription and found it unsuccessful. Because of these past experiences, monetary decisions depend on a broad range of factors, including: short-term interest rates; long term interest rate; velocity of money through the economy; exchange rate; credit quality; bonds and equities; government versus private sector spending; international capital flows; and, financial derivatives such as options, futures and swaps.

Under what exchange regime could a central bank operate a truly independent monetary policy? As earlier indicated, the central bank can influence interest rates by contracting or expanding the monetary base (money in circulation plus banks' reserves at the central bank), and there are three ways in which the monetary base can be changed. First is through open market operations or sales and purchases of second-hand government debt: if the central bank wants to lower interest rates, it purchases government debt and increases the amount of cash in circulation through payment for the purchases. Apart from the impact increased money supply would have on the cost of money (interest rate), the change (increase) in demand for government debt caused by the central bank purchases of securities already held by other market participants, would drive down the yield on government bonds, which should be expected to transmit to declining impact on market interest rates, in general. Second, the central bank can lower the interest rate it charges on overdrafts to the commercial banks, thereby encouraging them to borrow more from it: with such borrowing, commercial banks have enhanced reserves which enable them to make more credit available to the economy. Third, the central bank can lower the reserve requirement, thereby freeing up funds for banks to increase loans or buy other assets.

But a central bank can only operate such effective monetary policy when the exchange rate is floating. If the exchange rate is fixed, the central bank will have to purchase or sell foreign exchange, from time to time, to maintain the exchange rate target because demand for foreign currency is impacted by money supply. Essentially, the buying or selling of foreign exchange has a similar effect on the monetary base as open market operations through the buying and selling of government debt. Accordingly, under a fixed exchange rate, monetary policy cannot be independent because the monetary authority is also concerned about the impact of change in the monetary base on the exchange rate. The attention of the impact of changes in money supply is not unique but divided. To illustrate, if the central bank buys foreign exchange to prevent the local currency from appreciating the base money will increase. Suppose this is happening at a time when domestic economic realities dictate a tight monetary stance, the central bank must also sell government debt to contract the monetary base by an equal amount, in order to sterilize the increase in monetary base caused by the purchase of foreign exchange. In essence, if there is frequent volatility in the foreign exchange market which necessitates frequent attention and action by the central bank, it could lose the focus required in the conduct of domestic monetary policy.

The issue of independence of monetary policy discussed above is one of technical independence – whether and how a fixed exchange rate regime could compromise independence of monetary policy. But there is also concern about political independence: that is, how to avoid manipulation of the tools of monetary policy to achieve political goals, such as re-election of the party in power. There is a school of thought that subscribes to the logic that making a country's central bank independent of the rest of the executive arm is the best way to ensure an optimal monetary policy. The argument goes further to suggest that ensuring that members of the committee which conducts monetary policy have long, fixed and secure tenors, would uphold independence.

A practical step that has evolved in central banking towards enhancing independence is that which is based on a well-defined framework of operations. In particular, in this respect is the adoption of public inflation targets with the goal of making the outcome and process of monetary policy more transparent. Public inflation targeting started with New Zealand in 1990. A central bank would have an inflation target of $X\%$ for a given year and if actual inflation happens to be $(X + Y)\%$, the central bank would make an explanation. The Bank of England became independent of government, through the Bank of England Act of 1998 and adopted an inflation target of 2.5% RPI which was revised to 2% of CPI in 2003. In 1998, the European Central Bank adopted an inflation of under 2% HICP as the definition of price stability within the Eurozone; in 2003 this was revised to inflation below, but close to, 2% over the medium term. Similarly, the Federal Reserve Bank and the Bank of Japan adopted the 2% target in January 2012 and January, 2013, respectively.

In the case of developing countries, a number of factors constrain the establishment of effective monetary policy. A major difficulty is that only a few of those countries have a deep and liquid market for government securities. The development of a vibrant domestic government bond market is, therefore, an important challenge to address for effective monetary policy. A second constraint is that in those economies, there is serious difficulty in forecasting money demand and fiscal pressure for forced taxation by expanding the monetary base. The challenge of forecasting reflects, among other deficiencies, inadequate and unreliable database, which to some extent derive from the prevalent economic dualism, a large informal sector, weak institutions and poor organizational conditions of economic entities in both the public and private sectors of the economies. Further, monetary authorities in many developing countries are not independent of their governments; they are often subjected to the political preferences of the governments and even used to pursue non-monetary goals.

In Africa generally, South Africa, Nigeria, Kenya and Egypt are making relatively good progress towards viable financial systems. In Nigeria, starting from the early 2000s, laudable initiatives, including recapitalization of banks and other financial institutions were taken to improve the scope for implementing effective monetary policy. Indeed, there occurred what many analyst consider outstanding transformations in the Federal Government of Nigeria bond market since 2003, leading to the development of a yield curve of up to 20 years by 2008 (Table 7.1), a sustained secondary market for the sovereign debt instruments, which were listed on both the Nigerian Stock Exchange and the OTC trading platform - the FMDQ - as well as a well-functioning primary-dealing market-making system.

Table 7.1: Progression of Nigeria's Sovereign Yield Curve

TENOR	Testing Phase 2003	Smoothenin g Phase* 2004	Regular Monthly Issuance Phase					
			2005	2006	2007	2008	2009	2010
2-YEAR		-	√					
3-YEAR	√	-	√	√	√	√	√	√
5-YEAR	√	-		√	√	√	√	√
7-YEAR	√	-		√	√			
10-YEAR	√	-			√	√	√	√
20-YEAR		-				√	√	√

Source: Debt Management Office, Nigeria, working papers.

7.3   Monetary Policy Frameworks

Monetary policy framework could be defined as the configuration of tools, actions and flows of processes that lie in-between and inclusive of policy decision and ultimate objective in monetary policy management. In monetary policy, the gap between policy decision and ultimate objective could be long. In order not to lose orientation and momentum as a result of the long transmission lag, operating and intermediate targets are used. A target is a proximate goal but is not an objective in or of itself.   It works directly towards achieving the long-term objective of policy.

An operating target is a tactical goal that the monetary authority can influence in the short-run. These include the reserve money or monetary base which the central bank can control to influence its own balance sheet, although changing its balance sheet cannot constitute its objective. It also includes short-term interest rates (interbank rate or the federal funds rate in the United States), which are not the ultimate objectives but which are used to bring about changes that constitute the long-term objectives. The operating target of monetary policy is an economic variable, which the central bank wants to control, and indeed can control, to a very large extent on a day-to-day basis through the use of its monetary policy instruments. It is the variable whose level is the subject of decision of the monetary policy committee. It serves a crucial purpose in the making and management of monetary policy: (i) it guides the implementation officers of the central bank on the daily activities in-between the committee meetings; (ii) it serves to communicate the monetary policy stance to the public. On the basis of global experience of monetary policy over the years, there is an emerging understanding, more or less a consensus, that the appropriate operational target for a central bank is the short-term inter-bank interest rate. An operational target is a monetary policy objective specified by the central bank usually framed in terms of changes in money supply and non-borrowed reserves. A monetary policy instrument is a tool available to the central bank which can be used to attain the operational target. There are three such established tools: standing facilities (discount window); open market operations; and reserve requirement. However, between the 1930s and 1980s, an extended category of instruments - "direct methods" – of monetary control, such as deposit interest rate ceiling or margin requirements were introduced.

An intermediate target is an economic variable that the central bank can control with a reasonable time lag and significant precision and which is in a relatively stable or least unpredictable relationship with the final target of monetary policy – the ultimate objectives. The intermediate target is only a leading indicator of the ultimate target. The typical intermediate target is a monetary aggregate like M_1, M_3, exchange rate or some medium or longer-term interest rate. The assumption is that through the operational target, the intermediate target can be controlled or influenced significantly. Since the 1980s, the validity of attaching the "target" status to the intermediates has been questioned: the argument is that they are more of indicator variables which convey useful information to the central bank, but do not convincingly impact the ultimate target or policy objectives. But the argument is far from settled.

An intermediate target, according to Investopedia, is any economic variable that is not directly controlled by the central bank but which would, often quickly adjust to policy changes and behave in a predictable manner relative to the monetary authority's goals, and these targets pertain either to monetary growth or interest rates. Using the U.S. as an example, the Fed will, often, adjust the Fed Funds Rate to achieve desired intermediate targets. The Fed typically has three main tools for implementing its monetary policy; open market operations, discount window, and adjusting reserve requirement at depository institutions.

The essence of the intermediate targets is to provide links to the ultimate objectives. So what are the qualifications of good intermediate targets? Answer: consistency with the ultimate goal; accurate measurability; timeliness; and availability for use by the monetary authority. An intermediate target in a monetary framework serves as a nominal anchor. A nominal anchor is an intermediate target which helps to control inflationary expectations. The choice of the nominal anchor or intermediate target (for managing inflation) defines the monetary policy framework. These anchors could be: (i) exchange rate anchor; (ii) monetary aggregate target; or (iii) inflation targeting.

Sequentially, the flow of transmission is as follows: from *Policy Decision* to activation of *Policy Instrument*; from *Policy Instrument* to *Operating Target*; from *Operating Target* to *Intermediate Target*; and, from *Intermediate Target* to *Ultimate Target (Objective)*.

A relevant observation to be made at this point is that in the process of transmission of impact from policy decision to the ultimate objective, important information not originally taken into account could manifest itself. Under such a circumstance – usually at the Intermediate Target stage - instead of the flow of impact continuing as planned, it is diverted to carry the new information back to the policy decision stage. Policy decision is then beneficiated with the additional information and the flow of transmission to the ultimate objective re-starts. There will be detailed discussions on the various approaches to targeting in the next sections.

7.4   Monetary Targeting

In the 1970s and 1980s, many countries adopted monetary policy which relied on attempting to achieve desired level of inflation by maintaining a constant growth in money supply. The money supply aggregate used varied from country to country and even for the same country, the class of money and credit used was changed from time to time. In essence, for most, if not all the countries that tried money supply targeting it ended up being experimentation with various variables. In general, what central banks do is to set money supply growth target as a nominal anchor (intermediate target) in order to achieve long-term price stability. Accordingly, they rely on the quantity theory, which is a long-run model linking price levels to money supply and demand. The derived form of the quantity theory used is the one which specifies the rate of inflation (INFLr) to be equal to the rate of growth of money supply (MSg) minus the rate of growth of real output (ROg), thus:

$$INFLr = MSg - Rog \qquad (7.1)$$

This implies that price stability can be achieved in the long run by controlling the growth rate of money supply.

By implication, what a central bank would need to do is set INFLr equal to a constant and commit to that target. However, the assumption is that there is a stable relationship between the rate of growth of money supply and the rate of growth of real output; otherwise, even after the central bank has decided on INFLr, (MSg – ROg) will not be constant. Hence, the model collapses. In practice this failure is what often results because there is no way to target real output growth: it is not an instrument or tool within the control of the monetary authority. Therefore, money supply growth rate is considered a weak policy. Mishkin F. S. (2000) has a good documentation of experiences of industrialized countries with monetary targeting.

Mishkin notes that monetary targeting strategy has three elements, namely: reliance on information conveyed by a monetary aggregate to conduct monetary policy; announcement of targets for monetary aggregates; and, some accountability mechanism to preclude large and systematic deviations from the monetary targets. The United States and the United Kingdom introduced monetary targeting in the 1970s, while Canada did in the 1980s. The strategy was not a success in controlling inflation in the three countries. According to Mishkin, the failure was as a result of: inconsistency, including the focus on other goals such as output and employment, as well as the shifting of the money supply aggregate used as the anchor; and, the instability of the relationship between monetary aggregates and the goal variables such as inflation or nominal income.

On the other hand, monetary targeting proved successful in Germany and Switzerland, both of which adopted the strategy in 1974. In these countries, monetary targeting followed a pragmatic rather than a Friedman-type monetary targeting rule hinged on a constant-growth-rate path. They allowed money supply to overshoot the target for a period of two to three years and then skilfully reversed it towards the target. That is, it was flexible. However, the strategy was more problematic in Switzerland than in Germany, an observation Mishkin believes reflects the difficulties of targeting monetary aggregates in a small open economy.

Mishkin summarizes three lessons to be learnt from monetary targeting experience:

i.   The instability of the relationship between monetary aggregates and goal variables – inflation and nominal income;

ii. The key to success for monetary targeting is an active engagement in communication which enhances transparency and accountability of the central bank; and,

iii. Monetary targeting has been very flexible in practice and a rigid approach has not been necessary to obtain good inflation outcomes.

Referring back to the assumed quantity theory relationship, INFg = (MSg – ROg), it was observed that the assumption often fails because the relationship between the rate of growth of money supply and the rate of growth of real output is not stable. One would want to point out that one possible cause of this failure is the "Disaggregation Dissonsnance" which was theorized in Part I. For the same rate of growth of money supply, the relationship with a given real output growth will differ according to the composition of that underlying output. Hence, the relationship is unstable.

7.5 Inflation Targeting

When a monetary authority uses periodic adjustments of interest rate to keep inflation within a given range, it is said to be running an inflation targeting regime. The definition of inflation used could be the Consumer Price Index (CPI) or any other index that measures the movement of prices in the economy.

According to Mishkin (2000) inflation targeting involves five key elements:

i.   Publicly declared medium-term numerical targets for inflation;

ii.   Institutional commitment to price stability as the primary, long-run goal of monetary policy and commitment to achieve the inflation goal;

iii.   A strategy which includes as many variables beyond monetary aggregates are used in making decisions about monetary policy;

iv.   Increased transparency of the monetary policy strategy through communication with the markets and the general public about the plans and objective of monetary policy makers; and,

v.   Increased accountability of the Central Bank for attaining its inflation objectives.

The interest rate most often targeted is the overnight rate at which banks lend to each other overnight for cash flow purposes. The equation linking inflation with interest rates is derived from the Fisher Effect model. The Fisher Effect is the economic theory proposed by Irving Fisher which states that the real interest rate is equal to the nominal interest rate minus the expected inflation rate. Therefore, real interest rates would fall as inflation increases unless nominal interest rates increase at the same rate increase at the same rate as inflation.

What is the practical essence? The interest rate an investor has on a savings account is simply the nominal interest rate. If the interest on the deposit is 5% per annum and the expected rate of inflation is 3% per annum, then the money in the savings account is, in real terms, growing at 2% per annum and not 5% per annum. The smaller the real interest rate, the longer it will take for savings deposit to grow enough to be able to achieve a targeted or planned purchase of a good or service – the purchasing power explanation. A simple interpretation of this arithmetic is that, all things being equal, inflation slows down real savings and planned expenditure on durable goods by households. There is also a money-supply interpretation of the Fisher effect: it shows how money supply affects both nominal interest rate and inflation rate in a link. When a central bank's monetary policy pushes the inflation rate by X% points, then the nominal interest rate of the same economy will respond and increase by X% points as well. In that sense, it could be assumed that a change in money supply would not affect the real interest rate but would directly reflect in changes in the nominal interest rate.

Returning to the definition of the Fisher effect, we recapitulate that it states that "the real interest rate equals the nominal interest rate minus the expected inflation rate". This can be represented in notations as follows:

$$r = i - \pi \qquad (7.2)$$

Where r is the real rate of inflation, i is the nominal rate of interest, and π is the expected rate of inflation. To understand inflation targeting, the equation can be rearranged to become:

$$\pi = i - r \qquad (7.3)$$

Using i as an anchor, the central bank can influence π, on the assumption that r, the real interest rate, is constant. The central bank could choose to maintain a nominal interest rate at all times if it wishes to keep a targeted inflation rate. However, having chosen a targeted inflation rate for a given period, it must change the nominal interest rate if exogenous factors cause the real interest rate to change. The appropriate interest rate target is usually reviewed periodically (monthly or quarterly) by the policy committee of a central bank. Alterations to the interest rate target are made based on market indicators arising from the forecast of economic trends. Such alterations aim at keeping the system on track towards achieving the defined inflation target. A simple but popular method of inflation targeting is the Taylor Rule by which interest rate is adjusted in response to changes in inflation rate and output gap – when the latter two macro variables deviate from their policy target values. In formal terms, a Taylor Rule is a monetary policy rule that stipulates how much the central bank should change the nominal interest rate in response to changes in inflation, output, or other economic conditions. In specific terms the rule specifies that for each one percent increase in inflation, the central bank should raise the nominal interest rate by more than one percentage point. When it was proposed in 1933, the rule intended to foster price stability and full employment by reducing uncertainty and improving the credibility of future actions by the central bank, in a systematic manner. It also aimed at avoiding the inefficiencies of time inconsistency from the exercise of discretionary policy. Time inconsistency is the behavioural economic problem whereby a decision-maker's preferences change overtime in such a way that a preference can become inconsistent at another point in time. Tying preferences to a rule such as the Taylor Principle helps to eliminate such psychological deficiencies from policy.

Following the problems encountered with, and dissatisfaction experienced about, monetary targeting, inflation targeting in monetary policy was first used by New Zealand in 1990. Since then it has been used in Australia, Brazil, Canada, Chile, Colombia, the Czech Republic, Hungary, Norway, Iceland, India, Philippines, Poland, Sweden, South Africa, Turkey, the United Kingdom and Finland. The lessons from inflation targeting experience have been well documented by Mishkin (2000), based on his excellent studies of the cases of New Zealand, Australia, Canada and the United Kingdom. We will pick the essential conclusions from that research work starting from those relating to whether the strategy has been a success as follows:

i.   Inflation targeting has been successful in controlling inflation. It has helped the countries applying it to significantly reduce inflation rate from what might have been expected given their past experiences. Moreover, once inflation was reduced to levels acceptable for price stability, it remained low; and, after disinflation, the inflation rate does not bounce back up during subsequent cyclical expansion of the economy.

ii. Inflation targeting weakens the effects of inflationary shocks. A normal phenomenon in most economies is that following an inflation shock, for example a supply shock or a fiscal (tax shock), inflation would wave up into second- and third-round rises in wages and prices, which would generate a persistent rise in the inflation rate. But the evidence from Canada indicated that for an inflation-targeting economy, the shock does not enter a second phase. One can hazard, that this outcome reflects the fact that with a credible inflation targeting programme in place, economic agents trust that the policy-makers will bring back inflation to track and, therefore, do not build in a higher inflation expectation in their behaviours, particularly as regards wage contracts.

iii. Inflation targeting can promote growth and does not cause increased fluctuations in output. During the disinflationary phases in inflation-targeting economies, output will be below normal but this will be short-lived. When low inflation levels have been achieved, output and employment will return to levels as high as they were previously and output fluctuations do not get higher. The conclusion, therefore, is that inflation targeting promotes real economic growth in addition to maintaining price stability.

iv. But inflation targeting does not necessarily reduce the cost of reducing inflation as was hoped by industrialized countries. They had adopted the strategy thinking that the commitment of the central banks to control inflation would improve their credibility and reduce both inflation expectations and the output losses associated with disinflation. However, empirical studies show that inflation expectation did not speedily adjust downwards following the adoption of inflation targeting and there was little or no reduction in the output loss associated with disinflation (the sacrifice ratio) among countries adopting inflation targeting.

A second set of lessons relate to transparency and accountability.

As essential features of inflation targeting, they lead to the following lessons:

i). The success of inflation targeting derives mainly from its emphasis on transparency and effective communication with the public. This ingredient is well formalized and put in published documents, such as the Inflation Report published by the Bank of England. The reports are complemented with extensive speaking schedule used to explain the conduct of monetary policy to various stake holders. Other components of transparency include the publishing of minutes and proceedings of policy meetings without delay after such meetings: such speedy reporting helps to check speculations and harmonize behaviour of households and private corporations. This is important because the changes observed in macroeconomic indicators are a result of the behaviour of economic agents based on the latter's understanding or misunderstand of policy portends. The information available and their interpretation influence private sector planning and the more adequate and reliable they are, the more improved we expect private sector planning to be. Among the major items which communication by monetary authorities in inflation targeting economies would explain to the general public, financial market participants and the politicians are:

a)   The goals and limitations of monetary policy;

b)   Numerical values of inflation targets;

c)   How the inflation targets are to be achieved, given prevailing economic conditions; and,

d)   Reasons for any deviations from targets.

With such effective communication delivered, a central bank gains greater freedom of action, as it can more comfortably pursue expansionary monetary policy when faced with negative shocks without adverse effects on inflation expectations. Moreover, as has already been noted effective communication under inflation targeting improves private sector planning by reducing uncertainty about monetary policy while democratizing knowledge of monetary policy to the general public, encouraging public debate at all levels of society and using the environment of strategic engagement to educate all on what the monetary authority can and cannot be expected to achieve.

ii).   Inflation targeting helps ameliorate the time-inconsistency problem by increasing accountability. It reduces the chances that the Central Bank will succumb to the time-inconsistency temptation in which it tries to expand output and employment in the short-run by pursuing overly expansionary policy, whereas its focus should be on achieving long-term price stability, which would then be supportive of long-term achievement of the broader economy goals of growth and employment. Inflation targeting helps shift the orientation from political pressures on the central bank to engage in what it cannot do, which is using monetary policy to deal with immediate economic growth and job creation problems, to the more appropriate one of what the central bank can do in the long run, which is to control inflation. The change in political economy of monetary policy-making in inflation-targeting economies is, perhaps, the most important gain for the institutional relevance of central banks as it enhances their independence.

iii).   Of course, the forgoing point to the promotion of independence and goal autonomy of the central banks. It enables the monetary authorities to take a longer-run view and avoid time-inconsistency pressures from political authorities.

iv). Accountability to the general public in which sanctions for poor performance by the central bank is only in the form of the loss of pride and public disapproval, as well as accountability directly to government, in which failure to perform is met with real punishment for the central bank, both seem to work as well in encouraging good behaviour – delivering on inflation targeting. The New Zealand has the strong form of accountability of the central bank to the government: the government has the right to sack the governor of the Reserve Bank if the inflation target is breached. In other countries which practice inflation targeting such as Australia, Canada and the United Kingdom, the approach to accountability is less formal and consists more of acceptability and commendability or otherwise by the general public, of the performance of the central bank. The experience is that both approaches to sanctioning and rewarding the performance of the central bank have produced good results for inflation targeting.

v). Overall, therefore, inflation targeting is even consistent with democratic principles. A central bank cannot, for an extended period of time, pursue policies that are inconsistent with the interest of the society at large.

The third set of comments on experiences from inflation targeting regimes relate to their operational design as follows:

i) Inflation targeting is not meant to be a rigid rule. It is "rule-like" because it involves forward-looking behaviour which prevents or at least limits policymakers from systematically engaging in policies with long-run undesirable consequences. Such polices avoid the time-inconsistency problem and could better be described as "constrained discretion" (Bernanke and Mishkin, 1997). It requires central banks to use all available information to determine what are the appropriate policy actions to achieve the inflation target; yet inflation targeting is not based on policy discretion but is constrained by the predetermined goal of achieving the target to be forward-looking and not seduced by current economic conditions; hence avoiding the trap of time inconsistency.

ii)   Because inflation targets have been conventionally set above zero, they express the policymaker's concern that too low inflation could negatively impact real economic activity: Deflation can cause financial instability and precipitate serious economic contraction. Provided inflation targets are such that the resulting price dynamics does not warrant economic agents to build it into their decisions, then inflation targeting will not suffer credibility loss.

iii) Inflation targeting does ignore traditional stabilization goals but rather places them in the long-run context. That is why, for example, an inflation-targeting central bank emphasizes the floor of effective expansionary policy when there are negative shocks on aggregate demand.

iv)   For inflation targeting, undershoots of inflation are as important and unacceptable as overshoots. So both the floor and ceiling are important. Inflation targeting actually enhances the flexibility of the central bank to address contraction in aggregate spending: this is because declines in aggregate demand, which cause inflation to undershoot the target range would automatically stimulate the central bank to loosen monetary policy without worrying that inflation expectations would be triggered.

v)   It is not appropriate to introduce inflation targeting when inflation is initially high. During such a period, it is difficult for monetary authorities to control inflation: the likelihood of missing the mark is quite high; so is that of losing credibility. Therefore, inflation targeting should be introduced only after there has been disinflation.

vi)   Central banks should avoid too short a horizon and two narrow a range because these can create an appearance of failure and generate loss of credibility. A major consideration is that monetary policy impacts the economy and inflation with a time lag, sometimes quite long. A short horizon could, therefore, lead too frequent misses of the inflation target, which may be unreal because, with a little more time, the appropriate target might be achieved. Multi-year targets are more advisable. Similarly, for instrument stability, the range should not be too narrow.

vii) Targeting asset prices, such as exchange rate worsens performance under inflation targeting. Central Banks have reasons to be concerned about the value of the domestic currency. Particularly in small open economic depreciation would lead to a rise in inflation due to the pass-through from higher import prices and greater demand for exports. Pressure could also come from the public and politicians who have emotional interpretation of the value of the local currency.

Because of all these, exchange rate fluctuations raises the risk that even under inflation targeting regimes, central banks could put too much focus on limiting exchange rate movement. This leads to the risk of transforming the exchange rate into a nominal anchor that takes precedence over the inflation target. One would add here, that it all depends on the exchange rate and to what extent and in what direction the shock impacted on both the exchange rate and inflation in the first instance. Essentially, one imagines, that the appropriate policy response, even under inflation-targeting, would depend on the set of circumstances of the economy at the time of the exchange rate destabilization. But overall, targeting on an exchange rate is likely to worsen the performance of monetary policy; whereas, designing monetary policy instrument to achieve inflation targets should factor in exchange rate and other asset prices – perhaps by being complemented with fiscal and structural policies.

7.6 Fixed Exchange Rate Targeting

Fixed exchange rate targeting consists in maintaining a fixed exchange rate with a foreign currency under varying degrees of rigidity with the anchor currency. In a system of fiat fixed rates, the domestic monetary authority declares a fixed exchange rate but does not actively buy or sell currency to maintain the fixed rate. Instead, the rate is enforced by physical measures such as capital controls, import and export licenses, etc. These measures are also referred to as non-convertibility measures. Under this regime, there would be a black market where the currency trades at its market but unofficial rate.

In a system of fixed-convertibility, currency is bought and sold by the central bank on a daily basis to achieve the officially-fixed exchange rate. Sometimes, the target could be a range within which the exchange rate may fluctuate, rather than a point.

In a system of currency–board fixed exchange rate, every unit of local currency must be backed by a unit of foreign currency. This ensures that the local monetary base does not increase unless it is backed by hard currency; this eliminates any concerns about a long run on the local currency by those wishing to convert the local currency to the anchor currency.

In a system of dollarization, foreign currency, usually the United States dollar is used freely as the domestic medium of exchange either exclusively or in the parallel with the local currency. Dollarization is essentially a result of loss of faith in the local currency.

Countries may decide to use a fixed exchange rate monetary regime to take advantage of price stability and control inflation. But a corollary of a fixed exchange rate regime is that it requires the loss of capacity by the central bank to pursue independent domestic monetary policy. Rather, monetary policy is abdicated to the foreign monetary authority as the monetary policy in the pegging economy must align with monetary policy in the anchor economy for the exchange rate to be maintained. The degree of loss of domestic monetary independence would depend on such factors as capital mobility, openness, credit channels and other economic factors.

Deeper insight on the implications of fixed exchange rate in monetary policy could be gained from an examination of how exchange rate regimes relate to inflation targeting. The Asian currency and financial crises which engulfed much of East Asian economies began in July 1997. Before then many central banks in East Asia and other emerging economies, had maintained the fixed exchange rate regime. They considered that exchange rate stability is essential for growth of trade and investment. But fixed exchange rate became extremely difficult to maintain when capital accounts were liberalized: huge capital flows reversal led to speedy depletion of foreign exchange reserves and made the floating of the exchange rate inevitable. Which means that fixed exchange rate is incompatible with capital mobility; in addition, as earlier indicated the adoption of a fixed exchange rate regime leads to loss of domestic monetary policy capacity. Summing it all up, there is the impossibility of having an economy having capital mobility, the fixed exchange rate, and independent monetary policy – a conflict or (trilemma) described as the "impossible trinity". For any two of the three policies to be operational or effective, the third one must be abandoned.

As illustrated in Figure 7.1, if a country were to opt to operate along the side 'a' of the triangle it would maintain a fixed exchange rate and allows free capital flows but it would have to lose monetary sovereignty.

If it cannot afford the loss of monetary sovereignty and yet wants fixed exchange rate, then it must impose capital controls to block its monetary effects from hitting the exchange rate; which means it would opt to operate on the 'c' side of the triangle. This is because if for example, the central bank raised its interest rate above the world interest rate, it would experience net capital inflows which would cause appreciation of the currency, thereby challenging the fixed exchange rate policy and it would be forced to reverse the action it had taken on interest rate. So to prevent this monetary repercussion on the exchange rate, the solution is to block capital flows that would lead to currency appreciation. But capital controls reduce trade and foreign direct investment and create opportunities for corruption.

Figure 7.1: The Impossible Trinity

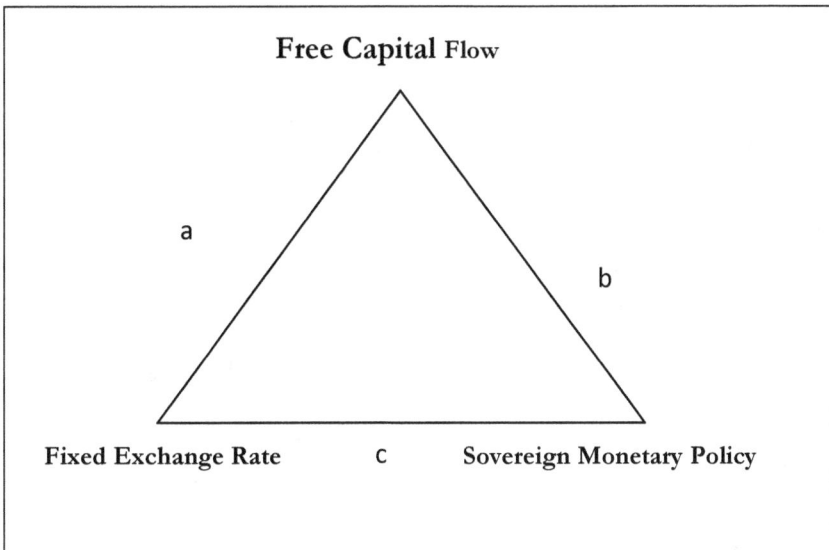

Alternatively, the country could opt to operate on the 'b' side of the triangle, meaning that it will forgo fixed exchange rate regime in favour of a combination of free capital flows and independent domestic monetary policy. Under this policy regime, the central bank can now fully employ money supply and interest rate instruments to influence the level of output and employment, as well as price stability.

This brings to the fore the nagging question of a choice between the flexible exchange rate regime, the fixed exchange rate regime and intermediate regimes. One strong position on the issue is based on the observation that during the international financial market crises in the 1990s, the economies most devastated were those involved in a fixed or pegged exchange rate regimes: these included Mexico in 1994, Thailand, Indonesia and Korea in 1997, Russia and Brazil in 1998 and Argentina and Turkey in 2000. On the other hand, countries that considerably avoided the crisis were those that did not have pegged rates. These included South Africa, Israel, and Mexico. This has led to a conclusion of some sort that countries open to international capital flows should keep off from pegged rates with an extension that intermediate regimes between hard pegs and floating rates are not sustainable. This line of thinking has evolved to the "two-corner" or "bipolar" solution view, namely: the choice of appropriate exchange rate for economies with access to international capital markets should be either flexible exchange rate or fixed exchange rate supported, where necessary, by a commitment to forgo independent monetary policy (Summers, 2000:8). In the view of the IMF, stable exchange rate is either the hard peg or the free float; the intermediates, such as the managed float or the fixed exchange rate regime without a currency board arrangement, would be inherently unstable. The IMF has subsequently recommended a combination of free float and inflation targeting as a way of reducing the probability of a currency crisis. One of the corners, free float, seems to have gained more popularity in combination with inflation targeting.

But in practice many inflation–targeting central banks, from time to time intervene in the foreign exchange market in order to influence the exchange rate movement. It has, therefore, been reconsidered that the managed exchange rate regime could be compatible with inflation targeting, contrary to the purist view that an inflation-targeting central bank should not attempt to manage the exchange rate. The pragmatic view has been strengthen by the argument that if both inflation targets and exchange rate targets are specified as a range of considerable width rather than a point, then it becomes conceivable that under certain economic conditions, a response to a shock on one of the policy targets may produce improvements in that target without jeopardizing the other target, more so if, for example, the inflation targeting is within the framework of an announced range in the medium term. Accordingly, Ito (2007) based on the study of exchange rate regimes practiced by many countries and the experiences of four Asian central banks, namely, Thailand, Korea, Indonesia, Philippines concludes: "Therefore, under usual circumstances, inflation targeting and the exchange rate management are not inconsistent, especially when both targets have reasonably wide ranges" (p.18).

7.7 Mixture of Exchange Rate and Monetary Policy Regimes

The exchange rate stance adopted could range from hard peg to free float, while the monetary policy framework could range from no-independence to total independence. In practice, countries adopt various combinations of an exchange rate regime and monetary policy framework. It is conceivable that from time to time, the actual mix in operation is different from the formally announced and documentarily articulated one; this is because when monetary authorities are faced with unexpected shocks, endogenous or exogenous, they would have no choice but to take practical steps to regain reasonable level of re-balance. Pragmatism dictates the implantation of adjustment actions outside the books, given that there are always new types of shocks entering the macroeconomic environment.

As regards exchange rate regimes, there are four broad types with their sub-categories: hard peg, with two categories; soft peg, with five categories; floating regimes with two categories; and, residual, with one category. The classes are further explained below.

7.7.1 Hard Pegs

7.7.1.1 Exchange Arrangement with no Separate Legal Tender (Dollarization)

The inhabitants of a country use foreign exchange in parallel to or instead of the domestic currency. The foreign (anchor) currency may or may not be the United States dollar, but the dollar is the most used foreign anchor currency. The foreign currency, also referred to as substitution currency is adopted most of the time after serious economic and financial crisis, as in the cases of Ecuador in 2000 and El Salvador in 2001. Both countries applied currency substitution with the United States dollar. Partial currency substitution could occur when residents prefer to hold significant share of their financial assets in foreign currency. Partial substitution could occur as a gradual process of full currency substitution as in the cases of Argentina and Peru with the United States dollar during the 1990s.

7.7.1.2 *Currency Board Arrangement*

Under this regime, the country has its own currency but the domestic currency is backed one-to-one by foreign reserves; that is, the local currency is linked by a fixed exchange rate to a foreign currency. For such a foreign-currency-dependent economy, there are no restrictions on current or capital accounts and there is absolute unlimited convertibility of domestic currency with the anchor currency. The dependent economy earns income in the form of interest on its foreign reserves but cannot acts as a lender of last resort to deposit money banks and cannot operate a fractional reserve system. Also it cannot lend to government which can only spend from tax revenue of from borrowing from the markets, to meet its needs. Pegging keeps interest rate and inflation rate very closely to the anchor country rate and the central bank cannot influence domestic interest rates with a policy rate or discount rate. In essence, the obvious drawback of the system is that monetary authority loses the capacity to set monetary policy to reflect domestic realities. In addition, such a fixed exchange rate system, to a high degree, also fixes a country's terms of trade so that differences between the dependents and anchor economies do not count. The advantage of the currency board system is that the problem of pursuing currency stability is eliminated. For small open economies, which would find independent monetary policy difficult and costly to sustain, it provides a simple alternative. Moreover, it implicitly conveys a credible commitment of the anchored-economy to low inflation.

7.7.2 Soft Pegs

7.7.2.1 *Conventional Pegs*

This is the arrangement whereby a country's currency is pegged to some band or value of another currency and the band or value is either fixed or periodically adjusted. An example is in the 1950s and 1960s when the United States pegged the dollar to gold at the rate of thirty five dollars to one ounce of gold (USD35:1oz of gold). Also Germany pegged the Deutsche Mark at the rate of four to one (4DM=1USD). The pegging of the subordinated currency could be to a basket of foreign currencies, particularly of major trading partners, with the weighting reflecting geographical distribution of trade, services and capital flows. The reference currency composition could also be standardized to a unique (artificial currency) such as the SDR. Usually, there is no irrevocable commitment to keep the parity but usually attempt is made to keep the fluctuation of the exchange rate within narrow margins of plus and minus 1 percent around a central rate. Alternatively, the maximum and minimum value of the exchange rate may remain within a narrow margin of 2 percent for at least three months. The monetary authority could endeavour to maintain the fixed priority through direct intervention - buying or selling of foreign currency in the market - or indirect intervention – e.g., aggressive use of interest rate policy in position of foreign exchange regulations, moral suasion or even through intervention by other institutions such as the fiscal authority. Unlike the hard peg categories, a conventional peg country has some, although limited, flexibility of monetary policy. It can still exercise traditional central banking functions and can adjust the level of the exchange rate.

7.7.2.2 Pegged Exchange Rate within Horizontal Bands

This arrangement maintains the value of the domestic currency within a band around a central exchange rate with reference to another currency or basket of currencies. But unlike the conventional peg, the fluctuation around the central reference rate is not required to be a maximum but a minimum. The margin of fluctuation will be at least plus or minus 1 percent around a fixed central rate, or, the margin between the maximum and minimum value of the exchange rate exceeds 2 percent. Within the band, the central bank could carry out traditional monetary policy and the band could be a crawling one.

7.7.2.3 Crawling Peg

The country fixes it currency exchange rate with another currency or basket of currencies. The exchange rate is adjusted periodically in small amounts at a fixed rate. Its adjustment could, alternatively, be dictated by changes in selective quantitative indicators such as past inflation differentials relative to major trading partners or differentials between inflation targets and expected inflation in major trading partners.

Running a crawling peg regime imposes constraints on monetary policy much like in a fixed peg system.

7.7.2.4 *Crawl-Like Arrangement*

This has then essential features of a crawling peg, plus the crawling is maintained within a certain fluctuation margins of at least plus or minus one percent around a central rate; or the margin between the maximum and minimum value of the exchange rate exceeds 2 percent. In either case, the central rate or the margins are adjusted periodically at a fixed rate or in response to selective quantitative indicators. The degree of flexibility which is certainly greater than in the case of straight crawling peg is the function of the band width. The band width could be symmetrical, around a crawling central parity or could be asymmetric. As should be expected, the monetary policy is constrained by the commitment to maintain the exchange rate within the band and the degree of policy independence is a direct function of the width of the band.

7.7.2.5 *Stabilized Arrangement*

This is a de facto soft peg but there is no de jure arrangement and no policy commitment is entailed. Statistically characterized, it would have a spot exchange rate that remains within 2 percent margin for at least six months. The margin of stability could be with respect to one currency or a basket of currencies. Exchange rate is not market determined but remains stable as a result of official action.

7.7.3   Floating regimes

7.7.3.1 *Floating*

Under this category, the exchange rate fluctuates from day to day, but in practice, the central bank attempts to influence the exchange rate without having a specific exchange rate path or target to pursue. It could be said that the motivation is to guide the market against violent and disruptive swings by the central bank buying or selling currencies. But interventions could also be indirect. The judgment to influence or intervene could be derived from desired values of: balance of payments, international reserve, parallel market developments, etc. This category is also called dirty float or managed float, and intervention could be frequent given the range of factors which trigger it.

7.7.3.2 Free Floating

Free floating countries allow the exchange rate of their currencies to fluctuate in response to foreign exchange market mechanisms. Virtually, there is no intervention by the central bank. An example is Canada since 1998. The United States comes second in this category of rare intervention to influence the currency exchange.

7.7.4   Residual

7.7.4.1 Other Managed Arrangement

These are other exchange rate regimes, which cannot be classified under the preceeding categorizes. As at 2014, this category included 18 of the 191 countries (inclusive of three territories) which made up the IMF Annual Report on Exchange Arrangements and Exchange Restrictions. Those 18 countries accounted for about 9.4 percent of the 191 countries. Most of the countries in this set have their de facto arrangements differing from their de jure; they manage their exchange rates in such a way that they exhibit frequent or irregular changes in policies.

The distribution of IMF's 191 members among the ten categories of exchange rate arrangements for 2014 is shown in the Table 7.2. An interesting observation is that there is concentration of the distribution at the extremes. The fixed regime extremes comprising of "no separate legal tender", "currency board" and "conventional peg", account for 69 out of the 191 countries, which translates to about 36% of the total. At the other extreme of the spectrum, that is the floating regimes, the ordinary "floating" and "free floating" includes 65 out of the 191 countries, translating to 34% of the total. These de facto situations seem to confirm that the two-corner or bipolar issue is not just a proposition for optimal positioning, but a practical outcome of global exchange rate policy experimentation. Indeed, the two corners taken together include 134 members out of the 191 members - that is, 70 percent. It is also interesting to note, that the fixed regime corner is dominated almost exclusively by the less developed economies of Africa, the Middle East,

Latin America, the small islands of the Atlantic and Pacific Ocean and the less advanced countries of Eastern Europe. It seems that these countries appreciate they have more than enough manifest economic management problems and would rather keep off from the fears of unpredictable foreign exchange market events. The only strange member in this set is the well-performing advanced economy of Denmark.

At the floating regimes corner, the dominant inhabitants in the free floaters category are a union of the European Monetary Union (EMU) members and the group of seven (G7), plus Australia, Poland, Norway, Sweden and the emerging economies Chile and Mexico. A strange member in this group is the African country of Somalia. The ordinary floating category hosts mostly developing and emerging economies but also advanced economies like Israel, New Zealand and Iceland.

Table 7.2: Defacto, Exchange Rate Arrangements, 2014

Category	Number of Countries	Percentage of Total
Separate Legal Tender	13	6.8
Currency Board	12	6.3
Conventional Peg	44	23.0
Crawling Peg	2	1.0
Crawl-like Peg	15	7.9
Stabilized Arrangement	21	11.0
Pegged Exchange Rate Within Horizontal Bands	1	0.5
Floating	36	18.8
Free Floating	29	15.2
Other Managed Arrangement	18	9.4
Total	**191**	**100**

Source: IMF Annual Report on Exchange Arrangements and Exchange Restrictions, 2014

In terms of the mix between exchange rate arrangements and monetary policy framework, most of the countries at the fixed exchange rate corner are, as expected by implication, exchange-rate anchored: the primary anchor currency being the dollar, followed by the euro. As has been noted in earlier discussions, these countries do not have a scope for domestic monetary policy. A notable feature in this group is the structure of a number of contiguous countries bonded together in a monetary union and then anchored as a group to foreign currency. These include the six-member West African Economic and Monetary Union (WAEMU) - consisting of former French colony countries of West Africa - anchored to the euro, and the six-member Central African Economic and Monetary Community (EMAC) - consisting of former French colony countries of Central Africa- also anchored to the euro monetary system.

At the other extreme corner, for the free floating exchange rate regimes, all the EMU countries plus the United States and Somalia do not explicitly submit to any nominal anchor in terms of monetary policy framework. Rather, they monitor various indicators in conducting monetary policy. The remaining free-floaters (Australia, Canada, Chile, Japan, Mexico, Norway, Poland, Sweden, and the United Kingdom) practice inflation targeting as their approach to monetary policy. The ordinary floaters' monetary policies are either monetary aggregate targeting or inflation targeting with a few members practicing the non-explicit nominal anchor option like most free-floaters do. A striking observation is that no free floaters is engaged in monetary aggregate targeting but ordinary floaters engage across monetary aggregate targeting, inflation targeting and non-explicit nominal anchor monetary management.

CHAPTER EIGHT

Bank of England and Monetary Policy

The Bank of England, the central bank of England founded in 1694, was originally designated to act as not only the government's banker but as the debt manager. But events and circumstances of more than 300 years have influenced the focus of the bank. Over time, the most crucial function of the Bank of England is that of monetary policy. The monetary policy objective is to deliver price stability, that is, low inflation. Subject to that the bank has the responsibility of supporting broader economic objectives, including growth and employment.

8.1   Evolution of Structure and Practice

It used to be the practice that the Treasury set the interest rates. But after the reforms of 1992, there was a growing acceptance of the views that there was undue political influence on what ought to be purely economic judgments on monetary policy. Accordingly, in 1997, the Chancellor of the Exchequer, Gordon Brown, granted the Bank of England operational responsibility to set interest rates. This was followed by the 1998 Banks of England Act which made the Bank independent to set interest rates. But it is important to note that while the Act states that the Bank is accountable to parliament and the wider public, "if in extreme circumstances, the national interest demands it, the Government has the power to give instructions to the Bank on interest rates for a limited period" (http//www.bankofengland.co.uk/monetary policy).

The 1998 Act also contained guidelines for the establishment of the Monetary Policy Committee and its responsibilities. The MPC consist of nine members, five from the Bank and four from outside, with the Governor of the Bank of England as Chairman. While the Act gave to the bank independence of instruments to pursue its objectives, it gave the government responsibility for specifying its price stability targets and growth and employment objectives, at least annually, while reserving the right to direct the Bank on what interest rate to set during times of emergency, as earlier observed.

The MPC is responsible for formulating the United Kingdom's monetary policy. Its major instrument is the setting of the Bank of England Base Rate (BOEBR) which is the rate at which the Bank lends to banks – with a primary aim of price stability, defined since 2011 by government's inflation target of 2 percent on the Consumer Price Index. The target takes the form of a "point" rather than a "band" used by the Treasury prior to 1997. It is important to point out that it is well understood that the remit for low inflation does not translate to a preference for the lowest inflation because an inflation rate below 2 percent is considered as bad as one above 2 percent; therefore, the target is symmetrical.

Under the Act, if inflation exceeds the target by more than one percent in either direction, the Governor must write an open letter of explanation to the Chancellor of the Exchequer, and is bound to do the same every three months thereafter, until inflation returns to within the allowed range. Such letter has to state measures being taken to return to the target and how long the derailment is expected to last.

Since interest rate is the main instrument used by the Bank to bring inflation into line, a target of 2 percent does not mean that inflation will be held constantly at this rate because that would imply changing interest rates all the time and conceivably by large amounts, causing too much uncertainty and wide fluctuations in the system. Rather, the MPC aims to set interest rates so that inflation can return to target within a reasonable time period without seriously destabilizing the economy.

The requirement of letter-writing from the Governor to the Chancellor has had opportunity to be demonstrated. In April 2007, the Governor (then Merlyn King) had to write the first MPC open letter of explanation to the Chancellor (then Gordon Brown), explaining why the inflation rate had deviated from the 2 percent target and reached 3.1 percent and had to write 14 such letters by February, 2013 because prices remained unstable. King's successor, Mark Carney who wrote his first open letter in February 2015, to explain why inflation had fallen below 1 percent for the first time in the MPC's history, had to write another in April 2015 to explain the first case of deflation of 0.1% in April 2015. By February 2016, Governor Carney had written five open letters to the Chancellor of the Exchequer.

To demonstrate how chasing inflation more or less dominates monetary policy and, indeed, central bank activities, while in the first ten years of the MPC interest rates were kept relatively stable between 3.5

percent and 7.5 percent, starting from October 2008 and up to March 2009, the base rate was cut six times to as low 0.5 percent in a bid to avoid deflation and stimulate growth.

8.2   The Workings of the Monetary Policy Committee

The MPC meeting used to hold once a month (for three days), that is twelve times a year; the rule was modified that from September 2016, it would hold only eight times a year. The Committee's decisions are announced to the public the same afternoon the meeting is concluded and since 2015, the minutes of the meeting, including the policy preferences of each member, are published on the Bank's website at the same time the decisions are announced. MPC members can be invited by Parliament to answer questions about their decisions. In addition to the MPC minutes, the Bank publishes its inflation Report every quarter. The report contains analysis of the economy, the factors influencing decisions, as well as the MPC's latest inflation and output growth forecasts, taking into account that monetary policy operates with a time lag of about two to two-and-a half years.

Although the MPC relies on a model of the economy to help it produce robust projections, it also understands the weight of uncertainties and unknowns of the future; hence, the need for a great deal of informed judgment. Members conduct a service of regional visits throughout the United Kingdom to engage stakeholders, individuals as well as businesses, on issues affecting businesses their economic lives. From these engagements, MPC members do gather first-hand intelligence about the economic conditions across the country. A particular formal arrangement is the existence of twelve regional agents (Bank's agents) who gather information following discussions with about 700 businesses around the country and submit monthly reports to the Bank, which the Committee also finds useful in judging the current and future economic conditions.

8.3   Quantitative Easing by the Bank of England

During the first quarter of 2009, it was becoming clear to the MPC that there was need to think outside the box - adapt unconventional tools – to manage inflation (and deflation). For a first reason, it was recognized that the effect of the deep cuts in the base rate and dependent interest rates would take up to two years to materialize. For another, with interest rates already at 0.5%, there was no plan to go below zero. Accordingly, by March 2009, the MPC voted to start the process of "quantitative easing" (QE). Money would be injected directly into the economy under the Asset Purchase Facility (APF). How it works: the Bank buys mainly government securities and a little of private sector high-quality bonds. The programme started with GBP 75 billion. As at February 2016, the total amount which the Bank dedicated to quantitative easing had risen to GBP 375 billion.

Another non-conventional tool introduced by the Bank of England was "Forward Guidance" (FG). The Bank committed itself to keeping interest rates low for a prolonged period of time as a way of giving assurance of the credibility of its stimulative stance. More importantly, in the FG statement the Bank pledged not to raise the Bank Rate from the 5 percent level and to stand ready to undertake further assets purchases (QE), while the unemployment level remained above 7 percent and if it judges that additional monetary stimulus was required. In particular, the Bank pledged not to reduce the stock of asset purchases financed by the issuance of central bank reserves and, would, therefore, re-invest the cash flows from maturing securities held in the APF. All these measures added up to give a clear picture of a stable future, thereby engendering confidence in the economy thereby reinforcing the essence of "forward guidance".

Yet an important subtle point lies behind all the inflation management manoeuvring. While price stability or low inflation is the primary target of monetary policy, it still revolves around the overall goal of the economy, which is sustained economic growth and higher employment. Therefore, the obsession of monetary policy with inflation is driven by the assumption that price stability is a most important condition for sustained economic growth. It is in this context that the then Chancellor of the Exchequer, George Osborne had in his March 2013 budget speech given the MPC more discretion to "trade off" inflation above the target rate, in the medium-term in order to boost other economic indicators.

8.4   More on Letters and Reports

The rituals of letters and reports are an integral part of the accountability, transparency and credibility credo of the Bank of England. First, at the beginning of each fiscal year, the Chancellor of the Exchequer writes letter to the Governor of the Bank of England confirming the inflation target and the Bank's remit for monetary policy. Second, if inflation deviates from the target by more than 1% in either direction, the Governor is required to send an open letter to the Chancellor explaining why the deviation occurred, what action the Bank is taking to bring inflation back to target and an estimate of the how long it will take to achieve the restoration to target. Thirdly, the Chancellor will reply the Governor with an open letter of his own. Samples of these letters in 2016 (the remit letter, one letter from the Governor explaining the deviation of inflation from target, and the response to it from the Chancellor) are shown in Appendices D, E, and F. In some years, there could be several such letters and replies about inflation. Indeed as at end of August 2016, there had been three sets of such to-and-fro letters on inflation.

CHAPTER NINE

The U.S.A Federal Reserve System and Monetary Policy

In the United States, the central bank is the Federal Reserve System, founded by Congress in 1913 and charged with the responsibility to provide safer, more flexible and more stable monetary and financial system. The Board of Governors, located in Washington D.C, provides leadership for the system. The Board consists of seven governors appointed by the President and confirmed by the Senate. The members serve 14-year terms which are staggered to ensure stability and continuity. Each of the chairman and vice-chairman is appointed from among the seven members for a four-year term and may be reappointed, subject to term limitations.

9.1 The Federal Reserve Network

The Federal Reserve System consists of twelve regional Reserve Banks and twenty-four branches. The Reserve Banks are the operating arms of the central bank and all under the general oversight of the Board of Governors. The Reserve Banks serve the banks, the treasury, and, indirectly the general public. The banks are named after the location of their headquarters, namely: Boston, New York, Philadelphia, Cleveland, Richmond, Atlanta, Chicago, St. Louis, Minneapolis, Kansas City, Dallas and San Francisco. The Reserve Banks supervise commercial banks in their regions, handle Treasury payments and sell government securities. They also assist the treasury with cash management and investment activities.

A striking characteristic of the Federal Reserve System's organisational architecture is that it captures private sector or business perspective. Each Reserve Bank has a board of directors which oversees the management of activities in the district and whose members contribute local business experience, as well as community involvement. The board of each Reserve Bank appoints its president and vice-president subject to approval by the Board of Governors. Another interesting entrepreneurial feature of the Federal Reserve System is that all member banks hold stock in the Reserve Banks (3 percent of their capital) and receive dividends. But the stocks are not traded. About 38 percent of the over 8,000 commercial banks in the US (as at 2016) are members of the Federal Reserve System. While national banks must be members, state chartered banks can only be members if they meet certain requirements.

9.2   Non-Member Financial Institutions

In addition to member banks of the Federal Reserve System, there are thousands of other depository institutions which provide checking and other banking services to the economy. These include non-member commercial banks, savings banks, savings and loans associations, and credit unions. These non-members are still subject to system regulation: they maintain reserve requirements and have access to the payment services of the Federal Reserve System.

9.3   Functions of the Board of Governors

The Board's most important responsibility is to participate in the Federal Open Market Committee (FOMC), which conducts the US monetary policy and consists of the seven governors and five presidents of the Reserve Banks. Other responsibilities of the Board apart from guiding monetary policy action, include: analyzing domestic and international economic and financial conditions; leading committees to conduct studies current issues such as consumer banking laws and electronic commerce; exercising supervision over the financial service industry; overseeing the payments system; overseeing activities of reserve banks, including approving the appointments of their presidents and some members of their boards of directors; setting reserve requirements for depository institutions; and, approving changes in discount rates recommended by Reserve Banks.

Board Members testify before Congress from time to time and maintain regular contact with other government agencies. The Chairman of the Board reports two times in a year to Congress on Fed's monetary policy objectives and meets periodically with the Secretary of the Treasury. The Federal Reserve Act requires the Federal Reserve Board to submit written reports to Congress on discussion of the conduct of monetary policy and economic development and future prospects. Such report is semi-annually to be submitted to the Senate Committee on Banking Housing and Urban Affairs and to the House Committee on Financial Services. The Monetary Policy Report is to be submitted with "Testimony" from the Chairman of the Federal Reserve Board.

9.4 The Federal Open Market Committee (FOMC)

The FOMC is the Fed's monetary policy making organ and its responsibility is to manage money supply in such a way as to promote stable prices and economic growth. The committee's voting members are the seven Governors of the Board, the president of the Federal Reserve Bank of New York, and four other presidents of the remaining Reserve Banks, who serve on a rotating basin. The Chairman of FOMC is the Chairman of the Board of Governors. All Reserve Bank presidents participate in FOMC policy discussions, whether or not they are current voting members. The FOMC meets eight times a year in Washington, D.C. to discuss the outlook for the US economy and monetary policy options. The interdependence and synergy arising from the Fed's governance structure – Board of Governors, twelve Reserve Banks, regional bank directors who are close to, and who gather invaluable information from, communities and private sectors – should be expected to produce robust and efficacious monetary policy decisions. By implementing effective monetary policy, the objective of the Fed is to maintain stable prices, thereby creating the conditions for long-term economic growth and maximum employment.

9.5 Process of FOMC Meetings

The routine steps are as follows:

i). A senior official of the Federal Reserve Bank of New York discusses developments in the financial and foreign exchange markets, along with the details of the activities of the New York Fed's Domestic and Foreign Trade Desks since the previous FOMC meeting.

ii). Senior staff members from the Board of Governors (BOG) present their economic and financial forecast.

iii). Governors and Reserve Bank presidents, including those who do not have current voting power present their views on the economic outlook.

iv). The BOG's director of monetary affairs discusses monetary policy options but without making a policy recommendation.

v). The FOMC members discuss their policy preferences.

vi). The FOMC votes.

While the presidents of the Federal Reserves discuss regional conditions in their presentations, when it comes to voting on policies, they base it on national rather than local conditions. After each FOMC meeting, the Committee issues a statement which includes the federal funds rate with an explanation of the decision. The statement also discloses the vote tally, including the names of the voters and the preferred actions of those who had dissenting votes. The minutes of the meetings are published three weeks after each meeting and are made public. While the FOMC meeting statutorily holds eight times in a year, developments may warrant it to make a change in monetary policy between meetings.

For implementation, the Committee issues a directive to the New York Fed's Domestic and Foreign Trade Desk to guide the implementation of the Committee's policy through open market operations. But before conducting the open market operations, the expert analysts at Federal Reserve Bank of New York need to have a reliable gauge of how much to be added to or drained from the reserves: for this purpose they hold talks with banks and other parties and collect and analyze data. They then proceed to confer with Fed officials at Washington, D.C., who do their own independent analysis to reach a consensus about the size and terms of the operations. Following this, a New York Fed official sends out messages to the primary dealers to indicate the Fed's intention to buy or sell securities, and the dealers submit bids or offers as may be applicable.

9.6 Inflation Management by FOMC

As in most economies, the most important decision of the FOMC has to do with the rate of inflation rate to be aimed at. The subsisting rate was decided by FOMC in January 2012, when it considered that an inflation rate of 2 percent (as measured by the annual change in the Personal

Consumption Expenditure, PCE) is most consistent over the longer-run with the Federal Reserve's mandate for price stability and maximum employment. A higher inflation rate would reduce the public's ability to make accurate longer-term economic and financial decisions, while a lower inflation rate would be associated with a heightened risk of falling into deflation. Therefore, the FOMC implements monetary policy to help maintain an inflation rate of 2 percent over the medium term.

9.7 Tools for Influencing Money Supply

The Fed has three main tools for influencing money supply: open market operations, the discount rate, and reserve requirements. The Fed buys and sells U.S. government securities in the financial market, thereby influencing the value of reserves in the banking system and, consequently, money supply. These operations also affect the volume and cost of credit, or interest rate. By setting the discount rate, which is the interest rate depository banks pay on short-term loans from the Fed, the Fed announces, by action, the change in its monetary policy – expansionary if the discount rate is lowered or contractionary, if the discount rate is raised. The Fed's goal in open market operations is to affect the federal funds rate – the rate at which banks borrows reserves from each other. The Federal Open Market Committee (FOMC) sets a target for this rate but the actual rate is determined in the open market. The discount rate is usually lower than the Fed Funds rate – the rate at which banks borrows from one another's reserve balances at the Fed, in order to satisfy the reserve requirement. The reserve requirement is the amount of physical funds that the depository institutions (banks and credit unions) are required to hold in reserve against deposits by customers in bank accounts. It requires a bank to hold only a fraction of its deposit liability in reserve and such a fraction or percentage is set by the Board of Governors of the Fed. Whatever is not in reserves can be lent out by banks. Therefore, by setting the reserve requirement and influencing credit, the Fed controls money supply.

9.8 Relationship between the Federal Reserve and the Treasury Department

While the Federal Reserve was established in 1913, the Department of the Treasury was established much earlier in 1789. According to Lisa Smith (2014), the Treasury's mission is to "serve the American people and strengthen national security by managing the U.S. government's finances effectively, promoting economic growth and stability and ensuring the safety, soundness and security of the U.S. safety, soundness and security of the U.S. and international financial system". It is a duty of the U.S. Treasury to advice the President of the U.S. The Treasury is responsible for printing currency and minting coins. So one can notice an area of close and special relationship with the Federal Reserve, which is responsible for monetary policy and for determining the level of money supply.

The Federal Reserve serves as a the central bank of the U.S., serves as the banker to the U.S. government and serves to keep the U.S. money valuable and the financial system healthy. Therefore, the Treasury and the Federal Reserve work together to maintain a stable economy. The two institutions work together to borrow money when government needs to raise cash: on behalf of the Treasury, the Federal Reserve issues U.S. Treasury securities, conducts the auction, sells the securities and effect the settlements involved in the transactions.

The Federal Reserve also serves as a revenue source for the Treasury. As the Federal Reserve is non-profit company, after meeting its expenses, operating surpluses are paid to the Department of Treasury, which then utilizes the funds to settle government spending. This source of funding for the Treasury is quite substantial and was about USD 26 billion in 2006.

To fight recession, the two entities cooperate to formulate and implement economic policies designed to stimulate the economy. The Federal Reserve would cut interest rates to make more money available to banks and consumers for increased lending and spending, thereby stimulating aggregate economic activity. At the micro-economic level, the Fed and the Treasury also do cooperate to help prevent the collapse of government-sponsored enterprises, such as was done in the cases of Fannie Mae and Freddie Mac, through bailout operations in September 2008. The Fed provides access to funds at a discounted borrowing rate, while the Treasury could provide a line of credit to them or even purchase their stocks. Such bailout support could also be extended to private corporations. An example was the loan of about USD 29 billion provided by the two entities to facilitate JP Morgan's purchase of Bear Sterns in March 2008.

9.9   Printing of Money and Money Supply

The Treasury Department, not the Federal Reserve Bank, is responsible for printing money and minting coins, using the Bureau of Engraving and Printing (BEP).

In a fractional reserve system, one of the expected business behaviours is that some depositors will request cash withdrawals. Accordingly, depository banks must keep a supply of cash available. When banks consider that they need more cash than they have in stock, they make requests for cash with the Federal Reserve. The Federal Reserve examines the requests and places an order for printed money with the Treasury Department. The Treasury Department submits the request to the Bureau of Engraving and Printing – to make the paper money – and the Bureau of the Mint – to stamp the coins. When the newly printed money is ready, the U.S. Treasury sells it to the Federal Reserve for the cost of printing. But part of the newly printed money is replacement for discarded old money (worn-out, counterfeit) while part is new money. For new money, in addition for cost of printing, the Treasury requires the Federal Reserve to pledge collateral (typically, government securities). The Fed then distributes the printed cash to the banks as needed.

Medium- and large-sized banks usually have reserve accounts with the Reserve Banks, and they pay for the cash they get from the Fed by having their accounts debited. The smaller banks usually have their required reserve at larger banks which act as their "correspondents". The smaller banks get their cash through the correspondent banks, which charge a fee for their service.

From the foregoing, it is evident that printing money is not a money supply operation. The Federal Reserve only plays the role of distributing currency (after having acted as the ordering agent on behalf of the depository banks that need it) for the Treasury Department which prints it. Depository institutions buy currency from the Federal Reserve Banks when they need it to meet customer demand, and they deposit cash at the Fed when they have more than they need to meet customer demand.

Given this type of close cooperation between them, one can understand the anonymous description of the Fed and the Treasury as "Partners in Protection". At the macro level they work in concert to address economic weaknesses through economic stimulus and at the micro level, they collaborate by bailing out failing corporations. By so doing, the moderate the impact financial troubles would have inflicted on the economy. It could, therefore, be highlighted that while the Treasury is part of the executive arm of the U.S. government and must follow the direction of The President of the United States, the Federal Reserve is independent of the executive arm, in much the same way as the Supreme Court is. Yet the two entities work cooperatively, even if largely independently, to ensure the achievement and sustenance of price stability, economic growth and maximum employment – a prosperous economy.

9.10   Independence of the Fed

The Board of Governors is independent and summarizes the independence of the Fed: the Board operates without official obligation to accept the request or advice of any elected official with regard to actions on money supply. While the Governors are nominated by the President of the United States, the nominations must be confirmed by the Senate.

The Fed also enjoys budgetary independence: it finances its operations by accessing the Federal Reserve Banks and does not depend on Congressional appropriation. But its financial accounts are audited annually by a public accounting firm and are subject to audit by The General Accounting Office.

There is another aspect of Fed's independence vis-a-vis the United States Treasury: although the Fed buys and sells Treasury securities to influence the level of money supply, it cannot conduct the transactions directly with the Treasury Department. The Federal Reserve Act specifies that the Fed may buy or sell Treasury securities only in the "Open Market", which means in the secondary market, and this happens mainly with major financial companies called primary dealers who buy from or sell directly to, the Treasury. The exclusion of direct securities transactions between the Fed and the Treasury supports the Fed's independence of the Treasury in the conduct of monetary policy.

9.11 Unconventional Monetary Policy in the United States

The rise of unconventional monetary policy in the United States of America could be traced to severe dislocations in the financial sector which led to the Great Recession from late 2007 to mid 2009. Weaknesses in the United Sates' financial regulation created problems in the mortgage market which spiralled into the global financial crisis.

There was general collapse in the prices of the United States real estate and a litter of mortgage defaults. Financial markets, which were tied to the mortgages, the so-called "mortgage-backed securities (MBS) became dysfunctional. The market had used the securities as collaterals and in derivatives. The headline impacts included the collapse of Lehman Brothers and the near-collapse of other United States financial institutions in the second half of 2008. The extreme challenges of the time stimulated new responses from the monetary authority in the United States. As Ben S. Bernanke, the Chairman of the Federal Reserve Bank from 2016 to 2014 noted in a 2015 article in Money and Banking magazine, what is different about unconventional monetary policy is that:

i). The new tools which leading central banks came to rely on since the Great Financial Crisis were introduced mainly because policymakers could no longer rely on short-term nominal interest rates.

ii). Despite the experiences gained in experimenting with the new tools over the years, certainty as to how the application of the new tools affects financial conditions and the overall economy is less compared to the case with conventional short-term interest rate policy.

The unconventional monetary policy tools fall into three categories:

i). Targeted Asset Purchases (TAP);
ii). Quantitative Easing (QE); and,
iii). Forward Guidance (FG).

9.11.1   TAP

TAP involves a change in the mix of central bank assets, while keeping the size of the balance sheet and supply of reserves unchanged. The aim is to alter the relative prices of different assets. Essentially, it involves shifting the traditional domination of the Federal Reserve's balance sheet by short-term government debts in favour of other assets.

Early in history in the 19th century, the Fed had intervened during crisis to prevent or moderate financial panic through central bank lending. But the Fed seemed to have failed to respond similarly during the Great Depression which started in 1929. Indeed, Milton Friedman and Anna Schwartz (1963) blame the Fed for not using their lending power in the 1933 banking crisis. So Fed did not want to repeat its mistake during the Great Recession. It responded aggressively in its lending to commercial banks and other financial institutions by buying securities off them, while not changing the size of its asset holdings. For example, in the aftermath of the run on Bear Sterns in March 2008, the Fed increased its lending to investment banks and other distressed financial institutions but at the same time lowered its holding of short-term Treasury securities. Also, between 2011 and 2012, the Fed executed its maturity extension programme, by which it sold short- and medium-term Treasuries and used the proceeds to purchase long-term treasuries in an attempt to flatten the yield curve.

Some deeper points of TAP include:

i). Apart from elongating the maturity profile of the markets, the operations demonstrated how a central bank can intermediate to substitute for the drop in private sector intermediation in times of crisis.

ii). The Fed's purchases of MBS injected much-needed liquidity in a market that had stopped working. These interventions from late 2008 to early 2009 narrowed the MBS yield spread above the yield on the Treasury securities; such a rotation of the relative yield path revived the MBS market. Bernanke (2015) has noted that similarly in the Eurozone, the European Central Bank's purchases (and promises to purchase) of debts of "peripheral sovereigns" under stress narrowed their yield spreads over German debt, from their peak in 2012: this significantly helped to prevent contagion, even when widespread expectation of the exit of Greece from the euro heightened uncertainty.

But as Bernanke aptly observed, TAP as a policy tool is not free of problems. First, by design it favours assets with one set of liquidity, maturity and default characteristics over others. In the United States, Fed favoured MBS; in Japan, the Bank of Japan favoured corporate liabilities; and, in the Eurozone, the ECB, favoured one country's sovereign debt over another. As a result, TAP has considerable distributional affects with significant fiscal policy impact. This poses a possible risk to central bank independence and could jeopardise, or at the minimum compromise, the monetary authority's long-run effectiveness of achieving economic stability objectives. Second, given that TAP involves the purchase of assets which are usually less liquid than short-term government securities, there is a risk that the assets could be difficult to sell when the central bank wishes to tighten monetary policy; what that means is that the new structure of the central bank's balance sheet could impair traditional open market operations.

Nevertheless, TAP seemed to have effectively run its course. Long-term lending under TAP increased sharply to a peak in 2008, then declined sharply. At the end of the Great Recession, total lending was about one-half of its level in the last quarter of 2008 and by the beginning of 2013, lending had tapered to return to the pre-Great Recession levels.

It should be noted that as the crisis lending proceeded, the Fed simultaneously used conventional interest rate policy to address the financial crisis. Commencing from late 2007, the Fed's target overnight rate was cut progressively to reach near-zero levels by the end of 2008 when the Federal Funds rate was set at a target range of 0 to 0.25 percent. By the end of Great Recession in mid-June 2009, both the financial crisis and the emerging lending that was pursuing its stoppage were over. However, given that the Great Recession was deep, recovery was going to take long. As a result, the interest rate policy was maintained at a target range of 0 to 0.25 percent. In addition, the Fed had begun experimenting with the two other unconventional policy tools: quantitative easing and forward guidance.

9.11.2 Quantitative Easing

Then TAP was followed by quantitative easing (QE) - rapid expansion of Fed's balance sheet - as follows: QE1 started around November 2008 and March 2009; QE2 in November 2010; and QE3 in September 2012. While QE1 and QE3 involved purchases of mortgage backed securities (MBS), QE2 focused on buying long-term securities. QE by the Fed involved expansion of its balance sheet through increased reserves beyond the level needed to attain the conventional target policy rate. The reserve of course, is simply the deposits of commercial banks at the central bank. As many analyses such as those by the Federal reserve bank of St. Louis have noted, the use of monetary authority's balance sheet to influence the quantity of money and credit in the system are as old as central banking. However, QE is different and new in the sense that it involves the purchase of unconventional assets aiming at goals that are more or less unconventional. Asset purchases per se had been conventional tools, since the founding of the FOMC in 1933. Open market operations (OMO) have been using the buying and selling of short-term government securities to guide the overnight federal funds rate towards the target set by the Committee. But QE was carried out when the federal funds interest rate are already near or at zero and involves the purchase, not of short-term government securities, but of long-term assets (including 30-year Treasury Bonds) some of which need not be government-issued, for example mortgage assets. The goal of QE is to lower interest rates on long-term assets, rather than lower short-term interest rates as is the case with conventional open market operations.

The Fed began QE1 in November 2008, that is, before the end of the Great Recession. Recovery from the Great Recession based on TAP interventions was slow. Compared to recovery following the recession of 1981-1982, the recovery from the Great Recession was 20 percent slower. (Federal Reserve Bank of St. Louis, 2015). This outlook, even after the initial application of some unconventional policies agitated the Fed to engage in further monetary accommodation. However, the federal funds rate was in the 0 to 0.25 percent range, so that there was no remaining accommodative options other than additional policies. The FOMC kept the federal funds rate close to zero for seven years under the zero-interest policy (ZIRP). The Great Recession officially ended in June 2009 but Fed continued with QE policies. QE1, which had started in

November 2008, continued until March 2010. In August 2010, the FOMC established the reinvestment programme replacing long-term assets in Fed's portfolio as they matured, so as to prevent undoing of the balance sheet restructuring. This policy subsisted into 2016. In November 2010, QE2 started and lasted to June 2011. It succeeded in purchasing USD600 billion in long-term treasuries. There was also the intrusion of the "Twist" programme from September 2011 to December 2012, under which the Fed sold short-term assets and bought long-term assts so as to lengthen the average maturity of the assets in its balance sheet. QE3 ran from September 2012 to October 2014. It conducted large-scale purchases of mortgage-backed securities and long-term Treasuries.

Prior to the QE operations, the Fed held one third of its total securities assets in the form of short-term Treasuries; by the end of the QE, the short-term Treasury holdings were zero. Before the 2007 financial crisis, reserve balances ranged between USD 5 billion and USD 10 billion but by January 2016, reserve balances were at a level of USD 2.4 trillion and bore interest at 0.25percent, initially and the rate was raised to 0.5 percent in December 2015. (Federal Reserve Bank of St. Louis, 2015)

It is worth highlighting that QE was first discussed and implemented in 2001 by the Bank of Japan (BOJ). In 2001, Japan had been operating zero interest rate policy (ZIRP). But BOJ discovered the liquidity trap, thus: with ZIRP in place, an open market purchase of short-term government debts by the central bank should have no effect because zero-interest bank reserves were replacing zero-interest government debt in the financial markets. Therefore, for the purchases to have the desired effect, they should target unconventional assets that are not liabilities of the government.

How big are the numbers of asset purchase under QE? Between 2008 and 2015, the United States Fed bought bonds worth USD 3.7 trillion. Between 2009 and 2012, the Bank of England bought bonds worth GBP 375 billion (USD 550 billion). Between January 2015 and August 2016, the European central Bank (ECB) bought bonds worth Euro 1.004 trillion. For an early-history assessment of and lessons from the exercise, Bernanke's remarks' are pertinent:

i). The fear and criticism that QE2 was risking currency debasement and high inflation has not been corroborated by the actual outcomes. By the end of QE3, although Fed's balance sheet was about five times as large as its mid-2007 size, as at 2015, the United States dollar's value was at its highest point in a decade; moreover, inflation remained below the 2 percent target.

ii). Where the central bank pays interest on reserves, as the Fed did since October 2008, the quantity of central bank money (sum of reserves and currency in circulation) becomes a poor indicator of broad money growth and inflation and value of the currency.

iii). When the financial system is under serious pressure, policymakers should not worry about inflation. Rather, they should saturate the banking system with reserves to prevent a collapse of credit to the real sector.

But Bernanke also widely indicated that those were still early days in the observation of the full ramifications of the implications of QE "consequences" for economic systems.

Indeed, it is plausible to contend that QE escalates the complexity of empirical investigation of, and policy design for, inflation. As unconventional monetary policy drags the monetary authority beyond price and macroeconomic stability into the sphere of direct real economy management, it will be confronted with challenges regarding the configuration of the aggregate output that results from such intervention. And, this is the set of issues that occupied the attention of Part I of the book.

9.11.3   Forward Guidance

Forward guidance is a form of communication by the central bank about its future path of policy rate. The message could range from a simple forecast about the economy to a strong statement about the trajectory of the economy. Unlike TAP and QE, forward guidance does not affect the size or mix of the monetary authority's balance sheet. Therefore, it could be regarded as the most conventional of the unconventional trio: it focuses on the policy rate. Unlike the other two, its use is not dependent on, and is not influenced by considerations for, the zero bound problem. Forward guidance assigns importance to, not only what the central bank is doing now, but also what it says it is going to do in the future. It has been acknowledged that even though forward guidance has been part of the Fed's policy for a long time, it was only during and after the financial crisis that it became increasingly important.

Forward guidance is essentially a tool of policy of promises by the central bank concerning its future actions. It is based on modern macroeconomic theory which postulates that monetary policy is more efficacious when the central bank behaves systematically, so that policy is well-understood by the public. The real challenge, therefore, is that Fed's promise must be credible.

An interesting perspective on forward guidance comes from the New Keynesian theory that the Fed has some policy leverage even when nominal interest rate is zero and can go no lower, since Fed can make a promise to keep interest rates lower in the future than it would otherwise be. If such a promise is credible, it would cause people to believe that inflation will be higher in the future, causing them to borrow more and spend more today to beat the more expensive future . Therefore, the New Keynesian theory recommends forward guidance as a means for central banks to stimulate the economy by promising to be "irresponsible in the future" , as the Federal Reserve Bank of St. Louis literature puts it.

CHAPTER TEN

The European Central Bank and Euro Area Monetary Policy

The European Central Bank (ECB) was established in 1998 as the monetary authority for the eurozone, which currently consists of 19 countries, namely: Austria, Belgium, Cyprus, Estonia, France, Finland, Germany, Greece, Iceland, Italy, Latvia, Lithuania, Luxemburg, Malta, Netherlands, Portugal, Slovakia, Slovenia and Spain. The Bank began to exercise its full powers on January 1, 1999 when the common currency, euro, was introduced. According to the Treaty of Maastricht which set it up, its primary purpose was to maintain price stability, while economic growth and financial stability were to be pursued as important but subsidiary goals (Micossi, 2015). Therefore, we note again that even in the case of a single monetary authority covering a diverse economic area or group of sovereign countries, the pre-eminence of price stability or control of inflation in monetary policy and duties of central banking, remains striking.

10.1 Organizational Architecture of the ECB

The Treaty of Maastritcht established the euro as the common currency of the Economic and Monetary Union under the eurozone monetary authority. The authority consists of: the National Central Banks (NCB's) of the constituent countries of the Union and the European Central Bank (ECB) at the centre; together, they constitute the European System of Central Banks (ESCB). The ECB is responsible for coordinating operations, while the NCBs are responsible for executing of transactions, such as the provision of funds to banks, settling cross-border transactions and managing foreign reserves. Subject to consultation with the European Parliament, the ECB can also exercise some prudential supervision of credit and other financial institution, with the exception of insurance companies. Based on this capacity, the Single Supervisory Mechanism (SSM) was established as a feature of the Eurosystem and consists of the ECB and the supervisory authorities of member countries.

The institutional arrangement of the monetary authority for the eurozone, apart from reflecting its primary goal which is to maintain price stability also re-echoes the cardinal principle of modern central banking of independence from political interference, in this case, by member states or supranational European institutions. In particular, it aims at avoiding connection with budgetary and other fiscal policies, to isolate it from the risk of monetization of public sector deficits. It would be pertinent to comment at this juncture, that there is a widely-shared view in monetary economic thought that independent monetary authority is an institutional correlate of price stability. The independence of the ESCB is additionally guaranteed with some specific legal and administrative provisions, viz:

i). The Treaty setting it up can only be amended by unanimous consensus of the member states;

ii). The monetary policy function is located outside national borders, thereby severing links with national fiscal policies and making the monetary authority inaccessible to national politicians.

iii). The ECB, the NCBs and members of their decision-making bodies are prohibited from seeking or receiving instructions from union institutions or national governments during their tenure of office;

iv). National legislatures are to ensure that NCBs enjoy similar independence from their respective national government;

v). The Treaty prohibits ECB from monetary financing of Union or government institutions.

Again this robust institutional configuration has its real meaning in the quest for price stability. When the monetary authority is considered as sufficiently truly independent, it will be trusted by private economic agents. Its policy pronouncements will be credible. Such credibility forms the basis for anchoring inflation expectations.

The administrative apex of the ECB, called the Executive Board consists of the President, the Vice-President and four other members appointed by the European Council. But the body responsible for the all-important monetary policy mandate is the Governing Council. It consists of the six members of the Executive Board and all the governors of the

NCBs; however, at any point in time, only 15 governors can have voting rights, meaning that since they are a total of 19 governors, a system of rotation for constituting the 15, is in place.

As the main decision-making body of the Eurosystem, the Governing Council of the ECB defines the inflation goal and the instruments of the single monetary policy of the eurozone.

10.2 Monetary Policy Instruments and Practice

ECB's monetary policy consists broadly of two components: the monetary policy strategy and the operational frameworks. The policy strategy is concerned with determining the interest rate appropriate for achieving price stability. For ECB, price stability is defined as a rate of inflation maintained below but close to 2 percent over the medium term. Inflation in the eurosystem is measured as movements in the Harmonized Index of Consumer Prices (HICP). Inflation is measured as the year-on-year increase in the HICP, which is calculated by Eurostate the eurozone statistical authority, in cooperation with member country statistical authorities. The definition of target inflation is symmetric, in the sense that it is not only inflation above 2% that is considered unacceptable but also excessively low inflation or deflations are considered incompatible with price stability. Therefore, preventing a self-sustaining fall in the HIPC is an objective of monetary policy.

As in other well-advanced central banking systems, the ECB's Governing Council attaches importance to communicating its policies and therefore, announced the above-stated quantitative definition of price stability states to the public and the expected benefits of the announcement include:

i).   To make monetary policy more transparent;
ii).   To provide a clear and measurable yardstick against which the European citizens can hold the ECB accountable;
iii).   To provide guidance to the public for forming expectations of future price developments.

In determining the policy-targeted state of inflation, the ECB considers that inflation rates of below, but close to 2% are low enough for the economy to reap the benefits of price stability. The chosen target underlines the ECB's commitment to:

i). Provide an adequate margin to avoid the risk of deflation because there are limits to how far interest rates can be cut. This makes it more difficult for monetary policy to fight deflation than to fight inflation.

ii). Take into account the possibility of HIPC inflation slightly overstating the true inflation position as a result of a small but positive bias in the measurement of price level changes using HIPC.

iii). Provide a sufficient margin to address the implications of inflation differentials in the euro area. It avoids the risk that individual countries in the zone have to structurally live with too low inflation rates or even deflation.

Before proceeding to discuss more on the monetary strategy of the ECB, it would be useful to note the economic-philosophical strands of thought on which it is based, thus:

i). As the sole issuer of bank notes and bank reserves, the ECB is the monopoly supplier of the monetary base in the eurozone. Therefore, it can set conditions at which banks can borrow from it and also influence the conditions at which banks can trade with each other in the money market.

ii). In the short-run, a change in money market interest rates induced by central bank action sets in motion a number of mechanism and reactions by economic agents, which ultimately impact developments in economic variables, prominently, output and prices, via the monetary policy transmission mechanism, a complex process that is yet to be fully understood.

iii). In the long run, that is after all relevant adjustments in the economy have worked themselves out, a change in the quantity of money in the economy will be reflected in a change in the level of prices – but will not cause permanent changes in real variables such as real output or unemployment. That is the principle of "the long-run neutrality of money", which states that real income or the level of employment are, in the long run determined by real factors such as technology, population growth or the portfolio preferences of economic agents.

iv). Inflation is, therefore, essentially a monetary phenomenon because in the long run, the central bank can only contribute to raising the growth potential of the economy by maintaining an environment of stable prices but cannot stimulate growth by expanding the money supply or keeping short-term interest rates at a level inconsistent with price stability. In the long run, it can only influence the general level of prices. Therefore, prolonged periods of high inflation are typically associated with high monetary growth and while other factors (such as changes in aggregate demand, technological changes, commodity price shocks, etc) can influence price developments over shorter horizon, over time their effect can be offset by a change in monetary policy.

The monetary strategy of ECB relies on the method of "anchoring": inflation expectations are anchored or guided by building trust and credibility around a consistent and systematic method for conducting monetary policy within a medium-term horizon. This is strengthened with "clear and open communication to the public of its goals and the underlying analysis" (Micossi, 2015:3). However, unlike the Bank of England, the ECB does not adhere to a formal inflation targeting strategy. Its response to deviations is flexible and depends on its assessment of the sources and nature of the shocks threatening the price stability. For example, recognizing that financial stability has implications for output and price stability, in responding to deviation from the inflation target, the ECB considers the implication of its response for financial stability as well.

The operational framework of the ECB consists of the set of instruments and procedures employed for achieving the desired interest rate. The instruments are:

i).   Open market operations;
ii). Standing facilities;
iii). Minimum reserve requirements for credit institutions.

However, since 2009, the ECB has implemented some unconventional monetary policy measures such as asset purchase programmes to complement the standard operations. All the instruments derive from the Legal Framework for Monetary Policy of the Eurosystem, which consists of series of guidelines and decisions.

The monetary policy framework encourages the participation of a broad range of counterparties. Therefore, for outright transactions, no restrictions are placed on the composition of counterparties. However, access to open market operations and standing facilities is available only to institutions which are subject to minimum reserve requirements. These transactions are based on standard tenders.

10.2.1 Open Market Operations

The ECB uses open market operations to guide interest rates, manage liquidity in the market and signal the monetary policy stance. The Eurosystem uses five financial instruments in the open market operations. These are: reverse transaction (conducted as repurchase agreement or collateralized loan) outright transaction, issuance of debt certificate, foreign exchange swaps and collection of fixed-term deposits.

There are four types of open market operations, which differ in terms of aims, regularity and procedure. Main refinancing operations (MROs) are regular liquidity-providing reverse transactions conducted by the Eurosystem. The frequency and maturity is usually one week. They are executed by the NCBs on the basis of standard tenders and based on indicative issuance calendar published on the ECB's website. It is the main source of providing refinancing to the financial sector. The MROs are the principal monetary policy instrument and their interest rate is the key official reference rate. Longer-term refinancing operations (LTROs) are similar to the MROs but with a longer maturity of usually three months. They are conducted monthly by the Eurosystem on the basis of standard tenders and in line with published indicative calendar. The Eurosystem could also conduct non-regular longer-term refinancing operations with maturities of up to 48 months (Targeted Longer Term Refinancing Operations – TLTROs, to serve special purposes. Fine-tuning operations (FTOs) are executed on ad-hoc basis to manage liquidity in the market and steer interest rates, mainly under conditions of unexpected fluctuations in interest rates. They are usually executed as reverse transactions or foreign exchange swaps or the collection of fixed deposits. The instrument and procedures of choice are detailed by the specific objectives being pursued. They are usually conducted through quick tenders or bilateral procedures.

Structural operations are executed whenever the ECB wishes to adjust the structural position of the Eurosystem vis-a-vis the financial sector. They are carried out by the Eurosystem through reverse transactions, and issuance of debt certificates, using standard tenders. Or, they could be executed through bilateral procedures if they are in the form of outright transactions.

10.2.2   Standing Facilities

The aim of standing facilities is to provide and absorb overnight liquidity, while signalling the general monetary policy stance and targeted overnight money market interest rates. The standing facilities are administered in a decentralized arrangement by the NCBs and are of two types: marginal lending facility and deposit facility. For marginal lending facility, counterparties obtain overnight liquidity from the NCBs against eligible assets. The interest rate on the marginal lending facility normally provides a ceiling for the overnight market interest rate. For Deposit facility, counterparties place their deposits overnight with the NCBs and earn an interest rate which normally provides a floor for the overnight market interest.

10.2.3   Minimum Reserves

Like in other central-banking jurisdictions, minimum reserves are an integral part of the operational framework for monetary policy in the eurozone. Accordingly, the European Central Bank requires credit institutions to hold compulsory deposits on accounts with the national central banks. The purpose of the minimum reserve system is to stabilize money market interest rates and to create a structural liquidity shortage in the banks so as to strengthen the ECB's ability to steer rates with open market operations. The reserve requirement of each financial institution is dependent on the elements of its balance sheet. The minimum reserve system of the Eurosystem enables institutions to make use of averaging positions: compliance with the reserve requirement is determined on the basis of the institutions average daily reserve holdings in current accounts with the NCBs over a maintenance period of about one month, the required reserve holding determined by multiplying the reserve base with the reserve ratio are remunerated at a level corresponding to the average interest rate of the MROs of the Eurosystem over the maintenance period; this rate is close to the short-term money market rates. With this near-market remuneration structure, the Eurosystem tries to ensure that the minimum reserve system does not put a pressure on the banking system but at the same time does not hinder efficient allocation of resources.

The reserve bases used to calculate the amount of required reserves include deposits of various maturities, debt securities, and money market papers. Categorized ratios or reserve coefficients are applied to liabilities of different maturities – short-term or long-term. For example, for the maintenance period starting January 18, 2012, the Eurosystem reserve requirement was as follows:

i). 1 percent for overnight deposits, deposit with agreed maturity or period of notice up to 2 years, debt securities issued with maturity up to 2 years and money market paper;

ii). 0 percent for deposits with agreed maturity or period of notice over 2 years, repos and debt securities issued with maturity over 2 years.

Interbank liabilities involving Eurosystem credit institutions, liabilities to the ECB and the euro area NCBs are excluded. It is apparent from the distribution of the reserve coefficient that the purpose of the requirement is to guarantee liquidity to satisfy obligations to depositors.

10.2.4   Overview

The Eurosystem monetary policy operations consist mainly of bank refinancing facilities dominated by reverse transactions, supported with eligible collaterals. The refinancing facilities comprise the short-term MROs and the long-term LTROs, fine-tuning operations, issuance of ECB debt certificates and standing facilities. Given the complex architecture of a 19-member monetary union, reliance on reverse transactions by the ECB in money policy operations helps it to minimize market and credit risks. As noted earlier, the MROs are the main monetary policy instrument and interest rates charged on them serve as the main official reference rates. The rate charged on marginal lending, which is the facility available overnight for unlimited amounts but against eligible and adequate collateral sets the ceiling for the overnight money rate; on the other hand, the rate paid on banks' deposits in the standing deposit facility sets the floor for the overnight money rate. These two limits provide the corridor within which the overnight money market rate fluctuates. The average of the overnight rates across the Eurozone, the Eurozone overnight index average (EONIA) is the reference overnight rate.

10.2.5   *Emergency Liquidity Assistance (ELA)*

In addition to the ECB-owned instruments, the NCBs establish and use lines of emerging liquidity assistance (ELA) to support individual banks facing temporary liquidity problems. This could be in the form of providing central bank money or any other assistance that may lead to an increase in central bank money. Such operation is not part of the single monetary policy. Therefore, responsibility for ELA rests on the respective NCB's who bear any costs and risk, therefrom. However, it is required of each NCB to fully and timely inform ECB of the beneficiaries, size and tenor of any ELA granted. Moreover, the Governing Council of the ECB has the power to restrict the operations of ELA if it is judged to be detrimental to monetary policy activities of the Eurosystem.

10.3 Issues in the Practice of Conventional Monetary Policy in Eurozone

An insightful account of the practice of monetary policy by the ECB has been provided by Stefano Micossi (2015). The overall lesson is that in addition to the usual challenges faced by monetary authorities in trying to attain their primary objectives, while not neglecting other objectives beyond acceptable limits, the ECB has had to grapple with the challenges of implementing a common set of policies, for a number of economies at varying stages of development, with a common currency, the euro, being perhaps the only common economic denominator.

The above assertion is supported by the highlights of the euro zone experience as follows:

i). Alternation of contractionary and expansionary monetary policy stances were deployed to influence interest rates and ultimately inflation, while not neglecting the goals of output growth and employment. For example, as inflation increased from below 1%

in the early 1999 to above 2%, and to over 3% in May 2001, the MRO reference rate was raised by 225 basis points to 4.75% from November 1999 to October, 2000. But when the dot.com stock market crash of early 2000s threw the world economy into a recession, the ECB monetary stance changed to expansionary up till 2006: between early 2001 and June 2003, the reference rate was lowered by 275 basis points. It was brought down to 2% despite rapid acceleration in the main monetary aggregate. Even though inflation tended to exceed its medium-term target of 2%, there was some policy attraction to easy money with the expectation it would help recovery. Thus, the provision of the Treaty on the Functioning of the European Union (TFEU), which requires that once price stability is assured, the ESCB "shall support the general economic policies in the Union" was put to practice.

ii). The development around monetary conditions differed between the core countries (such as Germany and France) and the periphery countries (such as Portugal, Ireland, Italy, Greece and Spain – PIIGIS) of the eurozone. Whether the eurozone is in the expansionary phase or the contractionary phase, the periphery exhibits much greater fluctuations than the core.

iii). The timing of ECB monetary policy stance tends to be biased in favour of the core, understandably, given that the core accounts for about 70% of the eurozone total economy.

Hence, Micossi (2015:9) speaks of:

> ....the main turning points of ECB policy stance, which clearly respond to monetary development in the centre, but on occasion, seem less felicitous in view of the periphery economic conditions. For instance, the turn to restriction in 2006 does not arrive till credit accelerates in Germany but probably too late to slow excessive credit growth in the periphery. In two instances in 2008 and 2011, the ECB raised interest rates at the wrong time, in view of rapidly falling credit growth in the periphery, but probably consistent with developments in Germany. Similarly, the decline in interest rates in 2011 and 2012 was less aggressive than would have been justified by plummeting credit growth in the periphery.

It is obvious that the ECB faces the challenge of using a single instrument in a particular period for at least two sets of economies with momentums that are not synchronized. The divergence could conceivably be as a result of structural differences, reflecting different stages of development, including institutions at different levels of technical maturity, as well as differences in the sophistication of behaviour of various economic agents. In addition, it would be a specific case, of information asymmetry in the markets in the two sets of economies.

Micossi concludes that while monetary policy was about right in the core of the Eurozone during much of the period, 2002 – 2015, it "was strongly pro-cyclical in the periphery, where it accommodated and indeed fed the build-up of imbalances up until mid 2000s, and then amplified deflationary forces after the inception of the financial crisis"(p.11).

A question that could be relevant is: if, and, to what extent, the pro-cyclical bias for the periphery, inherent in ECBs monetary stance, contributes to the "overshooting" of monetary aggregates in those disadvantaged economies. Although it is understandable to expect that the sharp variations should arise from the structural deficiencies, it is conceivable that the impact of repeated boots of pro-cyclicality would reinforce and exacerbate the divergence.

10.4 Unconventional Monetary Policies by the ECB

In his speech at the Central Bank Symposium in Jackson Hole on August 22, 2014, the President of the ECB, Mario Draghi signalled powerfully that the monetary authority was moving from passive monetary accommodation to active expansionary posture. The ECB had tended to be less aggressive compared to other major central banks as reflected in its consistently lower pace of interest rate reductions during the great financial crisis. In the speech, Draghi indicated that demand side policies were justified by among other conditions, the existence of hysteresis effect. Hysteresis is a condition of the possibility that periods of high unemployment tend to increase the rate-of-unemployment-below-which-inflation-begins-to-accelerate. In order words, it is a condition in which the existing depth of unemployment raises the natural rate of unemployment or the non-accelerating inflation rate of unemployment: while unemployment is still high, inflation will set in, in contradiction to the Phillips curve proposition. Draghi, then argued for monetary policy to play a central role in supporting demand.

In line with the new stance, over the summer of 2014, the ECB effected significant lowering of interest rates on MROs, deposit facilities and marginal lending facility. The ECB also announced a new series of Targeted Long-term Refinancing Operations (TLTROs), which were tied to the provision of credit to the real economy. These had a tenor of up to four years, hence signalling ECBs commitment to long-term goals of the monetary zone. But the result was unimpressive. The take-up was low such that by the fourth quarter of 2014, the total liquidity provided by the ECB to the banking system actually declined, demonstrating that demand for credit was still weak. Indeed, what happened was that the banks used the proceeds of the new facility to refinance existing financing lines at more favourable terms, while shying away from new borrowing from the ECB. Again, persistent on pursuing its new ambitious dream, the ECB took bold steps to encourage greater lending to the private sector: in the last quarter of 2014, it launched two private sector asset purchase programmes: an asset-backed securities purchase programme (ABSPP) and a new covered-bond purchase programme (CBPP3). The new programmes had a tenor of two years.

But the economy of the Eurozone continued to weaken while the inflation rate headed into a negative average for the zone in December 2014. Under this extreme condition, the ECB Governing Council was conditioned to foray into quantitative easing. In January 2015, it announced that under an expanded asset purchase programme, (EAPP) the ESCB would purchase private and government securities worth euro 60 billion per month. This evolution to radicalism of the ECB needs to be understood in its market-inducing context.

In the wake of the Lehman failure and the Eurozone sovereign debt crisis, such measures as the Securities Market Programme (SMP) and the Very Long-term Refinancing Operations (VLTROs), which were employed to repair segments of the market that had been impaired could be classified as "unconventional". But they were essentially an extension of the conventional lending-of-last-resort function of the central banks and would be more appropriately termed "credit easing" rather than quantitative easing (Bini Smaghi, 2009). The introduction had nothing to do with responding to lower bound interest rates, which had not yet occurred. On the other hand, the policies taken to address the challenge of lower interest rate bound fill squarely into the categorization of quantitative easing (Fawley and Neely, 2013).

The conventional logic of monetary policy is to set a target for the overnight interbank interest rate or money market rate and achieve that target simply by adjusting the supply of money by the central bank. However, when short-term interest rates have been pressed down to near zero, any further attempts to lower short rates will mean going into the region of negative short-term rates. Since the public would rather hold cash rather than accept negative yield on their deposits, the normal transmission mechanism from lower interest rates to higher aggregate demand for consumption and investment becomes impotent. The option left to the central bank stimulate the economy and inflation is to push down long-term interest rates, given that long-term rates would usually remain positive even after short-term rates have fallen to zero.

The transmission channels are essentially two. One is through forward guidance: by committing to a protracted period of low policy rates, the central bank influences both interest rate and inflation rate expectations. The second route is for the central bank to attempt to directly alter the price of long-term securities by purchasing them outright and thereby agitating asset substitution in private portfolios; hence portfolio balance effect. The overall impact in both cases is to flatten the yield curve because the price of the long-term assets rises, while their yields falls as more of them are purchased. The change in relative prices is sufficient to trigger asset substitution in line with the basic economic principle of marginal equivalence. Thus, activity returns to the financial market.

As noted earlier, the ECB's Mr. Draghi had in January 2016, announced the Governing Council's decision to embark on monetary expansion. The ECB stepped up purchases of asset-backed securities and covered bonds (which involved assets purchases worth euro 10 billion per month) and introduced the public sector bonds purchase programme (PSPP) under which the Eurosystem would purchase euro 50 billion of securities in the secondary market from March 2015 to September 2016. The new asset purchase package totalling euro 60 billion per month was known as expanded asset purchase programme (EAPP). More importantly, the ECB introduced an element of forward guidance into the expectations equation by committing to continue with the purchase if the rate of inflation did not adjust in a manner consistent with the medium-term target of "below, but close to, 2%". The planned public sector purchase is a total of euro 950billion over the 19-month period.

It is relevant to note that the refreshed euro 10 billion per month asset backed securities purchase programme (ABSPP) and covered bonds purchases programme (CBPP) are directed at private sector assets. They were meant to encourage greater lending to the private sector by providing affordable funds. The additional euro 50 billion per month purchase will be euro6 billion for debt securities of EU supranational and euro44 billion for debt securities of sovereigns, national agencies and national utilities. The national securities would be bought in proportion to the Eurozone's NCBs' shareholding of the ECB, which is actually in proportion to the size of the national economies.

On the asset side of the balance sheet the holdings and risk sharing of the new purchase under PSPP was structured as follows: ECB will hold 8% of sovereigns (euro4 billion) and 12% of securities of European institutions (euro 6 billion) and will, therefore be subject to risk-sharing by the entire Eurosystem banks. The NCBs will hold 80% national public securities (euro 40 billion), to be allocated to the NCBs on the basis of their shares in ECB's capital, and will not be subject to risk-sharing. The issuer, holding structure and risk sharing arrangement of the PSPP is summarized in Table 15.

Table 10.1: Allocation of Monthly Asset Purchases by the Eurosystem

Bonds	Bondholder	Monthly purchases	Total purchases	Notes
ABS & covered bonds	ECB	€10 bn	€190 bn	Risk on ECB
European institution	ECB	€6 bn (12% of 50)	€114 bn	Risk on ECB
Euro area central governments and agencies	ECB	€4 bn (8% of 50)	€76 bn	Risk on ECB
Euro area central governments and agencies	NCBs securities purchases allocated according to the ECB's capital key	€40 bn (80% of 50)	€760 bn	Risk on NCBs; purchases to be limited to 25% of new issues and 33% of total outstanding debt
Total		€60 bn	€1.14 tr	

Source: Micossi, S. (2015). The Monetary Policy of the European Central Bank (2002 – 2015). *Centre for European Policy Studies Special Report*, Number 109 (May).

In administering quantitative easing, a peculiar challenge faced by the ECB but not by the other major central banks is how to minimize risk spreads and fragmentation among union. In order words, how to use the instruments to engender homogeneity? It seems the formula the ECB has established for allocating bond holdings and risk-sharing is about optimal for responding to those challenges. They attempt to eliminate differentials and, therefore, preferences, by financial players for any of the countries. In addition, the allocation of most of the risk (80%) of the new bond purchases to NCBs, will discourage their governments from defaulting. With only 20% of the risk of default subject to risk sharing,

145

there would be little room for free-rider behaviour among the Eurozone countries and their NCBs. This safeguard is important for the all-important Eurozone member, Germany, which understandably is apprehensive of the dangers of some national Eurozone countries not living up to the responsibility of carrying out reforms that would ultimately determine the success of the monetary policies, conventional and unconventional.

Another point to note is that risk sharing also implies that coupon payments will remain within national borders so that quantitative easing does not produce significant capital flow problems across the Eurozone.

10.5 Recapitalization of the Banking System

The experience of the Eurozone sovereign debt crisis shows how monetary authorities could be transformed by challenges to view a wider range of activities as relevant to their mandates. Having settled on plans to for the ECB to act as a supranational banking regulator earlier on in the month, on June 28, 2012, the Eurozone leaders agreed to permit the European Stability Mechanism to make loans directly to ailing banks for recapitalization. By making the loans directly to the distressed banks rather than through Eurozone sovereigns, the programme avoided adding to sovereign debts. The countries affected were: Portugal (three banks); Ireland (three banks); Greece (four banks) and Spain (four banks).

10.6 ECB's Management of Crisis

Following the collapse of Lehman Brothers in the United States in September 2008, financial markets, all over the world experienced shock and uncertainty transmitted from the United States capital market. At the same time Eurozone sovereign debt crisis was taking root. Money Eurozone members were unable to repay or refinance their government debts. Nor would they bail out debt-burdened banks. The countries included Greece, Portugal, Ireland, Spain and Cyprus. What were the causes? These include:

    i).   Globalization of finance, that is, the phenomenal growth of cross-border networks of entities which enable massive and speedy flow of financial resources from their original homes to other destinations on the globe;

ii). Financialization, that is, the emergence of an economic system that attempts to reduce all value that is exchanged (goods or services, present or future promises), into a financial instrument or security – securitization of value – the purpose being to make it easier for people to trade in value;

iii). Easy credit conditions during 2002 – 2008, which encouraged high-risk lending and borrowing practices;

iv). The financial crisis of 2007 - 2008;

v). International trade imbalances;

vi). Real estate bubbles that eventually got burst;

vii). The Great Recession of 2008 – 2012;

viii). Defective fiscal policy choices related to government revenues and expenses; and,

ix). Approaches used by states to bail out troubled banks and private bondholders, which led to ballooning of public debt burdens or socialization of losses.

Under the 1992 Maastricht treaty, European Union members had signed to limit deficit spending and debt levels. But in the early 2000s many of the countries were breaching the criteria and adopted securitization of future government revenues to hide their debts and deficits, activities which were against best practice and international standards. They employed a combination of techniques to achieve this: inconsistent accounting, off-balance-sheet transactions and complex currency and credit derivatives. (Brown M. and Chambers, A.: 2005). When in late 2009 Greece's true indebtedness and budget deficit were unmasked, fears of sovereign defaults in some European countries beclouded the environment. Many government debts were downgraded. Ireland and Portugal were early victims, while Italy and Spain were wait-listed for the dangerous flight, to describe the situation dramatically. It was, therefore, obvious that the Eurozone faced serious imbalances (Belkin, Weiss, Nelson & Mix, 2012). The ECB reacted by lowering interest rates and aggressively expanded its refinancing operations for the banking system.

Between October 2008, and May 2009, the ECB cut its main refinancing rate by 325 basis points to 1%. From October 2008, demands for MROs and LTROs were granted in full at fixed rate basis, subject to availability of adequate collateral. In early May 2009, the Governing Council of the ECB decided to implement the first covered Bond Purchase Programme (CBPP1) and the actual purchase of the covered bonds started in July 2009. The purpose was to supply liquidity to the financial market segment which served the funding needs of banks but which had been adversely affected by the financial crisis. By June 30, 2010, the ECB had purchased euro 60 billion worth of securities from both the primary and secondary markets. The second covered bonds (CBPP2) amounting to euro 40 billion announced in October 2011, at the height of the Italian and Spanish sovereign market tension. In May 2010, the ECB introduced the security market programme (SMP) by which it bought sovereign bond in the secondary market in order to revive the market which had been impaired in depth and liquidity. An integral part of the scheme was the sterilization of the expanded liquidity by offsetting sales of interest–bearing deposits to the banking system. By re-absorbing the liquidity injected, the ECB ensured that the monetary policy stance was not jeopardized. The SMP was interrupted a couple of times and was finally discontinued in September 2012 having been issued to a maximum of euro 220 billion. Also in response to the Greek sovereign debt crisis in fall 2011, the ECB quickly accommodated the funding needs of banks by lowering the minimum ratio from 2% to 1% and by launching two very-long-term refinancing operations (VLTROs) in December 2011 and February 2012, with a maturity of three years. This move was meant to help break the "doom loop" which was the transmission of the uncertainty about sovereign crisis to banks as investors expected repercussions of sovereign default on banking institutions with large exposure to sovereign risks, while emerging banking crisis in turn worsened the market assessment of sovereign risk since sovereign were expected to bail out distressed banks. In order words, concerns regarding the solvency of banks and sovereigns became negatively reinforcing.

However, weakening confidence in the market persisted and showed up in huge balances, which the Eurosystem banks had with the ECB, amounting to about euro 600 billion. It also showed up in high government bond yields in many Eurozone countries, fuelled by the fear that some periphery countries might be forced to exit the Eurozone. About mid-June 2012, the ECB in conjunction with European leaders mapped out a plan for the ECB to become a bank regulator and to form a deposit insurance programme to augment national programmes. There is no doubt that the support for sovereigns was induced by the fear of the prospect of collapse of the entire Eurozone. This condition led the ECB President Mario Draghi in July 26, 2102 to announce that the ECB was "ready to do whatever it takes to preserve the euro". In addition in early September, the Outright Monetary Transaction (OMT) was announced. Under this, ECB and the NCBs would be prepared to intervene for unlimited amounts in secondary sovereign-bond markets. This announcement implies that the ECB accepted to play the role of lender of last resort for Eurozone sovereigns. The OMT is based on two arrangement set up by the Eurozone European Financial Stability Facility bailout funds and the European Stability mechanism. OMT is considered by the ECB when a Eurozone government asks for financial assistance, provided the bond-issuing country agrees to certain domestic economic measures. OMT operations are accompanied by full sterilization because their essence is not to provide liquidity but to:

i). Prevent divergence in short-term bond yields; and,
ii). Ensure that ECB's monetary policy is transmitted equally to all the Eurozone's member economies.

Evaluation of the OMT concludes that the mere announcement of the ECB caused a considerable narrowing of government bond spreads within the Eurozone (Grauwe, 2013; Saka, 2015).

A special development during the financial crisis demonstrated that the institutional arrangement of the Eurosystem is effective in handling balance of payments disequilibria among members based on the Target settlement system. Target, is the settlement system for euro transaction between banks of the eurozone - short for "Trans-European Automated Real-Time Gross Settlement Express Transfer System". It commenced operations in 1999 following the launch of the euro. When cross-border payments are executed between banks via Target, they result in change in the Target balances of individual NCBs. The transactions are channeled through the NCBs and give rise to net creditor and debtor positions of the NCBs and at the ECB. During the sovereign debt crisis in the Eurozone, the periphery economies suffered adverse cross-border financial flows. While the periphery registered huge current account deficits, Germany and other core countries experienced large increases in creditor balances as a counterpart in the form of current account surpluses and private capital account surpluses. Target became the compensating financing item in the external accounts of the Eurozone periphery members. The crisis in Ireland, Greece, Portugal and Spain also demonstrated that when a Eurozone member is under financial flows attack, private creditors can exit smoothly, provided the national banks can present eligible collateral to their NCBs, while Target adjusts the NCBs position at the ECB. Hence, creditor countries accumulated large claims on the ECB, mirroring the debt accumulated by the periphery with the ECB.

The crisis also brought out a major challenge for the eurosystem, which is that the structure of the eurozone as a currency zone, without fiscal union limits the ability of eurozone leaders to respond. Accordingly, one common currency, operating side by side with different tax and public pension rules, contributed to the crisis.

In comparison with the Federal Reserve Bank settlement system, the ECB system is more flexible. In the FRB system, balances similar to the Target balances must be settled annually, but the Target, balances in the Eurozone remain open. This means that under Target, the risk of default by a member is shared by the other members through their share in the ECB capital.

10.7 A Note on the Nature of Asset-Backed Securities (ABS) and Covered Bonds

It would be useful to understand the nature of two special securities which the ECB transacted on as it endeavoured to salvage banks and corporates: asset-backed securities and covered bonds. Asset backed securities (ABS) are created when a private bank combines different loans it is carrying into pools of different loans and sells them to new investors. The objective of the bank is to make its balance sheet lighter so that it has space to make new loans. The issue of bonds or securities generates cash which is used for more lending. The buyer of the portfolio of loans from the bank is a special purpose entity (SPE). The SPE finances the acquisition by issuing asset-backed bonds, which are secured notes. The SPE is a separate entity from the bank and has as its assets the loan portfolios and as it liabilities the notes it issues. The ABS holders have recourse over the SPE (that is the loan portfolio pool) but not over the original bank.

The SPE arranges the old loans into similar groups (called tranches) according to their degree of riskiness and issues bond-like obligations on each tranche it creates; the safest trances are called senior debts while the riskiest are the mezzanine debts. Those who buy the ABS, receive cash-flows from the underlying pool of original loans, which include standard loans, leases, or receivables against assets. The ECB investment guideline is to buy only senior ABS tranches and only if there is a guarantee. Overall, ECB purchases of ABS reflect its commitment to encourage credit flows.

Covered bonds are similar to ABS in that both are fixed income debt securities entitling their holders to recourse over an underlying portfolio of assets. But unlike ABS, covered bonds are issued directly by a credit institution (a bank) and no special purpose entity is involved, even though they are managed by a dedicated cover pool administrator. The bonds or notes issued by the bank are backed by a loan portfolio, called "cover pool", which remains on the balance sheet of the issuing bank. Investors in cover bonds enjoy a dual recourse: first, they have recourse over the issuer as the primary obligor, with who resides the obligation to pay; second, they have recourse over the covered pool cash flows, in case the issuer goes insolvent. The investor exercises the option either to liquidate the cover pool by selling it to another entity or to continue receiving coupon by the cover pool.

CHAPTER ELEVEN

Bank of Japan and Japan's Monetary Policy

The central bank for Japan is the Bank of Japan (BOJ). According to the Bank of Japan Act, which was first enacted in 1942 and revised in 1949, the Bank's monetary policy should be "aims at achieving price stability, thereby contributing to the sound development of the national economy". The revision of 1949 established the Policy Board and abolished an article which required the BOJ to seek the permission of the government to set or change the official discount rate.

11.1 Responsibility for Monetary Policy

Monetary policy is decided by the Policy Board at Monetary Policy Meetings (MPMs). Decisions are based on a majority vote of the nine members of the Policy Board, which includes the Governors, the two Deputy Governors and six other members. Meetings are held eight times a year. The BOJ makes use of its research findings for deciding monetary policy. The in-depth research covers economic and financial conditions, monetary policy strategy and instruments, as well as the financial system. It is the responsibility of the Policy Board to discuss economic and financial conditions, decide the guidelines for money market operations and the Bank's monetary policy stance for the immediate future. The discussions and the decisions of the meeting are also announced by the Board immediately after the meeting. Based on the guidelines announced, the Bank sets the amount of daily money market operations and chooses the operational instruments.

11.2 Price Stability Target and Rare Type of Cooperation between BOJ and the Fiscal Authority

Recognizing that in a market economy, individuals and firms find it difficult to make appropriate decisions on consumption and investment when prices are unstable, and that unstable prices distort income distribution, the BOJ accords premium to stable prices. Hence, in

January 2013 it set the "price stability target" at 2 percent in terms of the year-on-year rate of change in the consumer price index (CPI). It also made a commitment to achieving its set target at the earliest possible time. In announcing the price stability target, the BOJ defined it as "a state where various economic agents including households and firms may make decisions regarding such economic activities as consumption and investments without being concerned about the fluctuation in the general price level".

From its release titled': The "Price Stability Target" under the Framework for the Conduct of Monetary Policy, (Bank of Japan, 2013) the BOJ's concerns and priorities could be discerned from the following provisions:

i). Assessing, influencing and responding appropriately to inflation expectations of households and firms were considered central to price-stability management.

ii). The change from the pre-January 2013 "price stability goal in the medium to long term in the positive range of 2 percent or lower with an interim goal of 1 percent, to price stability targets at 2 percent in terms of the year-on-year rate of change in the CPI", reflects the position that as the strengthening of growth potential makes progress, the inflation rate consistent with price stability on a sustainable basis will rise. This also reflects increasing awareness of the importance of flexibility in the conduct of monetary policy in Japan, and that the appropriate target to anchor the sustainable rate of inflation will reflect new realities of the economy.

iii). The switching of the world "goal" for a new one "target" is also meant to signal that the BOJ's thinking on price stability is necessarily circumscribed by the responsibility to be flexible by considering other risk factors, such as the implications of financial sector imbalances and other forms of systemic or global crisis.

A notable development is what one could consider as the pursuit of trust and confidence in monetary policy through the joint declaration of commitment to the goal of macroeconomic coordination between the BOJ and the fiscal authority. On January 22, 2013, as the Bank was releasing "The Price Stability Target" under the Framework for the conduct of Monetary Policy, it was simultaneously releasing a joint declaration with the government titled, "Joint Statement of the Government and the Bank of Japan on Overcoming Deflation and achieving sustainable Economic Growth". This second paper repeated much of the objectives, logic and language of the first: monetary policy driven primarily to achieve price stability, so as to contribute to "sound development of the national economy"; recognition that inflation rate "consistent with price stability on a sustainable basis" will rise as efforts to strengthen competitiveness progress; "flexibility" in macroeconomic management; etc.

The opening clause of the joint statement declared: "In order to overcome deflation early and achieve sustainable economic growth with price stability, the Government and the Bank of Japan will strengthen their policy coordination and work together as follows ...." .

11.3 Money Market Operations

After each monetary policy meeting (MPM) by the Policy Board, the BOJ releases its assessment of economic activity, prices, and monetary policy stance in the immediate future. In addition it releases the guideline for money market operations. Based on the guidelines, the Bank controls the liquidity in the money market using money market operations. The mechanism starts in the guidelines where the Bank sets a target rate for uncollateralized overnight call rate. This is the rate at which the funds which financial institutions lend and borrow from one another are received and paid on a contract day and which reverse transactions are conducted on the business day following the contract day. To steer the uncollateralized overnight call rate to remain at the targeted level, The BOJ supplies funds to, or absorbs funds from, financial institutions.

The BOJ influences the supply and demand for funds and through it, the interest rate in the money market by adjusting financial institutions' current account balances at the Bank through open market operations. The total balance of each financial institution's account at The Bank is made up of (i) balances for settlement of transactions with other financial institutions, notably transactions in the call market; (ii) balances for settlement with other banks arising from private sector transactions; and, (iii) balances to satisfy the reserve requirement. The sum of the three components is what the BOJ counts for a bank as its "reserve".

Financial institutions borrow funds through the money market from each other in order to maintain their reserves at the Bank at a prudent level to meet their payment and settlement obligations, as well as to satisfy the reserve requirement. But when the BOJ through money market operations buys or sells securities, it adjusts the current account balances of the financial institutions. The quantum and direction of the adjustment triggered by the Bank influences the amount of funds borrowed or lent by the financial institutions in the call market and, in turn, the uncollateralized overnight call rate.

11.4 Independence and Accountability

The provision of Bank of Japan Act as regards independence of the BOJ, shows how delicate and complex the concept and exercise of independence of a central bank could be. On the one hand, the Act provides that "The Bank of Japan's autonomy regarding currency and monetary control must be respected". On the other hand, it also states that The BOJ shall "always maintain close contact with the government and exchange views sufficiently".

Related to the issue of BOJ's independence are those of accountability to the public and the role of communications in eliciting appropriate behaviour from private economic agents, such that they are consistent with the targets of monetary policy. Much in line with the standard practice among other advanced central banks, the BOJ satisfies this expectation by:

i). Releasing its decisions immediately after meetings regarding monetary policy, guidelines for money market operations and its view on economic and financial developments.

ii). The holding of regular press conferences by the Governor to explain details of monetary policy decisions.

iii). Releasing of summary of opinion at each monetary policy meeting.

iv). Submission of semi-annual Report on currency and Monetary Control to the Japanese parliament, in June and December each year.

v). Appearing before both houses of parliament, the Diet, when required, to answer questions on the conduct of the Bank's activities.

11.5 BOJ's Measures during the Financial Crisis

The Bank of Japan's monetary policy responses to the 2008 crisis in global financial markets were in three broad areas:

- i). Reductions in the policy rate;
- ii). Measures to ensure stability in the financial markets; and,
- iii). Steps to facilitate corporate financing.

Overall, the monetary policy stance was accommodative.

11.5.1 Use of Policy Rates

As regards policy interest rates, the target for the uncollateralized overnight call rate was reduced from around 0.5 percent which was decided in February 2007 to around 0.3 percent in October 2008 and further to around 0.1 percent in December 2008. Similarly, the basic loan rate, which is the official rate at which the BOJ provides loans to the banking system, was reduced from 0.75 percent in February 2007, to 0.5 percent in October 2008 and further to 0.3 percent in December 2008. The BOJ also responded through adjustments in the complementary deposit rate (CDR). The CDR facility was a temporary measure introduced by BOJ in October 2008, to pay interest on excess reserve balances of financial institution at their BOJ accounts. The purpose was to increase flexibility of money market operations by enabling sufficient liquidity, while maintaining policy interest rate at around its targeted level; the complementary deposit interest rate was set below the targeted policy rate and when it was introduced in 2008, it was set at 0.1 percent.

11.5.2 Stabilization of the Financial System

The BOJ also implemented many far-reaching measures to ensure stability of the financial system. Among them were the following:

- i). Securities lending and repos on Japanese Government Bonds (JGBs) were expanded, with softer terms; for example, lower rate was charged on securities lending facility.
- ii). Introduction of complementary deposit facility;

iii). Generous expansion of eligible collaterals to relatively riskier assets - for examples, real estate related instruments and other countries' government bonds (United States, U.K., Germany and France).

iv). Introduction of outright purchases of classes of JGBs hitherto excluded;

v). Inclusion of the Development Bank of Japan as a counter party in operations such as repo operations.

BOJ also undertake two particularly bold steps to support the financial markets. One, in October 2008, it suspended the selling of bank stocks held by it except in the case of buy-backs and at the request of the issuer and in February 2009, it resumed its purchases of stocks held by banks. These measures helped the financial institutions to reduce market risk associated with stock holding, particularly, under an environment of global financial market turbulence. Two, the BOJ decided in April 2009, to provide subordinated loans to financial institutions. Subordinated loans are loans whereby the creditor or lender has a lower priority than other creditors in the case of bankruptcy of the debtor or borrower. They are a quasi capital fund. The purpose was to ensure undisrupted intermediation and stability of the system. The measure enabled Japanese banks to maintain adequate capitalization even under the hostile economic and financial environment. While, the BOJ's measures regarding stockholding and subordinated loans protected the banks, they exposed the BOJ itself to risks that are unconventional for a central bank, namely, credit risks and stock-price fluctuation risks. Indeed, the entire miscellany of measures which the Bank took to ensure stability of the financial markets tantamount to a shift in the risk from the private players in the financial system to the regulatory authority.

11.5.3 *Steps to Facilitate Corporate Financing*

The Bank of Japan also took measures aimed generally at facilitating corporate financing. These measures included:

i). Increase in the size and frequency of commercial Paper repurchase operations;

ii). Expansion in the range of Asset Backed Commercial Papers acceptable as eligible collateral;

iii).   Introduction of special fund-supplying operations for corporate. Under this scheme, the BOJ extended loans to its counterparties for an unlimited amount against the value of corporate debt as collateral at an interest rate equivalent to the target for the uncollateralized call rate. Introduced in December 2008, this facility expired at the end of March, 2010.

iv).   Expansion in the range of corporate debt accepted as eligible collateral.

v).   Introduction of outright purchases of corporate bonds.

By foraying into the space of outright purchases of corporate securities, the Bank of Japan was assuming to itself the credit risk of individual firms. Even though these special interventions were preceded by the introduction of a set of guidelines that governed their implementation and while they were all temporary, having been expired by the first quarter of 2010, their introduction nevertheless, demonstrates how far severe economic and financial turbulence could radicalize a hitherto conservative monetary authority.

11.6 BOJ Stretches Monetary Policy: Yield Curve Control

In September 2016, the Bank of Japan extended yet further, the frontier of unconventional monetary policy. The Bank had in 2013 commenced the policy pursuit of a 2 percent inflation target through, mainly, massive asset purchases, which was expanded in 2014. It then followed with the introduction of negative interest rates in January 2016. But inflation remained below zero percent while prices were dropping. This was the situation prevailing when in September 2016, the BOJ introduced a new tool: control of the yield curve (Bajpai, 2016). The package was named, "Quantitative and Qualitative Easing (QQE) with Yield Curve Control. The yield curve is the relationship between yields across the different maturities of fixed income securities issued by a particular issuer. Under normal circumstances, shorter-term securities would have lower yields, while longer-term securities would have higher yields, reflecting that longer-term securities constitute higher-risk assets for the investor.

Under the policy of "Yield Curve Control", while leaving official interest rate unchanged at minus 0.1 percent, the BOJ adopted a target of around zero percent for the 10-year JGB yield, which were already trading at negative yields. Therefore, the Central bank was countering a problem of a flattened yield curve by engineering it to start sloping upwards from left to right, so as to avoid the negative effect on economic activity. BOJ's purchases of JGB's are at prices designed by the bank; hence, fixed-rate operations. The normal yield curve is positively sloping, that is, exhibits higher yield for longer-term securities because for a shorter period, investors can be fairly certain about the value of the money they receive back but over a longer period, inflation, currency fluctuations and the probability of default introduce significant level of uncertainty. That is, perception of risk is a positive function of time. At the macroeconomic level, a flatter yield curve generally means an outlook of weak growth and weak inflation and if the curve inverts, that is if the long-term yield is lower than the short-term yield, the economy might be heading to recession. Flattening of the yield curve could be because the shorter end is rising higher than normal or the longer end is falling lower than normal.

There are a number of specific ways in which the yield curve impacts the economy:

i). Banks and other financiers depend on the government securities yield in determining their risk mark-up and pricing for their borrowers; they charge their borrowers by marking up an appropriate risk premium on top of the yield on the government bond, which is usually considered to be risk-free.

ii). Banks make profits by arbitraging between the cheaper short-term funds which they access by either deposits from the public or borrowing from the central bank, and, higher rates they charge on longer term lending. Among other reasons, this is possible because in spite of the ordinary problem of asset-liability mismatch, there is often a hard-core (stable) component of short-term liabilities which could be safely deployed to longer term assets.

iii). Investors in other sectors can also gauge their investment decisions with the yield curve. Ceteris paribus, if a business estimates the return on an investment to be a couple of hundred basis points above, say a 5-year government bond yield, it would conclude that the investment is a good one.

When the BOJ introduced negative interest rate early 2016, the objective was to stimulate economic activity by encouraging spending, borrowing and investment with cheap money. But the actual results were the opposite of the expectation: bank margins shrank, and directly weakened their profits and share prices. Similarly, returns on insurance and pension products became lower, exposing them to challenges of meeting their obligations. To arrest this new source of stress for the financial system and the overall economy, the BOJ introduced the yield curve control; that is, propping up the longer end of the yield curve against the unintended consequences of negative interest rates.

As Fox (2016) has noted, the BOJ's yield curve control is similar to the exercise by the Federal Reserve in 2011 – 2012, the Operation Twist, in which the Fed was selling short-term Treasury securities and buying longer term ones in substitution with the aim of reducing the yield on 10–year Treasuries, thereby manipulating the yield curve. The aim was to lubricate the financial markets and encourage long-term investments for sustainable economic recovery by making investible funds cheaper. Indeed, there is even an older precedence at yield curve control: "From 1942 to 1951 the Fed capped the yield on long-term bonds to support government financing during World War II" (Reynolds, 2016).

11.7 Signals of Failed Central Banking from the Japanese Picture

The very-extended monetary policy experimentation by the BOJ highlights a major question which faces each of the other advanced economies to different degrees. Would quantitative easing and related unorthodox measures mutate into new monsters for the global economy? In the case of Japan, for example, after more than 20 years of experimentation with little or no success in restoring a healthy economy, the markets and the economy could be afflicted with an incurable sense of uncertainty. Indeed, one could hazard that monetary policy experimentation could degenerate to a state of addiction, thereby imparting continuous disequilibrium and crisis to the system. One also fears a far-reaching disorientation and degradation of the market, thus: private financial markets are fast loosing initiative and becoming more and more dependent on direct intervention of central banks. They are becoming more and more passive recipients and absorbers of external stimulus, rather than creative, imaginative and innovative drivers of business change and adaptation. Therefore, the market-economy strength of entrepreneurship may be at grave risk. Ironically, there are equally concerns that if recovery occurs, it might come with major disruptions. The pressures being piled on the economy by the central banks are so much that when the macroeconomic indicators such as interest rate and inflation begin to move in the required direction, the speed of unwinding would be so much that it would be certainly cause upheaval. If this concern is built into the expectation of the markets, it introduces enormous confusion into the system.

BOJ's quantitative and quantitative easing with yield curve control had a second component, namely: inflation-overshooting commitment. By this the central bank committed itself to maintain an increase in the monetary base until the annual rate of increase in the observed CPI exceeds the price stability target of 2 percent and stays above the target in a stable manner. It is noteworthy that at the time of this BOJ's commitment to expanding the monetary base, the amount outstanding was about 400 trillion yen or 80% of nominal GDP compared to 20 percent in both the United States and the euro area.

After many years of spectacular economic growth, Japan's economy slowed down drastically in the early 1980s. To stimulate recovery, Japan, as Sean Ross (2016a) put it, "deployed every conceivable Keynesian policy", which showed up in printing money, pursuit of low interest rates and huge fiscal deficits. Money stock grew by 10.5 percent between 1986 and 1990. Discount rate was adjusted from 5 percent in 1985 to 2.5 percent by 1987; easy money encouraged large-scale borrowing which Japanese investors used mainly to buy assets in other Asian economies. But cheap money failed to generate real sector growth at home, creating a scenario for a bubble-burst. The bubble burst in 1989 and 1999, closely corresponding to the raising of the discount rate between 1988 and 1990 from 2.5 percent to 6 percent.

In the 1990s, Bank of Japan applied as many as nine stimulus packages which were directed mainly at the buying of private sector assets with a view to recapitalizing business and propping up prices. By 2016, the injections by the Bank of Japan had reached a total 140.7 trillion, equivalent of USD 1.4 trillion, with virtually no impact on recovery. Faced with low growth, low interest rate, low inflation and a pile of bad debts among banks, the BOJ, in what could be considered the first phase of quantitative easing, helped banks in 1997 and 1998 by buying trillions of yen of their commercial papers. In the second phase of QE, between March 2001 and December 2004, Japanese banks received liquidity injection of about 35.5 trillion yen. The economy experienced a glimpse of recovery a couple of years up to 2007 but this was blocked by the worldwide Great Recession of 2008.

In 2013, BOJ launched Qualitative and Quantitative Easing (QQE) pumping in between 60 and 70 trillion yens in the following years. This was reinforced in October 2014 by the BOJ's announced commitment to inject 80 trillion yen per annum through asset purchases up till September 2015 (QQE2). In January 2016, the BOJ introduced negative interest rates (Ross, 2016b). A new source of worry is the negative effects of Japan's huge public and private debts: the public plus private sector debt-to-GDP ratio by the end of 2015 is estimated at 615% (Ross, 2016c). The alarming debt ratio placed side-by-side with virtually no economic gains since the early 1990s when the aggressive monetary intervention started, is instigating the question of whether the Bank of Japan is a failing central bank or even a failed central bank as it now seems to be "so ineffective and has so few options" (Ross, 2016d).

Indeed, according to Adams Hayes (2016), many people see negative interest rate policy as a signal of desperation by central bankers who have failed to stabilize macroeconomic activity via traditional monetary policy or even by quantitative easing. There is, therefore, a very dangerous prospect of the unconventional interventions by monetary authorities being adjudged as signals of failure rather than channels for recovery. Such a dysfunctional status if it takes root would effectively erode confidence in monetary policy and would have cataclysmic effects.

A related issue has been highlighted by financial market experts like Johnston (2016): by charging interest on reserve deposits, the BOJ causes yields on government debt to fall momentously; this even if only indirectly, amounts to monetization of government debt, which enables the government to service its debt more cheaply. By extension, it amounts to breaking of the independence of the central bank as it virtually hands over the money printing press to the fiscal authorities and politicians. Of course public debt monetization has adverse consequences in crowding out the private sector and triggering inflation and hyper-inflation. Johnston (2016) argues that by charging interest on reserves, the BOJ is effectively transferring wealth, and thereby, the ability to control economic resources from the private to the public sector.

The experience of the Bank of Japan demonstrates how dangerous monetary policy could get as a central bank attempts to address structural imbalances inherent in deflation, recession and depression. It shows how the pursuit of price stability could be a mirage because the overall macroeconomic topography more or less tends to disintegrate and fall apart, leaving no stable anchor for a focused pursuit of targets.

CHAPTER TWELVE

China's Central Banking and Monetary Policy

The old Peoples Bank of China (PBOC) was established in 1948 but was an omnibus institution performing not only central banking but also commercial banking functions and had subsidiary banking institutions. In 1984, the non-central banking aspects were stripped off PBOC and it began to focus on monetary policy and central banking responsibilities from January 1, 1984 "which marks the coming into implementation of modern monetary policies as well as the entry of Chinese government's macro-economic regulation into a new historical stage" (Zhou, 2015: 20).

12.1 Structure of the PBOC

The governing body of the PBOC is made of the governor and nine deputy governors. While the governor is appointed by the National People's Congress based on the nomination of the Premier of the State Council, the deputies are appointed by the Premier. The PBOC has 9 regional branches, 2 operation offices, 303 municipal sub-branches and 1809 county-level sub-branches. It is evident that the network of the PBOC reflects the physical and economic vastness of China, as well as its historical overwhelming presence when it was operating as an omnibus banking institution, and all that within an intensely socialist ideology. The Bank also has 6 overseas representative offices, – U.S.A. London, Tokyo, Frankfurt, Africa and the Caribbean. This is a feature hardly associated with other central banks.

The objective of the monetary policy of China's central bank as stated in Article 3 of the Law of the People's Bank of China, according to Zhou (2015) is "to maintain the stability of the value of currency and thereby promote economic growth" (p.20).   Other important functions of the PBOC apart from drafting and implementing monetary policy include: preventing or minimizing financial risk and safeguarding financial stability; issuing and administering the circulation of renminbi, which is the official currency; regulating the interbank bond market; managing official foreign currency and gold reserves; recording foreign currency and gold reserves; recording foreign exchange transactions and, regulating the interbank trade in foreign currencies; managing the State Treasury, calculating financial statistics and producing research analyses and forecasts.

12.2 Notable Peculiarities of the Chinese Economy

Compared to other major world economies which have been reviewed, China has significant peculiar economic characteristics which ought to be noted as a useful background to studying its central banking and monetary policy. As Michaels (2015) has well documented, the relevant elements include:

i). For about 30 years up to the 2010s, China was the fastest growing economy in the world, with its growth rates averaging 10 percent over the thirty years. It is the second largest economy, following the U.S.A., but in terms of purchasing power parity, it is the largest economy in the world according to the International Monetary Fund (IMF).

ii). While China has a gargantuan domestic market, being the most populated country in the world, it is also an export-oriented economy and is the largest exporter of goods. It is the world's fastest growing consumer market and second-largest importer of goods. Therefore, managing the growth as well as the balance between domestic and foreign demand for the economy's goods and services is an important issue.

iii). China operates a socialist-market-economy model. In the past two decades, it is relying more and more on the market to allocate resources and increasingly opening its resources to entry and exit of capital. Yet ownership and control of factors of production remain intensely public and social.

iv). China is not only the largest manufacturing country in the world; it has also become a global hub for manufacturing.

v). But China is also characterized by significant disparities in infrastructure, natural and human resources among different regions resulting in glaring differences in the comparative industrial output of the various regions. Economic development and rapid growth is highly concentrated in coastal regions of south east of China.

vi). Commodity exporters of Australia, Latin America, the Middle East and Africa are highly dependent on China's rapid growth and input-guzzling industrialization for their own economic performance. These include exporters of fossil oil of which China has become the biggest buyer. In essence, the economic fortunes of much of the world are tied to the continued growth and health of China's mega economy.

12.3 Independence

Monetary policy in China is not independently designed and conducted by the PBOC because as Geiger (2008) has observed, it is also influenced by other authorities, and notably by the central government in Beijing. Both in terms of goal and instrument, the PBOC needs approval of the State Council. In addition, there are in place in the Chinese economic arrangement, non-central bank instruments not controlled by the central bank, but which have direct and significant influence on the final targets of monetary policy. As Geiger notes, therefore, in China's context, when one talks of instruments of monetary policy one means both the instruments of the central bank and other non-central bank instruments.

12.4 The Two Sets of Monetary Policy Instruments

The two sets of monetary policy instrument in China as noted above are:

 i). Instruments of the Central bank;
 ii). Non-central bank instruments.

12.4.1 The instruments of the PBOC

These are of two types:

 a) Price-based indirect instruments;
 b) Quantity-based direct instruments.

The price-based indirect instruments include:

 i) Instruments with ratios – reserve requirement ratio;
 ii) Instruments with interest rates – central bank lending rate;

iii) Quantitative instruments – open market operations: in 1998 the use of "credit plan" was officially abolished and OMO was introduced as the main quantity based monetary instrument in the tool kit;

iv) Other instruments – such as bills issued and controlled by the PBOC.

The quantity-based instruments are those used for allocating credits in the Chinese financial system and include:

i) Window guidance under which the PBOC uses "benevolent compulsion" to persuade banks and other financial institutions to stick to official guidelines and encourages them to lend through certain windows to reflect national needs (Geiger, 2008). In essence, the window guidance is the Chinese version of sectoral allocation of credits.

ii) Direct PBOC lending, which is a legacy of the centrally-planned economy was used in its absolute form until 1994 as a way of administering fixed-quantity contribution from the central bank to the commercial banks. Thereafter, it has been used in various adapted forms to provide long-term central bank loans at low interest rates and which are not linked to the prevailing monetary policy stance. In recent times, the PBOC direct lending is in the form of subsidized, low-interest credit to rural credit cooperatives, and as lender-of-last-resort interventions to bail out financial institutions, local government, asset management companies and rural credit cooperatives – for dealing with the latter's of non-performing loans.

iii) Capital control for PBOC, essentially involves controlling financial flows between China and other economies, in order to influence money supply and liquidity under a de facto fixed exchange rate system. Given Padoa-Schioppa's "unholy trinity" or "inconsistency triangle", and given that maintaining the stability of the renminbi (RMB) could be taken as a doctrine for the Chinese type of economy management, an autonomous monetary policy system that addresses China's net-export based money supply dynamics, inevitably necessitates control of capital mobility.

12.4.2 Non-central bank Instruments

In China, the non-central bank instruments (of monetary policy) are price control and wage control. The use of these instruments in China are so extensive and effective that they constitute viable alternatives or at least strong complements to the conventional tools used in monetary policy to achieve price stability.

The system of prices in China is interestingly broadly of three categories:

i). Market-regulated prices;

ii). Government guidance prices, which could be in the form of a benchmark prices or a floating range of prices within which economic agents could undertake transactions for various goods and services;

iii). Government prices, which are fixed prices, set by government at various levels (central, provincial, regional, municipal) for goods, public utilities and services. Centrally, controlled prices need the approval of the State Council. It is important to note that China operates this complex price control system even after joining the World Trade Organisation (WTO) in October 2001, only that the defined scope of price controls was agreed.

It should be observed that the prominence and effectiveness of price and wage controls as monetary policy instruments is feasible because of the predominantly public and social ownership and coordination of economic activities.

12.5 Management of Money Supply and Exchange Rate in China

With its tremendous success as a manufacturing and export-driven economy, with the fastest growth rate in the world for more than two decades running, China became known for its huge trade surpluses. China foreign exchange reserves grew from a mere USD165.6 billion in 2000 to over USD3 trillion by 2012. The proportionate demand for the local currency by the exporters to defray wages and other expenses means rapid growth in money supply. Between 2009 and 2015, money supply in China grew by more than 225 percent; this loaded pressure on the local currency which could cause it to appreciate relative to the

United States dollar. In that case, China's exports would become costlier and lose their competitiveness. To prevent this, the PBOC intervenes to keep the renminbi (RMB) artificially low, with the result that the RMB remains stable within a narrow range.

Essentially, for the PBOC, money supply management and exchange rate management are inextricably linked through the trade-surplus nexus. A major task of the PBOC is to control the exchange rate of the RMB by absorbing the large inflows of trade surpluses and foreign capital arising from trade surplus by purchasing foreign currency of exporters and issuing them with RMB. But it purchases the foreign exchange at fixed rate within a narrow range. To prevent the monetization of foreign exchange from fuelling inflation, the PBOC then proceeds to sterilize money supply by selling appropriate amounts of domestic currency bonds, which takes away the excess cash from the open markets, which essentially constitutes one side of a classical open market operation; the PBOC also buys domestic currency bonds to infuse cash in the system if needed.

When the PBOC started open market operations, it relied on repos and outright bond purchases. But realizing that such operations were constrained by the limited holdings of the bonds by it, the PBOC began proactive issuance of central bank bills from 2003 when it issued 720 billion RMBs. By 2008 the annual volume of issuance had grown to 4.2 trillion RMBs. Again, the PBOC learnt fast from experience: it suffered the pressure of frequent redemption or refinancing of maturing short-term bills and, therefore, by the end of 2004, it began to issue 3-year bills, in addition to the existing 3-months, 6-months and 1-year bills. This move helped the Bank to freeze liquidity in a more effective way, while enabling the development of a longer risk-free yield curve which is a good foundation for market-based interest rate reform and for the development of more sophisticated bond market.

In order to maintain price stability, the PBOC also uses the conventional instruments – changes in the reserve ratio; changes in the discount rate; as well as changes in the levels of subsidies and direct price controls.

In respect of the use of the required reserve ratio, Xaochuan (2012) has argued that in contradistinction to the conventional practice of using it sparingly because it is considered to be overly aggressive, it was considered appropriate for China's circumstances. The first reason is that China's foreign exchange reserve build-up and the growth of the money supply base was enormous and required the application of high-impact instruments alongside open market operations. The second reason is that "the effectiveness and sustainability of open market operations are limited by the willingness of commercial banks to buy as the size of sterilization grows". It is, therefore, more suited for controlling liquidity in the medium-term.

These arguments explain why from September 2003 to June 2011, the PBOC adjusted the reserve requirement ratio for an unprecedented 36 times, including 32 hikes and 4 reductions. The reductions were executed in the second half of 2008 to counter the impact of the Global Financial Crisis.

A deeper appreciation of China's monetary policy would be engendered by understanding the broader macroeconomic and structural context. A number of these conditions are ably articulated in a 2012 speech by Xiaochuan who became the governor of PBOC since 2002 – in a speech titled, "China Monetary Policy Since The turn of the Century". The insights from the speech include:

i). Given a condition of accelerated urbanization, industrialization and strong motivation to achieve rapid growth in all regions of the large country, monetary policy faces the challenge of striking an appropriate balance between growth and inflation.

ii). The transition to a market-based economy with consequent reforms in interest rate and exchange rate regimes is bound to be very difficult given the dominance of state-owned banks embedded in operating in a planned economy under largely-substandard regulatory requirements.

iii). Global imbalances such as that caused by a combination of overconsumption in the U.S.A and high savings in emerging Asian economies in the period 2008 - 2010, challenges China to balance its three (transition) priorities of reform, development and stability.

iv). The emergence of new types of, largely global, challenges such as the priority of reserve-build up after the Asian Financial Crisis and overheating of the real estate sector from oversupply, has led China to conclude that the traditional single-objective monetary policy framework must be expanded to incorporate macro-prudential policies.

v). China's monetary policy faces an environment quite different from other countries because it is transiting to a market-driven system from a centrally-planned one, though the economy remains dominantly socialist in ownership and control of enterprises. The old, traditional expectations of localities for soft fiscal conditions to enable them undertake big projects with correlated big borrowings, as they aspire to urbanise and raise per capital income, remains. Yet, this expectation may not be consistent with the measures required from the global reality.

12.6 China's Response to the Global Financial Crisis

In view of its export dependency of 35% of the GDP, the global financial crisis of 2008 impacted China through the fall in global demand for exports,. The fact that fixed asset investment (FAI) plus net exports were growing at a rate 60 percent greater than the GDP growth rate meant that overcapacity would result in FAI as export capacity shrunk. (Yongding, 2010). The PBOC responded quickly to the global financial crisis by using moderately easy money to complement government stimulus packages. It cut the benchmark deposit rate to 2.25 percent and also aggressively cut the deposit reserve requirement between October and December 2008. According to Xiaochuan (2012) the PBOC encouraged banks to lend more by keeping the benchmark interest rates unchanged and preventing the occurrence of liquidity trap and maintaining interest rate spread within a certain range. In essence, the PBOC reflected the understanding that as far as the economy is concerned, the lowest interest rate may not be the most beneficial.

In November 2008, the Chinese government introduced a 4 trillion RMB stimulus package, including direct grants and interest rate subsidies. Some analysts like Yongding (2010) have observed that China's stimulus package succeeded because there was plenty of spare capacity in industry and infrastructure available to use fiscal policy to fill the gap created by drop in exports. And as noted earlier, the PBOC effectively supported the fiscal stimulus with smooth monetary expansion which led to 7.3 trillion RMB increase in bank credit in the first half of 2009. It has also been noted that compared with other advanced economies whose banking systems were in crisis during this periods, China's banking system was healthy and had adequate liquidity (Yongying:2010).

The PBOC's easy monetary policy continued generally but with some cautious normalization slant up to 2012 when the spread of sovereign debt crisis across Europe and the spectre of high unemployment and high debt in the U.S.A, enveloped the global economy with a new cloud of uncertainty about economic recovery.

It can be demonstrated that the PBOC indeed proactively deployed its monetary policy instruments to counter the global crisis. The base discount rate which was 6.310 percent in July 2011 was reduced to 6.00 percent in July 2012 and was subjected to consistent reduction to 4.600 percent in August 2015 and further to 4.350 percent by October 2015. Similarly, the required reserve ratio was continuously reduced from 21 percent in August 2008 to 18 percent in August 2015.

However, a school of thought argues that PBOCs loose monetary policy did not qualify to be designated as Quantitative Easing. According to the Economist (2015) the reasons are as follows:

i). The use of quantitative easing was the norm with the PBOC even before the global and local crisis that stimulated it in other advanced economy; the regulators had for long used lending quotas to influence the behaviour of banks.

ii). More often than not, the PBOC adjusts reserve ratio to determine what is available to banks to lend, rather than interest rates.

iii). The QE analogy is deficient and exaggerated because the monetary stimulus of 2008 was mainly intended to replace cash that had left the Chinese system through fall in external demand, rather than to pump extra money into the economy; in the past, the PBOC relied on foreign exchange inflows to generate money supply growth; it printed a steady stream of RMB to buy up the dollars flowing in from both trade and investment. With capital flows reversing, the PBOC created base money through alternative channels.

iv). Unlike the Bank of Japan or the ECB, where conventional monetary policy had run out of room and lost steam, conventional monetary policy still had a lot of room in China.

v). PBOC uses relending through China Development Bank not because of concern over bank sector liquidity but because it does not trust the formal markets to allocate credit to the sectors which policymakers are targeting.

Accordingly, the Economist concludes, thus:

> Easing has always been quantitative in China. The point is to get away from it because as bond markets displace banks, it is for more effective for central banks to focus on the price of credit (interest rate) rather than its volume.

CHAPTER THIRTEEN

India's Central Banking and Monetary Policy

Based on the Reserve Bank of India (RBI) Act of 1934, the RBI is charged with the responsibility for conducting monetary policy for India. The Act states the primary objective of monetary policy as "maintaining price stability, while keeping in mind the objective of growth".

Under the RBI Amendment Act of 2016, inflation target is to be set by the government of India in consultation with the RBI, once every five years. Accordingly, on August 5, 2016, the RBI announced an inflation target of 4 percent CPI, with symmetric upper and lower limits of plus or minus 2 percent. Although flexible inflation targeting was practiced hitherto, the new policy gave it a statutory basis.

13.1 The Monetary Policy Committee and its Activities

Section 45 ZB of the amended RBI Act provides for a six member Monetary Policy Committee (MPC) to be constituted by the central government, thus: the Governor of the RBI as the chairman; the Deputy-Governor in charge of Monetary Policy; one officer of the RBI to be nominated by the central board; three other experts from outside the RBI who serve for a 4-year tenor. The MPC determines the policy interest rate needed to achieve the inflation target. The Monetary Policy Department (MPD) assists the MPC in formulating monetary policy by gathering the inputs and views of stakeholders and carrying out analytical work required for arriving at decisions on the policy repo rate, which is the primary policy instrument. The Financial Markets Committee (FMC) meets daily to review liquidity conditions so as to ensure the operating target of monetary policy (weighted average lending rate) is kept close to the policy repo rate.

In respect of openness and transparency, the RBI, under the amended Act has the following features:

i.   The MPC meets at least four times in a year.
ii. The quorum for the MPC is four

iii. Decisions are taken on the basis of one member, one vote, but when there is a tie, the Governor will exercise a second casting vote.

iv. Resolutions adopted, by the MPC are published after every meeting.

v. On the 14th day after each MPC meeting, the minutes of the meeting are published and include: resolutions adopted, how each member voted on each issue, and the statement of each member on the resolution adopted.

vi. RBI is required to publish, in every six months, a report explaining: (a) sources of inflation; (b) the forecast of inflation for the next 6 - 18 months.

13.2 Independence of the RBI

The RBI is not statutorily independent because the 1934 Act which governs its operations gives the central government powers to direct it and to appoint the governors. The central government's direction of the Bank though, is to be after consultation with the Governor of the Bank. Therefore, from a technical point of view the government could supersede the Bank if it considers that the Bank has not carried out its obligation in the public interest. From the practical point of view, however, the liberalization of the central banking function and more reliance on indirect controls, the stripping out of direct developmental activities and the focus on traditional central banking functions means that the areas of interest to the government have been diluted. Hence, more independence for the RBI even though routine consultation with the fiscal authorities continues. It could also be said that while no legal instrument conferred autonomy on the RBI, major actors in the system understand that independence is healthy for the RBI and the entire economic system. This is more so as India continues to evolve as a major global emerging market and expectations from it become higher.

But the condition of non-statutorily conferred independence leaves room for tensions to arise from time to time. Sometimes these could be pronounced, reflecting the fact that while, in general, the RBI is biased in favour of anti-inflation policies and the government is biased in favour of pro-growth policies. Another consequence of the arrangement is that the personality of the governor of the RBI becomes a factor. This factor seemed to have played out in 2016 when the incumbent governor,

Raghuram Rajan, came under political attack, and chose to quit the office rather than seek a second term which, he was eligible for.

13.3 Framework of Monetary Policy

The RBI Act mandates the Bank to operate the monetary policy framework (MPF). The MPF aims at setting the policy (repo) rate based on the assessment of current and evolving economic conditions. Market liquidity conditions are modulated to anchor money market rates at or near the repo rate. Repo rate changes transmit through the money market to the entire system; aggregate demand in the economy is influenced by the market rates and is itself a major determinant of inflation and growth, which are the ultimate foci of monetary policy. Day-to-day liquidity management is based on the announced policy repo rate. The MPF itself is subject to fine-tuning and revision to reflect changing financial and economic conditions.

13.4 Instruments of Monetary Policy

The **repo rate** is the rate at which the RBI provides overnight liquidity to banks against the collateral of government and other approved securities specified in the liquidity adjustment facility (LAF). On the other hand, when the RBI wants to absorb liquidity away from the system, it uses the reverse repo. The **reverse repo rate** is the interest rate at which the RBI absorbs liquidity on overnight basis from banks against eligible collaterals under LAF.

As noted by Das (2015) the **liquidity adjustment facility** (LAF) "is the key element in the operating framework of the RBI and is meant to operate in a deficit liquidity mode to ensure more effective monetary transmission (p.9)". Essentially, it has played the major role in developing policy interest rates (repo and reverse repo) as the main monetary policy instrument. It consists of overnight auctions as well as term repo auctions of up to 56 days as at 2016. The aim of extending the term of repo transactions is to help develop the interbank term money market, so as to generate market-based benchmarks for pricing loans and deposits on a fairly stable basis. It is expected that such a condition will improve the transmission of monetary policy. LAF has experienced improvements over the years. For example in 2004, "fixed" rate repos and reverse repos were introduced. In May 2011, among other innovations, the weighted average overnight call rate was explicitly recognized as the operating target of monetary policy (Das, 2015). At the same time, there was the shift from overnight repos to term repos of varying maturities of up to 56 days.

Marginal Standing Facility (MSF) is the arrangement under which commercial banks borrow additional amounts of overnight money from the RBI. It allows a bank to utilize part of the statutory liquidity ratio (SLR) portfolio up to a limit while paying a penal rate of interest. It enables the commercial banks to have a safety cushion against unanticipated shocks. The MSF rate and the reverse repo rate define the corridor (upper limit and lower limit, respectively) for the daily movement in the weighted average call rate.

The **bank rate** is the rate at which the RBI is ready to buy or rediscount bills of exchange or other commercial papers. It is aligned to the MSF rate and changes automatically as and when the MSF rate changes alongside the policy repo rate.

The RBI also employs other ratio-based and non-ratio based instruments common to central banks all over the world. These include the cash reserve ratio (CRR), the statutory liquidity ratio (SLR), and the open market operations (OMO).

13.5 Market Stabilization Scheme

This instrument was introduced in 2004 to absorb surplus liquidity of a sustained nature arising from huge capital flows. It relies on the use of sales of short-dated government securities. The emergence and importance of stabilization securities reflects the growing importance of India, globally, which enables it to experience net positive trade and capital flow balances, which in turn stimulate expansion in domestic money supply that needs to be appropriately sterilized to avert excessive inflation.

13.6 RBI's Response to the Global Financial Crisis

Given its size, compared to western economies, India's economy was less adversely affected by the global financial crisis of 2008 – 2010. Even then, India's financial markets (money market, equity market, forex market and credit market) were significantly stressed as a result of the shrinking of overseas financing owing to reversal of capital flows. It was also negatively impacted by the fall in exports through the export multiplier on the GDP. Indeed, economic growth which registered 9 percent and above for each of the three previous fiscal years, slowed down to 6.7 percent in the 2008 – 2009 fiscal year. The increasing risk of an open economy in a globalized era was aptly described for the Indian case by Bajpai (2011) thus: "India could not insulate itself from the adverse developments in the international financial markets, despite having a banking and financial system that had little or nothing to do with investments in structured financial instruments carved out of subprime mortgages, whose failure had set off a global crisis" (p.2).

The RBI undertook a battery of measures to stabilize the economy. Apart from significant slashing of the policy repo and reverse repo rates by 400 and 250 basis points, respectively the rupees liquidity was shored up by the reduction of the CRR by 400 basis points, raising the export credit refinance limit for commercial banks from 15 percent to 50 percent of outstanding exports, and enhancement of other refinancing facilities. Forex liquidity was also enhanced by RBI selling foreign exchange and availing forex swap facilities to commercial banks. To ensure capital inflows, interest ceiling rates on non-resident India deposits were raised. There was also regulatory forbearance as the risk-weighted and provisioning requirements were relaxed while restructuring of weakened assets was allowed. The monetary initiatives were supported with fiscal stimulus measures: tax relief was provided, while expenditure on public projects was expanded in order to boost domestic aggregate demand.

Beyond the core years of the global financial crisis, most central banks were confronted with deciding on whether and how to engage in quantitative easing. In the case of India, a pertinent view on the situation seems to be one expressed by Shetty (2016) thus: "Countries like India and China are already doing quantitative easing in a small way every year, which essentially means increasing the central bank's balance sheets (increasing liabilities) and printing money and increasing the monetary base. But they do not do super propaganda like the US. The reason for this is our bonds are not sold in the international markets so we do not have to announce to the world loudly and buy back our debt".

This view could also be understood in the context of the special development role the RBI played for most of its years – starting from inception to the 1990s when liberalization enabled it to focus on core central banking activities. The RBI was activist in supporting schemes for agricultural development and establishment of financial infrastructure and institutions. It spearheaded the establishment of the Deposit Insurance and Credit Guarantee Corporation of India, the Unit Trust of India, the Industrial Development Bank of India, the National Bank of Agriculture and the Rural Development and the Discount and Finance House of India.

CHAPTER FOURTEEN

Nigeria's Central Banking and Monetary Policy

The Central Bank of Nigeria (CBN) is responsible for the country's monetary policy formulation and implementation. This mandate is backed by the Central bank of Nigeria Act, 1958 which has undergone many amendments, the last being in 2007. The CBN commenced operations in July 1959. The CBN lists its mandate as: ensuring legal tender currency and price stability; issuing legal tender currency in Nigeria; maintaining external reserves to safeguard the international value of the legal tender currency; promoting a sound financial system in Nigerian; and, acting as banker and providing economic and financial advice to the Federal Government.

Section 12, sub-sections 1 to 5 of the CBN Act, 2007 (amended) states: "In order to facilitate the attainment of price stability, and to support economic policy of the Federal Government, there shall be a Committee of the Bank known as the Monetary Policy Committee". Therefore, the Monetary Policy Committee (MPC) is responsible for carrying out the monetary policy job of the CBN. The composition of the MPC is as follows: The Governor, who is the chairperson; the four Deputy Governors; two members of the board of directors; two members appointed by the President of the country; and two members appointed by the Governor.

14.1 Independence

The Central Bank of Nigeria has had fluctuating experiences with the independence to carry out its responsibility of formulating monetary and credit policy towards achieving its goals of price stability and supporting national economic policies. Between 1968 and 1970, the various amendments to the Act curtailed the CBN's power by subjugating it to the supervision of the Federal Ministry of Finance. In 1991, the Bank's operational autonomy was restored by the Banking Act amendment of that year but the 1997 amendment brought the Bank back to the supervision of the fiscal authority. The amendment of 1998 again reversed the subjugation and this reversal was confirmed by the Central Bank of Nigeria Act, 2007. It was under the 2007 Act that the monetary Policy Committee was created, to be responsible for monetary policy decisions.

14.2 Institutional Arrangement

The eleven-member MPC meets bi-monthly under the chairmanship of the Governor of the Bank. The committee is supported by four sub-committees. (Central Bank of Nigeria, 2011). These are:

i). The Monetary Policy Technical Committee (MPTC) which monitors economic and financial system developments and, on a monthly basis, provides technical documents on issues relevant to the work of the MPC. The MPTC is chaired by the Deputy Governor, Economic Policy.

ii). The Monetary Policy Implementation Committee (MPIC), which is the implementation arm of the MPC, is also chaired by the Deputy Governor, Economic Policy. Other members are from ten relevant departments of the CBN, including Policy, Operations and Surveillance. The MPIC meets weekly to assess. The liquidity position of the banking system; it also reviews issues relating to banking system infrastructure and the health of the system.

iii). The Liquidity Assessment Group (LAG) is the subcommittee which meets daily to assess the liquidity situation and to suggest policy actions to be taken each day in the foreign exchange and domestic money markets; it follows up the implementation of monetary policy measures and reports to the MPIC. It members include Monetary Policy Department; Banking and Payment System Department, Trade and Exchange Department and Reserve Department. It is chaired by the Financial Markets Department.

iv). The Fiscal Liquidity Assessment Committee (FLAC) is responsible for: providing information on the operations of the Treasury to the LAG for forecasting the level of liquidity in the economy; providing policy advice on fiscal issues to the management of the Bank; and, generating reliable database on the operations of the Treasury, which have implications for domestic liquidity. The committee meets weekly and is chaired by the Monetary Policy Department.

14.3 The Monetary Policy Process

The CBN's monetary policy process consists of a complex set of interrelated activities which includes: setting of objectives, choosing the operating and intermediate targets, preparing the monetary programme, selecting appropriate policy instruments, implementation of day-to-day routine activities such as liquidity management, adjusting policy rates, communicating policy actions, as well as evaluating outcomes and policy review (Central Bank of Nigeria, 2011)

At the centre of CBN's monetary policy is monetary programming: that is, the process which enables the CBN to determine the level of money supply and credit considered adequate for the achievement of the objectives of monetary policy. The macro-economic objectives pursued in the financial programming are those which would help achieve internal and external balance. Monetary programming is a comprehensive and consistent set of policy measures aimed at achieving certain desired macroeconomic objectives in a forward-looking time-frame. It is used to evaluate macroeconomic and structural conditions of an economy, for the purpose of determining and designing a monetary programme for achieving policy objectives. The financial programming is comprehensive because it captures all the four sector macroeconomic accounts: the real sector (national accounts); the external sector (balance of payment accounts); the fiscal sector (government finance accounts); and, the monetary sector (monetary accounts). The CBN uses the four sector economy-wide financial programming framework to derive the operating target (reserve money) and intermediate target (broad money supply – M2). Based on a comprehensive review of developments in the economy, the CBN sets quarterly and annual targets of reserve money that are consistent with the policy of non-inflationary growth rate, that is, low and stable inflation rate. As part of the process of generating inputs for the programming, liquidity assessment and forecasting are carried out daily, weekly and monthly to determine the current liquidity position and its future trend.

Monetary and financial programming is a critical component of the CBN regime of monetary targeting. One has no doubt that monetary programming framework would greatly enhance the effectiveness of

CBN's monetary policy. But the challenge is that practical conditions of the Nigerian economy may not be conducive to the realization of its full contributions yet. Indeed this is the conclusion of the CBN itself (2011), thus: The programme has been quite useful in the conduct of policy in Nigeria in a number of ways. Precisely, it is used to set targets on various macroeconomics indicators; it ensures consistency among the four sector macroeconomic accounts; it provides information to all stakeholders; it safeguards against economic shocks. It has contributed immensely to the formulation and implementation of monetary policy in Nigeria. Despite the advantages of monetary programme, its preparation and implementation have not been without some challenges. Some of the major challenges include: poor quality of data; considerable lag in data generation; constant revision of Federal Government budget; lack of effective coordination between the fiscal and monetary authorities; late approval of Federal Government Budget and extra budgetary spending.

14.4 CBN's Monetary Policy Framework

The CBN has employed two monetary policy frameworks in its 58-year history up to 2016. It used exchange rate targeting between 1959 and 1973 and monetary targeting from 1974 onwards.

14.4.1 Exchange Rate Targeting Periods

During colonial rule, the Nigeria pound was fixed in relation to the British pound as the fixed exchange rate option was the global practice then. The fixed parity continued after Nigeria gained political independence in 1960 until 1967 when the British pound was devalued. Nigeria resisted devaluing its national currency, first because the Nigerian civil war started in the same year and a high proportion of the country's resources was used to finance the war (and, therefore, concerns about external balance could not have been a priority) and second because there were concerns that devaluation of the Nigerian pound would cause importation of inflation without significant increase in exports. Therefore, the country took leave of parity-fixing of the local pound to the imperial pound. As an alternative, the Nigerian authorities decided to peg the Nigerian currency to the U.S dollar and propped up the value of the currency with strict restriction of imports using direct administrative control of foreign exchange transactions.

But in the 1970s global crisis put enormous pressure on the global fixed exchange rate system leading to the devaluation of the U.S. dollar and the collapse of the Breton Woods exchange rate regime in 1974. The new Breton Woods recipe was the adjustable peg and so Nigeria had its currency (the Naira) pegged to the U.S. dollar. However, recognizing the complications of adjustable-pegging to a particular currency, the Nigeria monetary authority decided in 1978 to peg the Naira to a basket of the currencies of Nigeria's 12 major trading partners. (Central Bank of Nigeria, 2011)

Another factor that influenced the direction of Nigeria's monetary policy at this time was the domination of the country's export by crude oil. In 1960 oil contributed only N8.8 million or about 2.6% to total export earnings; by 1970, it contributed N509 million or about 57% of total export earnings; and, by 1980, it contributed N13,632 million or about 96% of total export earnings. Oil and other mineral resources are public-owned assets. As a result, Nigeria's external reserves rose rapidly; the favourable terms of trade fuelled growth in public expenditure; and, inflationary pressures intensified. An added factor is the provision in the constitution of the Federal Republic to the effect that all revenue accruing to the three ties of government (Federal, States and Local Government) should be fully shared among them in line with a predetermined revenue allocation formula. This provision meant uncontrolled monetization of the foreign exchange earnings with direct implications for money supply. In view of this emerging reality of an oil-export dominated economy, it was obvious that a new monetary policy framework focused on money supply was needed; hence, Monetary Targeting.

Before we discuss the period of monetary targeting, it is relevant to note that under both major monetary policy frameworks, both direct and indirect monetary controls were adopted and used for implementation of the frameworks. Throughout the exchange rate targeting framework period, direct controls were the option in use; even after the change to monetary targeting in 1974, direct control continued into 1985. Under the direct control regime, the following condition and practices applied:

i). The size of the fiscal deficit to be financed by the banking system determined credit allocated to the government.
i). Allocation to the private sector was determined through credit ceiling.

ii). The direct policy instruments used included: credit ceilings imposed on banks; administratively fixed interest rates administratively fixed exchange rates; specified maximum or minimum sectoral credit allocation.

Among other objectives, the level and structure of interest rates administered were aimed at ensuring desired allocation of resources, promoting growth of the preferred sectors, achieving orderly development of the financial market and subduing inflation. Moreover, and notably they also aimed at lessening the burden of debt servicing on the government. In this context, it should be noted that during the period under discussion, Nigeria's debt management agency, the Debt Management Office had not been established; it was established only in 2000. During the period, the CBN acted as the government borrowing agent and actually underwrote much of government borrowing offers. It is, therefore, clear that there was a case of conflict of interest on the part of the monetary authority which also acted as government's debt manager, to a certain extent; hence, the temptation to suppress market interest rates to favour government borrowing, with consequent distortions on the financial markets.

This situation also points to a practical manifestation and consequences of the non-independence of the central bank. This type of relationship is far-reaching in understanding the complications and distortions that could arise in a monetary policy arrangement. Consider, for example, that a primary objective of the CBN is to ensure low and stable price levels. Yet, by guaranteeing cheap or subsidized debts for the government, what the CBN did was to encourage uncontrolled government spending through deficit financing with no negative trade-off for the fiscal authorities. It could be argued that the CBN would, and did, under such circumstances apply other instruments to absorb the shock, or to bear the transferred cost of the policy favouritism. But such self-induced complications can only, in the last analysis, induce avoidable volatilities, distortions and inefficiencies in the macroeconomic system.

14.4.2 Monetary Targeting Regime

As already observed, the rapid money supply growth caused by rapidly growing foreign exchange inflows from oil export catalyzed the switch from foreign exchange targeting to monetary targeting by 1974. The

186

focus on control of monetary aggregates reflects the conclusion that inflation was essentially a monetary phenomenon and, therefore, if money supply could be controlled to remain at levels required to sustain output growth, inflation would be controlled. Again, as has already been noted, direct controls continued well into the regime of monetary targeting until 1985, the only difference being that such controls were in the circumstances applied from the standpoint of controlling inflation and impacting on the level of foreign exchange reserves through controlling the monetary aggregates. In addition to the use of direct credit controls and changes in cash reserve ratios, stabilization securities were introduced in an attempt to reduce the liquidity of the commercial banks, by unilaterally debiting the accounts of the deposit money banks at the central bank and issuing them with CBN securities in exchange.

As the conditions in the economy and the complications of the direct controls worsened, the need to eliminate unnecessary economic controls was appreciated. This led to the introduction of the Structural Adjustment Programme (SAP) in July 1986. SAP accepted the need to rely on the market system for the allocation of resources: the overreaching direct controls of about twenty past years would be progressively removed to remove constraints on growth and development. SAP heralded exchange control liberalization, adoption of appropriate pricing policies in all sectors of the economy and rationalization and restructuring of public expenditure. By October 1996, all mandatory credit allocation mechanisms by the CBN were abolished and interest rates were also deregulated; but the transition was not smooth: for example, stabilization securities were re-introduced in 1990. However, about the most important signal of the move towards reliance on indirect controls was the shift to the use of open market operations (OMO) in 1993 by issuing Nigerian Treasury Bills (NTBs). This was complemented by the cash reserve requirement (CRR) and liquidity ratio (LR).

Another major introduction was the Monetary Policy Rate (MPR) to replace the Minimum Rediscount Rate (MRR) as the nominal anchors in November, 2006. The MPR operates an interest rate corridor with the lending and deposit facilities rates as the upper and lower corridor, respectively. The purpose is to have a policy rate which will effectively signal the direction of monetary policy and minimize the volatility in the money market rates, since the MPR is designed to be the mid-point of the corridor (Gbadebo & Mohammed, 2015).

At this juncture, it would be relevant to observe that following the resuscitation of the sovereign bond market between 2002 and 2004, the scope for more effective monetary policy became greatly enhanced because government financing of fiscal deficits began to rely on auctions in the competitive open market. The development of a sovereign yield curve of up to 20 years as at 2008, as well as the development of a deep and dependable secondary market for fixed-income securities driven by a primary-dealer market-marker system, liberated the CBN from monetary financing of fiscal deficits and underwriting of issuances of government securities.

14.5 Tracking the Activities of the CBN's MPC

Since its establishment in 2007, the MPC has been quite active in applying the monetary policy rate (MPR), the cash reserve requirement (CRR) and the liquidity ratio (LR) to manage money supply, price stability and overall macroeconomic stability in the Nigerian economy. For example, as Appendix G shows, over the 10-year period, 2007 – 2016, the MPC was changed 18 times. There were complementary changes in the CRR and LR, as well. The rigorous process of the MPC is also evidenced in the considerations and decisions of the committee from 2003 to 2016 as detailed in Appendix H. Overall, it could be concluded that Nigeria's monetary authority has been operating at technical and analytical standards which compare favourably with what obtains among monetary authorities of the advanced economies.

14.6 How the CBN Responded to the Global Financial and Economic Crisis of 2007/2008

The impact of the 2008 global crisis was transmitted to Nigeria, mainly via the collapse of commodity prices, specifically oil which accounted for over 90 percent of the country foreign exchange earnings and over 75 percent of public revenue. Public revenue dropped drastically and affected government expenditure. Decline of capital and current account inflows led to shrinking of foreign reserves and pressure on the exchange rate. The exchange rate was allowed to reflect the market pressure by adjusting from N117 per dollar to N135 per dollar as at 2008. Limited foreign trade finances for Nigerian banks impacted negatively on the real sector. But Nigerian banks remained relatively strong, having undergone recapitalization in 2000.

In term of the use of conventional monetary policy tools, the CBN did the following:

i). Reduced the MPR from 10.25 percent to 9.75 percent;
ii). Reduced the CPC from 4 percent to 3 percent;
iii). Reduced LR from 40 percent to 30 percent;
iv). Gave banks the option to restructure margin loans into 2009;
v). Expanded lending facilities to banks up to 360 days;
vi). Introduced expanded discount windows;
vii). Stopped liquidity mopping-up operations from September, 2008.

These measures were meant to counter the exogenously induced contractionary pressure on the economy.

14.7 Special Development Interventions by the CBN

Since 2010, the Central Bank of Nigeria, citing the development provision in the CBN Act, has been proactive in financing various sectors of the economy, including agriculture, manufacturing, micro, small and medium enterprises, electricity industry and aviation. Apart from the variety of sectors of intervention, many of the interventions seem to be more or less direct rather than intermediated. As at September 2015, the number of such real sector intervention financing by the CBN was about twelve with total seed money amounting to about 1.8 trillion Naira, of which about 65 percent had been disbursed – as shown in Appendix I.

The issues of concern regarding the CBN's foray into real sector financing include:

i). Intrusion into the fiscal operation space;
ii). Weakening of focus on core mandate of monetary policy;
iii). Creating a conducive atmosphere for conflict of interest and compromise of standards and principles;
iv). The nature of intervention inevitably brings the CBN dangerously close to politicians who must be involved in the "officially" sponsored real sector projects, thereby breaking the

thin barrier protecting the central bank from the predation of the politicians.

Unfortunately, therefore, there are indications that the CBN is facing self-inflicted erosion of the invaluable attribute of independence. The dilemma is similar to the one faced by a number of advanced economy central banks who have undertaken unconventional monetary policies. It seems that central banks all over the world tend to be carried away by the sheer size of financial power under their control, to arrogate to themselves the responsibility of solving all the economy's problems, without due regard to the macro division of labour, with its implicit "separation of powers" that helps maintain sanity and stability.

CHAPTER FIFTEEN

Summary and Conclusions

This book focuses on how the composition of output and the interaction between the agricultural and non-agricultural sectors affect the general price level. In particular, it investigates the possibility that the growth of some components of output could accentuate, rather than dampen inflation and the condition for inter-temporal stability of the parameter estimate of the marginal effect of aggregate output on the average price level. An examination of the characteristics of the Nigerian economy leads to the conclusion that a lot of inflationary impulses are embedded in the structure of the economy. A survey of the literature on inflation reveals that the problem has not been investigated within the context of the structural composition of output.

15.1 Validation of the New Thinking

For the purpose of explaining inflation, the analysis that has been undertaken in this book confirms that from the inflation-study point of view, aggregate output consists of two groups: those components that influence the price level inversely and those components that influence the price level positively. This is the essence of the *Disaggregation Dissonance Hypothesis*. Error correction mechanism regression results for the period covered by the analysis show that:

(i)   Aggregate output, agriculture output, manufacturing output, construction output and, wholesale-and-retail output influence the average price level inversely;

(ii) Non-agricultural output (taken together) and petroleum exports influence the price level positively;

(iii) The non-agricultural-agricultural output ratio, which is a measure of sectoral interaction and structural tension, affects the price level positively.

In addition, import price index and money supply also affect the price level positively.

The theoretical and policy implications of the results have been discussed. The fact that components of aggregate output affect the price level diversely – some positively, others inversely – implies that it is inappropriate to use aggregate output as an explanatory variable for the price level.

15.2 Further New Intellectual Windows

This conclusion is further used to advance the following arguments.

(i)   For the coefficient representing the marginal effect of aggregate output on the average price level to be temporally stable, the relative weights of the inflation-accentuating components and the inflation-dampening components of the GDP must remain constant over time.

(ii)   To improve the optimality of partitioning of an aggregate regressor (as a way of reducing aggregation bias), the coefficients of the components in each partition should have the same algebraic sign.

(iii) One of the reasons for the appearance of 'wrongly' signed regressor coefficients in regression models, is the misconception of an explanatory macro variable as influencing a dependent variable in a particular direction, whereas, such an explanatory macro variable, is actually made up of components which influence the dependent variable in opposing directions.

(iv)   At any given rate of unemployment and given the expected rate of inflation, the actual rate of inflation will vary directly with the proportion of the GDP that is made up of inflation-accentuating components. Thus, the non-uniformity of the directions of the impacts of changes in the components of the GDP on the average price level is a reason for the instability of the Phillips Curve.

The above findings constitute the *Disaggregation Dissonance Effects* derived from the *Disaggregation Dissonance Hypothesis* and are the thrust of the contribution which the empirical study underlying this book would make to economic theory.

Policy-wise, inflation can be mitigated through efficient use of resources, through appropriate output mix, and through paying attention to the issue of sectoral imbalance, particularly between agriculture and non-agricultural, in the process of economic growth. However, some measure of inflation seems to be an inevitable cost for structural transformation and growth. The empirical investigation demonstrates the theoretical and policy relevance of the structure-of-the-economy approach to the study of inflation. Inflation being a complex problem, the analysis herein does not provide a complete solution of the riddle but it demonstrates, more or less powerfully, that in the design and execution of anti-inflation policy, all of monetary, fiscal and structural dimensions must be brought into play.

Indeed, this conclusion is well-corroborated by the rich insights gained from the case studies of central banking and monetary policy-making presented in Part II of the book. From the seven country case studies, it could be observed that in their use of monetary policy to achieve price stability, central banks recognize the need to simultaneously focus on the behaviour of aggregate output   for two reasons. The first is that economic growth is also a priority objective of macroeconomic policy. The second is that monetary policy impacts aggregate economic activity. Following through on these two dimensions, it is obvious that central banks could significantly enhance the efficacy of policy design, analysis and implementation by taking into account the far-reaching insights about the relationship between inflation and the structure of output which was discussed in Part I.

Moreover, the findings from the analyses do open plausible new windows. In particular, the theoretical revelations, particularly, those embodied in the *Disaggregation Dissonance Effects*, could provide an agenda for further research.

References

Aboagye, A.A. (1982). *Rising World Prices and Inflation in Ghana.* Paper presented at the 3rd Biennial Meeting and Conference of the West African Economic Association, 7th – 10th April, 1982, Freetown, Sierra Leone.

Adejugbe, M. (1982a). Nigeria's Industrial Development Goals, Strategies and Performance, 1946-1980. *The Political Economy of Nigeria.* 1982 Annual Conference of the Nigerian Economic Society, Port Harcourt.

Adejugbe, M. (1982b). The Mechanics and Dynamics of Inflation in Nigeria: 1961-1972. In K. Awosika & H.M. Onitiri (eds.), *Inflation in Nigeria.* (Proceedings of a National Conference). Ibadan: NISER, 47-74.

Adelina-Genina, I. (2011). Monetary Policy and Economic Policy. *Journal of Knowledge Management, Economics and Information Technology,* 1(2), 1 – 20.

Adeyeye, E.O. & Fakiyesi, T.O. (1980). Productivity, Prices and Incomes Board and Anti-Inflation Policy in Nigeria. *The Nigerian Economy under the Military.* Proceedings of the 1980 Annual Conference of the Nigerian Economic Society, 309 – 320.

Adeyokunnu, T. & Ladipo, O. (1982). The Causes of Inflation in Nigeria: Quantitative Assessment. In K. Awosika & H.M. Onitiri (eds.), *Inflation in Nigeria.* Proceedings of a National Conference, 141 – 155. Ibadan: NISER.

Ahmed, A.E.M. & Suliman, S.Z. (2011). The Long–Run Relationship between Money Supply, Real GDP, and Price Level: Empirical Evidence from Sudan. *Journal of Business Studies Quarterly,* 2(2), pp. 68-79. ISSN 2152-1034

Ajayi, S.I. (1978). *Money in a Developing Economy.* Ibadan: Ibadan University Press.

Akinnifesi, E. O. & Phillips, T. (1978). Determinants and Control of the Monetary Stock in Nigeria. *Economic and Financial Review,* 16(1), 26 – 38.

Anders, J. & Hernando, I. (1997). Does Inflation Harm Growth? *National Bureau of Economic Research,* Working Paper, 6062, Cambridge: M.A.

Argy, V. (1970). Structural Inflation in Developing Countries, *Oxford Economic Papers*, March, 73 – 85.

Awogbemi, C.A. & Taiwo, J.K. (2012). Empirical Analysis of the Causes and Effects of Inflation in Nigeria. *Journal of Economics and Sustainable Development*, 3(11), 35 – 41.

Awosika, K. (1980). Nigeria's Anti-Inflation Policies in the 1970's. *The Nigerian Economy Under the Military*. Proceedings of the 1980 Annual Conference of the Nigerian Economic Society, 276 – 279.

Bacon, R.W. & Eltis, W.A. (1975). The Implications for Inflation, Employment and Growth of a fall in the Share of Output that is Marketed. *Oxford Bulletin of Economics and Statistics*, 37(4), 269 – 296.

Bajpai, N. (2011). Global Financial Crisis, its Impact on India and the Policy Response. *Columbia Global Centres/South Asia, Columbia University*, Mumbai, Working Papers, No.5.

Bajpai, P. (2016). *Bank of Japan Tweaks Its Monetary Policy Stance*. Retrieved from http://www.investopedia.com.news/bank-japan-tweak-its-monetary-policy-stance/.

Ball, L., Mankiv, N.G., & Romer D. (1988). The New Keynesian Economics and the Output-Inflation Trade-Off. *Brookings papers on Economic Activity*, 1.

Banerjee, A., Dolado, J., Hendry, D.F., & Smith, G. (1986). Exploring Equilibrium Relationships in Econometrics through Static Models. *Oxford Bulletin of Economics and Statistics*, 48, 253 – 77.

Bank of Japan. (2013). *Monetary Policy*. Retrieved from http://www.boj.or.jp/en/mopo/index/html/.

Bank of Japan. (2013). *The Price "Stability Target" Under the Framework for the Conduct of Monetary Policy*. BOJ Policy papers.

Belkin, P., Weiss, M.A., Nelson, R.M. & Mix, D.E. (2012). The Eurozone Crisis: Overview and Issues for Congress. *Congressional Research Service Report*, R 42377.

Bernanke, B.S. & Mishkin, F.S. (1997). Inflation Targeting: A Framework for Monetary Policy. *Journal of Economic Perspectives*, II(2).

Bernanke, B.S. (2015). Unconventional Monetary Policy through the Fed's Rear View Mirror. Retrieved from http://www.moneyandbanking.com/commentary/2015/12/7/unconvetional-monetary-policy-through-the-feds-rear-view-mirrow.

Blass, W. (1982). Institutional Analysis of Stagflation: The Interaction of Institutional Changes. *Journal of Economic Issues*, XVI(4), 955 – 971.

Brecher, R.A. & Heady, C.J. (1979). Stagflation in an Open Economy. *Oxford Economic Papers*, 31(2), 165 – 176.

Bronfenbrenner, M. & Holzman, F.D. (1963). A Survey of Inflation Theory. *American Economic Review*, LIII(4), 593 – 661.

Brown, M. & Chambers, A. (2005). How Europe's Governments have Euronized their debts. *Euromoney*, (September).

Bulir, A. (2001). Income Inequity: Does Inflation Matter? *IMF Staff Papers*, 48(1), 139 – 159.

Cagan, P. (1956). The Monetary Dynamics of Hyper-Inflation. In M. Friedman (eds.), *Studies in the Quantity Theory of Money*. Chicago: Chicago University Press.

Campos, O. (1967). *Reflections on Latin American Development*. Austin: Texas, University of Texas Press.

Central Bank of Nigeria (2011). Central Bank of Nigeria Monetary Programme._*Understanding Monetary Policy Series*, Number 2. Abuja: Central Bank of Nigeria.

Central Bank of Nigeria. (2011). Central Bank of Nigeria Monetary Policy Framework. *Understanding Monetary Policy Series*, No.3. Abuja, Central Bank of Nigeria.

Chimobi, O.P. (2010). Inflation and Economic Growth in Nigeria. *Journal of Sustainable Economics and Sustainable Development*, 3(2), 159 – 166.

Clark, P.K. (1982). Inflation and the Productivity Decline. *The American Economic Association*, Papers and Proceedings of the 94th Annual Meeting, Washington, D.C., 28-30 May, 1981, 149 – 154.

Cox, J. (2016). *CNBC Explains: The Bank of Japan's 'yield curve control*. Retrieved from http:/www.cnbc.com/2016/09/21/cnbc-explains-the-bank-of-japan-yield-curve-control.html.

Crockett, D.C. (1981). Stabilization Policies in Development Countries: Some Policy Considerations. *IMF Staff Papers*, 28(1), 54 – 79.

Curwen, J.P. (1976). *Inflation*. London and Basingstoke, Macmillan Press Ltd.

Das, S. (2015). Monetary Policy in India: Transmission to Bank Interest Rates. *IMF Working Paper, WP/15/129*. (June).

Davidson J.E.H., Hendry D.F., Sbra, F, & Yeo S. (1978). "Econometric Modelling of Aggregate Time-series Relationship between Consumers Expenditure and Income in the United Kingdom". Economic Journal. 88, pp. 661- 692.

De Grauwe, P. & Ji, Y. (2013). Panic-driven austerity in the Eurozone and its implications. *Vox EU*, Paper on voxeu.org. (Feb. 21).

Dew-Becker, I. And Gordon, J. (2005). Where did the Productivity Growth Go? *National Bureau of Economic Research*. Working Paper, 11842, Cambridge, M.A. (Dec.).

Diaz-Alejandro, C.F. (1965). *Exchange Rate Devaluation in a Semi-Industrial Country: The Experience of Argentina 1955-1961*. Cambridge: Cambridge University Press.

Dickey, D.A. & Fuller, W. (1981). Likelihood Ratio Statistics for Autoregressive Time-series with a Unit Root. *Econometrica*, 49, 1057 – 1072.

Diz, A.C. (1970). Money and Prices in Argentina, 1935-1962. In D. Meilselman (ed.), *Varieties of Monetary Experience*. Chicago: Chicago University Press, 111 – 122.

Doguwa, S.I. (2013). Inflation and Economic Growth in Nigeria: Detecting the Threshold Level. *CBN Journal of Statistics*, 3(2), 99 – 124.

Draghi, M. (2014). *Unemployment in the euro area*. Speech presented at the Annual Central Bank Symposium in Jackson Hole. (Aug. 22).

Economist (2015). *China's Monetary Policy*. Retrieved from http://www.economist.com/blogs/freeexchange/2015/04/chinas-monetary -policy.

Einchengreen, B. (1992). The Origins and Nature of the Great Slump. Economic History Review, XLV(2), 213 – 239.

Engle, R. & Granger, C. (1987). Co-integration and Error Correction: Representation, Estimation and Testing. *Econometrica*, 55, 251 – 276.

Falegan, S.B. & Ogundare, S.O. (1982). Causes of Inflation including the Relative Importance of Internal and External Causes. In K. Awosika & H.M. Onitiri (eds.) *Inflation in Nigeria*, Proceedings of a National Conference. Ibadan, NISER, 126 – 146.

Fawley, B.W. & Neely, C.J. (2013). Four Stories of Quantitative Easing. *Federal Reserve Bank of St. Louis*, 95(1), 51 – 88.

Federal Republic of Nigeria (1970). *Second National Development Plan 1970-74*. Lagos, Federal Ministry of Economic Development.

Federal Republic of Nigeria (1975). *First Report of the Anti-Inflation Task Force*. Lagos, Federal Ministry of Information.

Federal Reserve Bank of St. Louis. (2015). The Origin of Unconventional Monetary Policy in the U.S. *Annual Report*, Retrieved from www.stlouisfed.org

Fei, J.C. and Ranis, G. (1964). *Development of the Labour Surplus Economy: Theory and Policy.* Homewood, Illinois: Richard D. Irwin, pp. 7-20.

Forder, J. (2004). "Credibility" in Context: Do Central Bankers and Economists Interpret the Term Differently?. *Economics Journal Watch.* 1(3), 413 – 426.

Fox, T. (2016). *Market Analysis: Focus in Japan turns to yield curve policy.* Retrieved from http:/www.thenational.ae/business/markets/20160925/market-analysis-focus-in-japan-turns-to-yield-curve-policy

Friedman, I.S. (1973). *Inflation, A Worldwide Disaster.* (New ed.) Boston, Hughton and Mifftin Company.

Friedman, M. (1948). A Monetary and Fiscal Framework for Economic Stability. *American Economic Review*, 38(3), 245 – 264.

Friedman, M. (1968). The Role of Monetary Policy, *American Economic Review,* 58(1), 1 – 17.

Friedman, M. (1956). *Studies in the Quantity Theory of Money.* Chicago: Chicago University Press.

Friedman, M. (1960). *A Programme for Monetary Stability.* Chicago: Chicago University Press.

Friedman, M. & Schwartz, A. (1963). A Monetary History of the United States, 1867 – 1960. Princeton, N.J.: Princeton University Press.

Frisch, H. (1877). Inflation Theory 1963-1975: A Second Generation Survey. *Journal of Economic Literature*, XV(4), 1289 – 1317.

Garber, G.A. (1982). Tests of Monetary Neutrality for the United Kingdom. *Quarterly Review of Economics and Business.* 22(3), 81 – 95.

Gbadebo, A.D. & Mohammed, N. (2015). Monetary Policy and Inflation Control in Nigeria. *Journal of Economics and Sustainable Development.* 6(8).

Geiger, M. (2008). Instruments of Monetary Policy in China and their Effectiveness: 1994 – 2006. *UNCTAD Discussion Papers*, Number 187.

Ghosh, R.N. (1982). Economic Growth with Controlled Inflation. *Economic Affairs*, 27(4-6), 387 – 392.

Granger, C.W.J. & Newbold, P. (1974). Spurious Regressions in Econometrics. *Journal of Econometrics.* 2, 111 – 120.

Granger, C.W.J. (1981). Some Properties of Time Series Data and Their Use in Econometric Model Specification. *Journal of Econometrics.* 16, 121 – 130.

Gregorio, Jose (1996). Inflation, Growth and Central Banks. *World Bank Policy Research Working Paper, 1575.* (February).

Grunfeld, Y. & Griliches, Z. (1960). Is Aggregation Necessarily Bad? *Review of Economics and Statistics*. 42 (1).

Guildord, G. (2014). *The Mystery of China's fading inflation, explained.* Retrieved from https:/qz.com/169958/the-mystery-of-chnas-fading-inflation-explained/

Gupta, K.L (1969). *Aggregation in Economics.* Rotterdam: Rotterdam University Press.

Gyebi, F., & Boafo, G. K. (2013). Macroeconomic determinants of inflation in Ghana from 1990–2009. *International Journal of Business and Social Research*, 3(6), 81-93.

Harberger, A.C. (1963). The Dynamics of Inflation in Chile. In C. Christ (ed.), *Measurement in Economics.* Standford: Standford University Press, 219 – 250.

Hayes, A. (2016). *Negative Interest Rates: 4 Unintended Consequences.* Retrieved from http://investopedia.com/articles/investing/022616/negative-interst-rates-4-unintended-consequences.asp

Heller, P. (1980). "Impact of Inflation on Fiscal Policy in Developing Countries", *IMF Staff Papers._* 22(4), 712 – 748.

Hicks, J. (1974). *Crisis in Keynesian Economics.* Oxford: Basil Blackwell.

Hines, A.G. (1964). Trade Unions and Wage Inflation in the United Kingdom, 1893-1961. *Review of Economic Studies.* 221 – 252.

Hogan, T.G. (2015). *Understanding Japan's Heavy Exposure to Rising Rates.* Retrieved from http:/www.investopedia.com/articles/investing/050815/understanding-japans-heavy-exposure-rising-rates.asp

Hopkins, A. G. (1973). An Economic History of West Africa. London: Longmans.

Humphrey, T.M. (1975). A Monetary Model of the Inflationary Process. *Federal Reserve Bank of Richmond Economic Review*, 13 – 23.

IMF. (2014). *Annual Report on Exchange Arrangements and Exchange Restrictions.* Washington, D.C.: IMF.

Imimole, B., & Enoma, A. (2011). Exchange rate depreciation and inflation in Nigeria (1986–2008). *Business and Economics Journal*, 28, 1-11.

Ito, T. (2007). The Role of Exchange Rate in Inflation Targeting. Post-Conference Version of Paper presented at the November, *2006 Bank of Thailand Conference on The Challenges to Inflation Targeting in Emerging Economies* (May).

Johnston, M. (2016). *How Central Banks Monetize Government Debt.* Retrieved from http:/www.investopedia.com/articles/investing/032 516/how-central-banks-monetize-government-debt.asp.

Kaldor, N. (1980). *Essays on Economic Policy, Volume 1.* London: Gerald Dulkworth and Co. Ltd.

Kennedy, J. (2015). *3 Economic Challenges Japan Faces in 2016.* Retrieved from http:/www.investopedia.com/investing/123015/3-economic-challenges-japan-faces-2016.asp.

Keynes, J.M. (1936). *The General Theory of Employment, Interest and Money.* New York: Harcourt Brace.

Khan, M.S. and Senhadji. A.S. (2001). Threshold Effects in the Relationship Between Inflation And Growth. *IMF Staff Papers*, 48 (1), 1 – 21.

Kirkpatrick, C.H. & Nixon, F.I. (1976). The Origin of Inflation in Less Developed Countries: A Selective Review. In M. Parkin & C. Zis (eds.), *Inflation in Open Economies.* Manchester, Manchester University Press, 131 – 149.

Koutsoyiannis, A. (1977). *Theory of Econometrics.* London and Basingstoke: The Macmillan Press.

Levison, C. (1971). *Capital, Inflation and the Multinationals.* London, Allen and Unwin.

Lewis, W.A. (1954). Development with Unlimited Supplies of Labour. *Manchester School of Economics and Social Studies*, 20, 139 – 192.

Lewis, W.A. (1971). Education and Economic Development. In UNESCO, *Readings in the Economics of Education.* Paris, UNESCO, pp. 135-147.

Lioi, V.C. (1974). *Inflation in Developing Countries: An Econometric Study of Chilean Inflation.* New York: El Servier Publishing Company.

Maddala, G.S. (1977). *Econometrics.* New York, McGraw-Hill.

Maskowitz, D. (2016). How to Go Long or Short Japan via ETFs. Retrieved from http:/www.investopedia.com/articles/markets/041316/how-to-go-long-or-short-japan-etfs-ewjdx.asp

Maynard, G. (1961). Inflation and Growth: Some Lessons to be Drawn from the Latin American Experience. *Oxford Economic Papers*, (New Series). 13(1), 184 – 202.

Michaels, R. (2015). *Chinese Monetary Policy.* Retrieved from http://international banker.com/finance/Chinese-monetary-policy/

Micossi, S. (2015). The Monetary Policy of the European Central Bank (2002 – 2015). *Centre for European Policy Studies Special Report*, Number 109 (May).

Mishkin, F.S. (2000). From Monetary Targeting to Inflation Targeting: Lessons from Industrialized Countries. Prepared for the Mexico Conference, *Stabilization and Monetary Policy: The International Experience*. Mexico City, Nov. 14 – 15.

Musgrave, R.A. & Musgrave, P.B. (1982). *Public Finance in Theory and Practice* (3rd Ed.). Auckland:McGraw-Hill Book Co.

Muth, J. F. (1961). Rational Expectations and the Theory of Price Movement. *Econometrica.* 29(3), 315 – 338.

Myint, H. (1965). Economic Theory and Underdeveloped Countries. *Journal of Political Economy.* 73(5), 477 – 491.

Nwankwo, G.O. (1984). *The Role and Impact of the Central Bank of Nigeria on Economic Development.* Paper delivered at the National Seminar on the Revitalization of the Nigerian Economy and Economic Development, Nigerian Institute of Legal Studies, Lagos, February 1 – 3.

Obadan, M.I & Ihimodu, I. I. (1980). Balance of Payments Policies Under The Military, *The Nigerian Economy Under The Military*, Proceedings of the 1980 Annual Conference of the Nigerian Economic Society, 243 – 276.

Obinna, O. E. (1981). *The Concept of Fiscal Policy.* Lecture Presented at the Economics Week of the Department of Economics, University of Nigeria Nsukka.

Ojo, A. T. (1976). *The Nigerian Financial System.* University of Wales Press.

Okun, A. (1970). *The Political Economy of Prosperity.* New York: Norton.

Okurounmu, T. O. (1969). Analysis of Consumer Price Movement in Nigeria. *Central Bank of Nigeria Economic and Financial Review*, 14(1), 5 – 14.

Olayide, O. (1980). Agricultural Policy of the Military Era, 1966-1979, *The Nigerian Economy Under the Military*, Proceedings of the 1980 Annual Conference of the Nigeria Economic Society. Nigerian Economic Society, pp. 159-180.

Onah, J.O. (1980). Uniform Pricing and Retailing of Petroleum in Nigeria. *Oil and The New International Economic Order*, Proceedings of the 1980 Annual Conference of the Nigerian Economic Society, 213 – 229.

Osagie, E. (1982). Macro-economic Relations in an Oil Producing LDC – Implications for Inflation Policy. In K. Awosika & M.A. Onitiri (eds.), *Inflation in Nigeria*, Proceedings of a National Conference. Ibadan: NISER, 176 – 186.

Owosekun, A. and Odama, O. (1982). The Causes of Inflation in Nigeria – Some Empirical Evidence. In K. Awosika & H.M. Onitiri (eds.), *Inflation in Nigeria*, Proceedings of a National Conference, Ibadan: NISER, 98 – 111.

Parker, T. (2016). *Will Quantitative Easing Be Japan's Saviour?* Retrieved from http:/www.investopedia.com/articles/investing/047913/will-quantitative-easing-be-japans-saviour.asp

Phelps, E. (1972). *Inflation Policy and Unemployment: Cost-benefit Approach to Monetary Planning.* New York: Norton.

Phillips, A.W. (1958). The Relationship between Unemployment and the Rate of Change of Money Wage Rates in the United Kingdom, 1962-1957. *Economica*, November, 282-299.

Rao, P. & Miller, R.L. (1972). *Applied Econometrics.* New Delhi: Prentice-Hall of India Private Ltd.

Ratnasiri, H. P. G. S. (2011). The main determinants of inflation in Sri Lanka: A VAR based analysis. *Staff studies*, 39(1).

Reese, J. E. (1977). The New Inflation, *Journal of Economic Issues*, XI(2), 285-297.

Reynolds, G.C. (2016). *Quick Take Q & A: Why Japan's Central Bank Targeted the Yield Curve.* Retrieved from http:/www.bloomberg.com/news/articles/2016-09-21/quicktake-q-a-what-s-a-yield-curve-and-why-boj-targeting-it

Ross, S. (2016a). *Japan's Case Study: Diminished Effects on QE.* Retrieved from http://www.investopedia.com/articles/markets/052516/japans-case-study-diminished-effects-qe.asp

Ross, S. (2016b). *Why Negative Interest Rates Are Still Not Working In Japan.* http://www.investopedia.com/articles/markets/080716/why-interst-rates-are-still-not-working-japan.asp

Ross, S. (2016c). *Deflation and Debt: Is the Unites States the New Japan?* Retrieved from http://www.investopedia.com/articles/markets/052816/deflation-and –debt-united-states-new-japan.asp

Ross, S. (2016d). *Is the Bank of Japan Failing as a Central Bank?* Retrieved from http://www.investopedia.com/articles/politics-money/0630/bank-japan-failing-central-bank.asp

Saka, O., Fuertes, A.M. & Kalotychou E. (2015). How did the ECB save the Eurozone without spending a single euro?. *Vox EU*, March 26. Retrieved from voxeu.org

Samuelson, P. & Solow, R. (1960). Analytical Aspects of Anti-Inflation Policy. *American Economic Review*, 50(2), 177 – 194.

Schultz, C.L (1969). Sectoral Shifts and Inflation. In R.J. Ball & P. Doyle (eds.), *Inflation*. Harmondsworth: Penguin Books.

Shetty, R. (2016). *The Economy of India: Why doesn't the RBI adopt Quantitative Easing like US is?* Retrieved from https://www.quora.com/Economy-of-India-Why-doesn't-the-RBI-adopt-Quantitative-Easing-like- US-is

Shobhit, S. (2015). *How Does China Manage its Money Supply?* Retrieved from http:/www.investopedia.com/articles/investigation/072815/how-does-china-manage-its-money

Smaghi, L.B. (2009). *Conventional and unconventional monetary policy*. Keynote lecture at the International Center for Monetary and Banking Studies, Paris. December 4.

Smith, L. (2014). *The treasury and the Federal Reserve*. Retrieved from http://www.investopedia.com/articles/08/treasury-fed-reserve-asp

Summers, L.H. (2000). International Financial Crisis: Causes, Prevention and Cures. *American Economic Review*, Papers and Proceedings, No. 2 (May).

Sunkel, O. (1960). Inflation of Chile: an Unorthodox Approach, *International Economic Papers*. 10, 107 – 131.

Systemic Risk and Systemic Value (Editorial). (2016). *Japan's yield curve control: the basics*. Retrieved from http:/www.sr-sv.com/japan-yield-curve-control-a-brief-review/

Teriba, O., Edozien, E. & Kayode, M. (1981). *The Structure of Manufacturing in Nigeria*. Ibadan: Ibadan University Press.

Thei l, H. (1954). *Linear Aggregation of Economic Relations*. Amsterdam: North-Holland.

Thirwall, A. P. (1974). *Inflation, Savings and Growth in Developing Economies*. London and Basingstoke: Macmillan.

Tobin, J. (1972). Inflation and Unemployment. *American Economic Review*,1, 1 – 18.

Tomori, S. & Fajana, F.O. (1979). Development Planning. In Olaloku, F. A. (ed.), *Structure of the Nigerian Economy*, 131– 146. London and Basingstoke: Macmillan Press Ltd.

Totonchi, J. (2011). Macroeconomics Theory of Inflation. *International Conference on Economics and Finance Research*, 4, 459 – 462.

Turnovsky, S.J. (1977). *Macroeconomic Analysis and Stabilization Policy*. Cambridge: Cambridge University Press.

Ukpong, I.I. (1979). Social and Economic Infrastructure. In Olaloku, F. A. (ed.), *Structure of the Nigerian Economy*, 68 – 99. London and Basingstoke: Macmillan Press Ltd.

Vogel, R.C. (1974). The Dynamics of Inflation in Latin America. 1950 – 1969. *American Economic Review*, 64(1), 102 – 114.

Wang, J. (n.d.). *Why does the Federal Reserve prefer to control money supply indirectly with interest rates instead of directly with reserve requirements (like China)?* Retrieved from https:/www.quora.com/why-does-the-Federal-Reserve-prefer-to-control-money-supply-indirectly-with-interest-rates-instead-of-directly-with-reserve-requirements-like-china

Weintraub, E.R. (1977). The Microfoundations of Macroeconomics: A Critical Survey. *The Journal of Economic Literature*, 15, 1 – 23.

Xiaochuan, Z. (2012). *China's Monetary Policy since the Turn of the Century*. Retrieved from http:/m.english.caixin.com/m/2012-11-30/1004675 22.html

Yongding, Y. (2010). *China's Response to the Global Financial Crisis*. Retrieved from http:/eastasiaforum.org/2010/01/24/Chinese-response-to-the-global.financial.crisis/

Zhou, H. (2015). *China's Monetary Policy Regulation and Financial Risk Prevention*. Berlin: SpringerBerlin Heidelberg.

Appendices

Appendix A: Data Used For Estimation of the Error Correction Equations

Year	Agric GDP	Construction GDP	Consumer price index	GDP	Import price index	Manufacturing GDP
1960	13208	883.27	0.107329	20805.3	61.0236	1006.26
1961	12769.6	931.03	0.114068	20700	60.7696	1076.55
1962	13373.4	939.419	0.120074	21633.3	62.8581	1219.25
1963	14325.7	1008.23	0.116839	23586.4	66.1367	1480.67
1964	14226.1	1162.6	0.11784	24562.2	63.5437	1473.19
1965	13789.3	1452.62	0.122675	25351.5	68.4779	1749.33
1966	13785.4	1340.64	0.134563	25079.7	72.8826	1731.53
1967	11793.3	1194.92	0.129549	21247.6	72.6572	1499.05
1968	10976.3	1019.14	0.128932	20601.6	72.4776	1540.35
1969	12052	1348.34	0.142026	24990.5	77.8039	1984.14
1970	15946.5	1670.54	0.161565	32687.2	74.7821	2342.09
1971	16187.2	2195.68	0.187414	35487.8	75.5938	2218.62
1972	15950.5	2682.4	0.193894	37069.3	82.025	2635.98
1973	15957.4	2832.62	0.204369	42229.9	90.1754	3045.47
1974	19012.3	7282.51	0.230272	81743	106.671	6900.61
1975	19038.1	5882.26	0.308482	69615.9	78.9783	3794.19
1976	15965.8	6795.82	0.383443	69517	78.662	3818.82
1977	16772.5	6777.4	0.441296	71426.7	71.8538	3842.27
1978	14957.3	5729.29	0.537098	64308.7	58.8981	5428.84
1979	15355.5	5320.61	0.599991	69958.9	82.0639	6359.38
1980	15172.9	5563.87	0.659824	75220.6	84.4848	7823.62
1981	17036.1	3478.64	0.797152	59737.3	64.0489	5895.93
1982	18526.8	2898.03	0.858514	57156.1	59.9584	5879.47
1983	17808	2132.74	1.0578	50205.7	63.4046	5240.11
1984	19096.1	1529.33	1.2463	47839.6	77.4645	3889.52
1985	19884.9	1144.17	1.33897	50717.1	86.5179	4796.71

Appendix A continued....1

Year	Agric GDP	Construction GDP	Consumer price index	GDP	Import price index	Manufacturing GDP
1986	19701.2	1356.39	1.41552	48849.3	82.9867	4656.33
1987	24886.3	1380.66	1.57533	66794	87.2942	4740.87
1988	23797.4	1013.53	2.43407	57141.1	82.1625	4526.49
1989	19034.5	1052.42	3.66246	59194.5	90.4834	3406.32
1990	21449.8	1106.45	3.93218	68041.1	97.914	3738.99
1991	21933.4	1102.77	4.44364	70244.2	79.8536	4355.89
1992	22603.1	950.929	6.425	82897	81.7411	4202.96
1993	22958.6	794.138	10.0979	67724.1	78.9093	3860.93
1994	22024.8	651.112	15.8569	56749.1	77.4582	3966.59
1995	22615.5	502.964	27.4063	70539	77.2722	3841.8
1996	23751.4	452.816	35.4276	76288.4	96.9834	3751.23
1997	24800	488.321	38.4496	72874	82.4755	3747.95
1998	25006	588.224	42.2931	64039.5	65.5932	3345.61
1999	25008.6	610.471	45.0923	70832.9	80.3573	3347.5
2000	24739.6	634.691	48.2186	95028.1	92.0504	3484.9
2001	27824.8	710.828	57.3193	82434.5	80.2799	3473.17
2002	51886.6	741.66	64.7	106837	74.2528	3660.36
2003	49127.8	798.408	73.7786	115034	82.8422	3900.04
2004	46011.1	1957.46	84.8439	134495	96.8432	4117.16
2005	47732	2157.86	100	145722	100	4127.07
2006	54880.5	2312.76	108.24	171514	97.3406	4420.97
2007	59245.6	2336.07	114.065	181101	94.2713	4566.54
2008	62711.5	2408.88	127.272	190901	91.7773	4600.97
2009	64712.4	2449.29	141.956	174662	86.0857	4313.38
2010	63869.8	2444.78	161.432	210520	83.5103	3983.52
2011	64773.5	2548.66	178.933	209820	80.6403	3882.58

Appendix A continued...2

Year	Nominal Money supply	Non-agric/Agric GDP ratio	Non-agric GDP	Non-agric GDP(excluding petroleum)	Petroleum export value	Wholesale and Retail GDP
1960	267.6	57.5198	7597.24	7532	251.117	2642.35
1961	287.4	62.1035	7930.37	7744.5	277.624	2566.89
1962	302.742	61.7636	8259.89	8018.4	274.547	2606.72
1963	315.75	64.6433	9260.64	9014.1	318.884	2966.48
1964	363.683	72.6557	10336.1	9978	393.738	3229.81
1965	410.667	83.8496	11562.2	10691.6	390.266	3311.18
1966	456.158	81.9299	11294.4	10335.7	163.805	3235.66
1967	453.517	80.1676	9454.37	8900.1	179.3	2752.64
1968	420.475	87.6908	9625.24	9291.7	307.465	2654.12
1969	548.408	107.355	12938.5	11315.5	301.114	3217.01
1970	789.558	104.98	16740.7	13710.3	239.545	4149.42
1971	971.925	119.234	19300.6	14262.6	268.924	4291.04
1972	1055.82	132.402	21118.8	15218.6	233.117	4190.95
1973	1265.99	164.642	26272.5	16979.6	200.617	4547.16
1974	1753.72	329.948	62730.7	44887.8	227.557	16614.8
1975	3031.33	265.665	50577.8	37074.5	382.519	14033.8
1976	4510.55	335.413	53551.2	37627.3	247.755	14348.4
1977	6147	325.856	54654.2	38629.6	231.591	15345
1978	7392.76	329.948	49351.4	35314.1	204.804	13071.2
1979	9185.8	355.596	54603.4	36790.4	383.339	14543.2
1980	11856.6	395.755	60047.7	38621.7	344.638	14575.4
1981	14471.2	250.652	42701.2	29880.8	150.285	8102.19
1982	15786.7	208.505	38629.3	28713.4	262.663	7708.56
1983	17687.9	181.928	32397.8	25412.7	162.224	7854.28
1984	20105.9	150.521	28743.6	21492.1	226.591	6897.93
1985	22299.2	155.054	30832.2	22336.8	38.6865	6861

Appendix A continued...3

Year	Nominal Money supply	Non-agric/Agric GDP ratio	Non-agric GDP	Non-agric GDP(excluding petroleum)	Petroleum export value	Wholesale and Retail GDP
1986	24001.13	147.95	29148	22395.1	645.63	6704.84
1987	27573.6	168.397	41907.7	24944.4	2012.34	9404.85
1988	38356.8	140.115	33343.7	21076.5	1562.45	8524.12
1989	45902.9	210.986	40160	19264.2	1275.54	8837.73
1990	52857	217.211	46591.3	21103.3	1544.46	9113.94
1991	75401.2	220.261	48310.8	22087.7	1749.06	9404.95
1992	111112	266.75	60293.9	21877.1	3044.59	9695.91
1993	165339	194.984	44765.6	20789.3	4073.74	9987.14
1994	230293	157.66	34724.3	20906.3	2670.74	9989.02
1995	289091	211.905	47923.5	19954.8	5685.77	9994.52
1996	345854	221.195	52537	19853.2	4577.74	10078.4
1997	413280	193.847	48074	20271.9	4340.81	10204.1
1998	488146	156.096	39033.4	21612.3	4157.98	10509.6
1999	628952	183.234	45824.3	23105	4693.97	10770.5
2000	878457	284.113	70288.5	24939.2	4579.51	10939.5
2001	1300000	196.263	54609.8	25492.1	4136.6	11212.6
2002	1500000	105.906	54950.8	27148.3	5590.57	11938.7
2003	2000000	134.152	65906	28746.8	5407.02	12498.9
2004	2100000	192.31	88483.8	38418.7	3749.41	17495.9
2005	2600000	205.293	97990.4	41341.6	7972.99	18682.5
2006	3800000	212.523	116634	52119.8	6565.84	25330.8
2007	5100000	205.678	121855	55813.7	6734.98	26693.3
2008	8000000	204.412	128190	56706.9	10895.8	27525.2
2009	9400000	169.904	109949	57692.5	7492.08	28757.9
2010	11000000	229.608	146650	56793.6	10882.1	28796.5
2011	12000000	223.928	145046	58332.4	17005.2	30111.9

Source: Central Bank of Nigeria, Statistical Bulletin (Various Issues)

Appendix B: Federal Government Domestic Debt Outstanding By Holder Category, 1960 – 2011

	CBN				Non-Bank Public			
	Amt (N'm)	% of Total	Amt (N'm)	% of Total	Amt (N'm)	% of Total	Total (N'm)
1960	4.60	15.33	3.70	12.33	21.70	72.33	**30.00**
1961	17.20	32.27	5.90	11.07	30.20	56.66	**53.30**
1962	32.60	38.44	6.70	7.90	45.50	53.66	**84.80**
1963	61.20	60.12	2.40	2.36	38.20	37.52	**101.80**
1964	46.30	33.97	10.70	7.85	79.30	58.18	**136.30**
1965	30.80	16.78	12.90	7.03	139.80	76.19	**183.50**
1966	72.70	31.91	22.50	9.88	132.60	58.21	**227.80**
1967	101.70	42.77	28.50	11.98	107.60	45.25	**237.80**
1968	76.10	16.88	195.70	43.42	178.90	39.69	**450.70**
1969	104.80	15.74	334.50	50.23	226.60	34.03	**665.90**
1970	102.70	9.41	500.20	45.85	488.10	44.74	**1,091.00**
1971	149.50	12.18	290.80	23.70	786.70	64.12	**1,227.00**
1972	37.10	3.76	382.70	38.76	567.50	57.48	**987.30**
1973	102.70	9.71	389.90	36.88	564.60	53.41	**1,057.20**
1974	28.60	2.27	767.40	60.79	466.40	36.95	**1,262.40**
1975	4.00	0.24	741.40	44.25	930.10	55.51	**1,675.50**
1976	59.90	2.28	1,082.20	41.20	1,484.80	56.52	**2,626.90**
1977	240.60	7.06	1,217.10	35.73	1,949.00	57.21	**3,406.70**
1978	1,204.30	25.02	978.50	20.33	2,630.90	54.65	**4,813.70**
1979	1,109.90	15.39	2,204.60	30.56	3,899.50	54.05	**7,214.00**

1980	1,592.40	19.38	2,502.40	30.46	4,120.80	50.16	**8,215.60**
1981	4,523.60	40.42	1,843.30	16.47	4,825.70	43.12	**11,192.60**
1982	6,488.90	43.24	2,993.30	19.95	5,525.40	36.82	**15,007.60**
1983	10,402.20	46.81	5,525.90	24.87	6,293.30	28.32	**22,221.40**
1984	9,531.70	37.13	9,620.10	37.47	6,520.30	25.40	**25,672.10**
1985	9,905.50	35.44	11,388.80	40.75	6,654.80	23.81	**27,949.10**
1986	16,103.30	56.62	4,570.20	16.07	7,765.20	27.31	**28,438.70**
1987	17,646.90	47.97	7,858.10	21.36	11,284.10	30.67	**36,789.10**
1988	26,636.00	56.64	7,477.50	15.90	12,916.10	27.46	**47,029.60**
1989	15,647.70	33.26	3,698.60	7.86	27,703.30	58.88	**47,049.60**
1990	27,380.80	32.56	9,064.50	10.78	47,647.80	56.66	**84,093.10**
1991	62,294.30	53.61	7,486.50	6.44	46,417.90	39.95	**116,198.70**
1992	138,769.60	77.98	6,228.40	3.50	32,963.70	18.52	**177,961.70**
1993	202,434.70	73.93	38,879.40	14.20	32,522.30	11.88	**273,836.40**
1994	308,440.80	75.68	47,272.10	11.60	51,869.80	12.73	**407,582.70**
1995	414,285.90	86.72	22,295.60	4.67	41,152.40	8.61	**477,733.90**
1996	312,804.30	74.48	56,065.20	13.35	51,106.10	12.17	**419,975.60**
1997	403,301.50	80.38	45,100.10	8.99	53,349.50	10.63	**501,751.10**
1998	454,910.50	81.11	57,675.00	10.28	48,244.70	8.60	**560,830.20**
1999	530,420.80	66.74	201,490.80	25.35	62,895.00	7.91	**794,806.60**
2000	511,445.80	56.94	292,056.80	32.51	94,751.30	10.55	**898,253.90**
2001	738,585.40	72.63	202,966.20	19.96	75,422.40	7.42	**1,016,974.00**
2002	532,453.20	45.66	461,357.00	39.57	172,190.50	14.77	**1,166,000.70**
2003	613,800.00	46.16	500,430.00	37.64	215,460.00	16.20	**1,329,690.00**

2004	403,490.00	29.44	669,070.00	48.83	297,760.00	21.73	**1,370,320.00**
2005	501,970.00	32.90	759,610.00	49.78	264,330.00	17.32	**1,525,910.00**
2006	335,530.00	19.14	882,850.00	50.36	534,870.00	30.51	**1,753,250.00**
2007	290,590.00	13.39	1,394,750.00	64.29	484,290.00	22.32	**2,169,630.00**
2008	289,370.00	12.47	1,482,160.00	63.88	548,780.00	23.65	**2,320,310.00**
2009	323,180.00	10.01	1,274,580.00	39.48	1,630,270.00	50.50	**3,228,030.00**
2010	343,140.00	7.54	2,605,010.00	57.23	1,603,670.00	35.23	**4,551,820.00**
2011	348,840.00	6.20	3,790,900.00	67.42	1,483,100.00	26.38	**5,622,840.00**

Sources:
i. Debt data for the period, 1960 to 1999 from the CBN (Several Annual Reports, including CBN's Statistical Bulletin)
ii. Debt data for the period, 2000 to 2011 from the DMO's Annual Reports and Publications

213

Appendix C1: Summary of the long run analysis of price-output relationship.

Eq Name:	EQ01	EQ02	EQ03	EQ04	EQ06
LOG(GDP)	-1.239				
	(0.247)*				
LOG(MS)	0.982	1.014	0.794	0.727	0.719
	(0.047)*	(0.054)*	(0.007)*	(0.019)*	(0.032)*
C	4.410	4.048	-0.862	-2.913	-2.720
	(2.283)	(2.829)	(0.322)**	(0.758)*	(1.066)**
LOG(AGDP)		-0.482	-0.089	-0.182	
		(0.305)	(0.037)**	(0.074)**	
LOG(NAGDP)		-0.837			
		(0.155)*			
LOG(IMPX)				0.426	0.211
				(0.092)*	(0.204)
LOG(PEXP)			0.154	0.010	0.052
			(0.011)*	(0.021)	(0.047)
LOG(NAGDPN)			-0.654		

				(0.022)*	
LOG(MGDP)				-0.513	-0.621
				(0.052)*	(0.130)*
LOG(CGDP)				-0.449	-0.422
				(0.041)*	(0.082)*
LOG(WRGDP)				0.410	0.179
				(0.076)*	(0.187)
LOG(NAAGR)					0.289
					(0.123)**
R-squared:	0.987	0.987	0.994	0.995	0.995

*significant at 1% level
** significant at 5% level

Appendix C2: Summary of the short run analysis of price-output relationship

Eq Name:	EQ01	EQ02	EQ03	EQ04	EQ05
ΔLOG(CPI(-1))	0.598 (0.069)*	0.608 (0.089)*	0.430 (0.056)*	0.547 (0.055)*	0.540 (0.055)*
Δ(LOG(GDP))	-0.124 (0.056)**				
Δ(LOG(MS))	0.491 (0.076)*			0.502 (0.060)*	0.487 (0.058)*
Δ(LOG(MS(-1)))		0.297 0.073)*	0.405 (0.067)*		
Δ(LOG(AGDP))		-0.167 (0.082)**	-0.184 (0.052)*	-0.209 (0.061)*	
ΔLOG(NAGDP)(-1))		0.155 (0.055)*			
ΔLOG(NAGDPN(-2))			-0.134 (0.047)*		
Δ(LOG(NAAGR))					0.149 (0.038)*
Δ(LOG(PEXP(-1)))			0.035 (0.011)*		
Δ(LOG(MGDP))				-0.078 (0.044)	-0.154 (0.046)*
Δ(LOG(CGDP))				-0.010 (0.034)	-0.063 (0.035)
Δ(LOG(WRGDP(-2)))				-0.149 (0.037)*	-0.134 (0.036)*
Δ(LOG(PEXP(-2)))				0.031 (0.011)**	0.042 (0.011)*
Δ(LOG(IMPX(-2)))				0.164 (0.062)**	0.189 (0.063)*
MODEL_ECM(-1)	-0.107 (0.034)*	-0.136 (0.042)*	-0.153 (0.034)*	-0.159 (0.039)*	-0.175 (0.039)*
C	-0.038		0.010	-0.025	-0.029

	(0.020)		(0.013)	(0.016)	(0.016)
R-*squared:*	0.643	0.525	0.567	0.714	0.719

*significant at 1% level
** significant at 5% level

Appendix D: Remit Letter from the Chancellor of the Exchequer to the Governor of the Bank of England

HM Treasury, 1 Horse Guards Road, London, SW1A 2HQ

Mark Carney
Governor
Bank of England
Threadneedle Street
London
EC2R 8AH

16 March 2016

REMIT FOR THE MONETARY POLICY COMMITTEE

The Bank of England Act (1998) requires that I specify the definition of price stability and the Government's economy policy objectives at least once in every period of 12 months beginning on the anniversary of the day the Act came into force.

I hereby re-confirm the inflation target as 2 per cent as measured by the 12-month increase in the Consumer Prices Index (CPI). The inflation target of 2 per cent applies at all times. This reflects the primacy of price stability and the inflation target in the UK monetary policy framework. Price stability represents an essential pre-requisite for economic prosperity.

The Government's commitment to medium-term price stability remains absolute. The inflation target is symmetric: deviations below the target are treated in the same way as deviations above the target. This ensures the framework does not have a deflationary bias, given the risks such as bias would pose to achieving the Government's economy policy objective, which, in accordance with the Act, I confirm is to achieve strong sustainable and balanced growth that is more evenly shared across the country and between industries.

Monetary policy has a critical role to play in supporting the economy as the Government delivers on its commitment to necessary fiscal consolidation. Over this Parliament the Government and the Bank of England have taken a number of important steps to enhance transparency and accountability and to ensure that monetary policy can continue to play its role fully.

The Bank of England and Financial Services Bill will implement the remaining recommendations from Governor Warsh's review on *Transparency and the Bank of England's Monetary Policy Committee* and will ensure that the Bank of England is well equipped to fulfil its vital role of overseeing monetary policy and financial stability, a key part of the government's long term plan to build a resilient economy.

I updated the Monetary Policy Committee remit on 14 January 2015 to ensure that, if inflation moves away from target by more than 1 percentage point in either direction, the open letter will be published alongside the first routine publication after the meeting of the Committee that follows the release of the CPI data. This is a key element of the Committee's transparency and accountability in communicating its strategy at times when inflation deviates from target.

Alongside fiscal credibility and comprehensive reforms of the UK's regulatory architecture, of which the Financial Policy Committee is a key element, these steps have enhanced the strength and resilience of the UK's macroeconomic framework. This framework has performed well through testing times, and is now well-equipped to address future challenges. The Financial Policy Committee and the Monetary Policy Committee should continue to have regard to each other's actions, to enhance coordination between monetary and macroprudential policy

Finally, I also confirm that the Asset Purchase Facility, created on 29 January 2009, will remain in place for the financial year 2016-17.

A copy of the remit is attached.

GEORGE OSBORNE

REMIT FOR THE MONETARY POLICY COMMITTEE

The Bank of England Act came into effect on 1 June 1998. The Act states that in relation to monetary policy, the objectives of the Bank of England shall be:

a. To maintain price stability; and

b. Subject to that, to support the economic policy of Her Majesty's Government, including its objectives for growth and employment.

In order to comply with the Act, this remit sets out what price stability shall be taken to consist of and what the economic policy of the Government shall be taken to be.

Price stability

I confirm that the operational target for monetary policy remains an inflation rate of 2 per cent, measured by the 12-month increase in the Consumer Prices Index. The inflation target of 2 per cent applies at all times. This reflects the primacy of price stability and the inflation target in the UK monetary policy framework.

The inflation target is forward-looking to ensure inflation expectations are firmly anchored in the medium term. The Government believes that low and stable medium-term inflation is an essential pre-requisite for economic prosperity.

The framework is based on the recognition that the actual inflation rate will on occasion depart from its target as a result of shocks and disturbances. Such factors will typically move inflation away from the target temporarily. Attempts to keep inflation at the inflation target in these circumstances may cause undesirable volatility in output due to the short-term trade-offs involved, and the Monetary Policy Committee may therefore wish to allow inflation to deviate from the target temporarily.

Circumstances may also arise in which attempts to keep inflation at the inflation target could exacerbate the development of imbalances that the Financial Policy Committee may judge to represent a potential risk to financial stability. The Financial Policy Committee's macroprudential tools are the first line of defence against such risks, but in these circumstances the Monetary Policy Committee may wish to allow inflation to deviate from the target temporarily, consistent with its need to have regard to the policy actions of the Financial Policy Committee.

In exceptional circumstances, shocks to the economy may be particularly large or the effects of shocks may persist over an extended period, or both. In such circumstances, the Monetary Policy Committee is likely to be faced with more significant trade-offs between the speed with which it aims to bring inflation back to the target and the consideration that should be placed on the variability of output.

In forming and communicating its judgements the Committee should promote understanding of the trade-offs inherent in setting monetary policy to meet a forward-looking inflation target while giving due consideration to output volatility. It should set out in its communication:

- The outlook for inflation and, if relevant, the reasons why inflation has moved away from the target or is expected to move away from the target;

- The policy action the Committee is taking in response;

- The horizon over which the Committee judges it is appropriate to return inflation to the target;

- The trade-off that has been made with regard to inflation and output variability in determining the scale and duration of any expected deviation of inflation from the target; and

- How this approach meets the Government's monetary policy objectives.

If inflation moves away from the target by more than 1 percentage point in either direction, I shall expect you to send an open letter to me, covering the same considerations set out above and referring as necessary to the Bank's latest Inflation Report and forecasts, alongside whichever is the earlier of (a) the minutes of the Monetary Policy Committee meeting that followed the publication of the CPI data, or (b) the Inflation Report that followed the publication of the CPI data. The reason for publishing the open letter at that time is to allow the Committee time to form and communicate its strategy towards returning inflation to the target after consideration of the trade-offs.

You would send a further letter after three months, sent, as before, alongside whichever is the earlier of the minutes of the third subsequent Monetary Policy Committee meeting or the Inflation Report, if inflation remained more than 1 percentage point above or below the target.

In keeping with the principles underpinning the monetary policy framework, and the practice followed in previous inflation open letter exchanges, I suggest that you copy your letters to the Chair of the Treasury Committee.

In responding to your letter and confirming whether an appropriate balance has been struck in the judgements the Committee has made, I shall, of course, have regard to the circumstances prevailing at the time.

The thresholds do not define a target range. Their function is to define the points at which I shall expect an explanatory letter from you because the actual inflation rate is appreciably away from its target.

Unconventional policy instruments

In the event of exceptional shocks that result in the Monetary Policy Committee's conventional policy instrument having approached its effective lower bound, as has been the case since March 2009, the Committee may judge it necessary to deploy unconventional policy instruments in order to set monetary policy consistent with the requirements of this remit.

Where those instruments involve unconventional interventions in specific markets or activities, with implications for credit risk or credit allocation, I shall expect the Committee to work with the Government to ensure the appropriate governance arrangements are in place to ensure accountability in the deployment of such instruments. This was the case with the Bank of England and the Treasury in establishing the Asset Purchase Facility in 2009 and the Funding for Lending Scheme in 2012.

The Committee may also judge it to be appropriate to deploy forward guidance in order to influence expectations and thereby meet its objectives more effectively. The Government considers any use of this to be a matter subject to the Committee's operational independence in setting policy.

Government's economic policy objectives

The Government's economic policy objective is to achieve strong, sustainable and balanced growth that is more evenly shared across the country and between industries. This objective recognises that over a number of years preceding the recent financial crisis, economic growth in the UK was driven by unsustainable levels of private sector debt and rising public sector debt. This pattern of unbalanced growth and excessive debt helped to create exceptional economic challenges in the UK.

The Government's economic strategy consists of four key pillars:

- Monetary activism and credit easing, stimulating demand, maintaining price stability and supporting the flow of credit in the economy;

- Deficit reduction, returning the public finances to a sustainable position and ensuring that sound public finances and fiscal credibility underpin low long-term interest rates;

- Reform of the financial system, improving the regulatory framework to reduce risks to the taxpayer and build the resilience of the system; and

- A comprehensive package of structural reforms, rebalancing and strengthening the economy for the future, including a package of measures to support businesses to invest and export.

Accountability

The Monetary Policy Committee is accountable to the Government for the remit set out in this letter. The Committee's performance and procedures will be reviewed by the Oversight Committee of the Court on an ongoing basis (with particular regard to ensuring the Bank is collecting proper regional and sectoral information). The Bank will be accountable to Parliament through regular reports and evidence given to the Treasury Committee. Finally, through the publication of the minutes of the Monetary Policy Committee meetings and the Inflation Report, the Bank will be accountable to the public at large.

Restatement of the Remit

The inflation target will be confirmed in each Budget. There is a value in continuity and I will have proper regard to that, but I will also need to consider the case for a revised target at these times on its merits. Any changes to this remit will be set out in the Budget. The Budget will also contain a statement of the Government's economic policy objectives.

Coordination between monetary policy and macroprudential policy

In order to foster coordination between monetary and macroprudential policy, there is overlap between the membership of the Monetary Policy Committee and the Financial Policy Committee. To enhance that coordination, where appropriate, the Monetary Policy Committee should reflect, in any statements on its decisions, the minutes of its meetings and its Inflation Reports, how it has had regard to the policy actions of the Financial Policy Committee. In the same way, the Government had also asked the Financial Policy Committee to note in the records of its meetings, its policy statements and its Financial Stability Reports how it has had regard to the policy settings and forecasts of the Monetary Policy Committee.

Appendix E: Sample of Letter Conveying the Inflation Report from the Governor of the Bank of England to the Chancellor of the Exchequer

BANK OF ENGLAND

Mark Carney
Governor

The Rt Hon George Osborne
Chancellor of the Exchequer
HM Treasury
1 Horse Guards Road
London
SW1A 2HQ

12 May 2016

Dear Chancellor

On 12 April, the Office for National Statistics (ONS) published data showing that twelve-month CPI inflation was 0.5% in March. As required by the Remit of the Monetary Policy Committee, this letter – which will be published alongside the May Inflation Report – addresses the following.

- The reasons why inflation has moved away from the target and the outlook for inflation.
- The horizon over which the MPC judges it appropriate to return inflation to the target.
- The trade-off that has been made with regard to inflation and output variability in determining the scale and duration of any expected deviation of inflation from the target.
- The policy action that the MPC is taking in response.
- How this approach meets the Government's monetary policy objective.

The forthcoming referendum on the United Kingdom's membership of the European Union makes addressing a number of these issues more challenging than usual.

Why has inflation moved away from the target?

Twelve-month CPI inflation stood at 0.5% in March, 1.5 percentage points below the target. As in my previous letters to you, Table 1 shows a breakdown of the arithmetic contributions of different components of CPI inflation to the deviation from the target.

Table 1: Arithmetic contributions to March 2016 CPI inflation relative to the pre-crisis average

Percentage points	1997-2007 average	March 2016	March 2016 difference from average	Memo: difference in February 2015 open letter(b)
Energy	0.3	-0.5	-0.8	-0.8
Food, non-alcoholic bevs.	0.2	-0.3	-0.5	-0.4
Other goods(a)	-0.1	-0.1	0.0	0.2
Services	1.6	1.3	-0.2	-0.5
Total	2.0	0.5	-1.5	-1.4

(a) Adjusted for the close to 0.4 percentage point downward bias from clothing that existed until 2010.
(b) Relates to the December 2014 CPI release.

2

As I have noted in previous letters, the underlying causes of the below-target inflation of the past year and a half have been: sharp falls in commodity prices, the past appreciation of sterling, and to a lesser degree the subdued pace of domestic cost growth.

In fact, as Table 1 indicates, more than four-fifths of the deviation is accounted for by food and energy prices alone, with the most quantitatively significant factor remaining the sharp fall in energy prices between the middle of 2014 and beginning of 2016. Notwithstanding the most recent increase in the sterling price of oil, on average in March it stood around 25% below the level of a year earlier. Similarly, while the sterling price of wholesale gas has risen during the past two weeks, it had declined by almost 40% in the twelve months to March. These movements have resulted in a contribution of domestic energy prices to the latest CPI inflation figure some 0.8 percentage points lower than seen on average in the decade preceding the financial crisis and, on its own, this accounts for roughly a half of the deviation of inflation from the target.

A further third of the deviation of inflation from the target reflects the continued decline in food prices, itself a consequence of reductions in the prices of the underlying commodities, the past appreciation of sterling and continued intense competition amongst food retailers.

The sterling effective exchange rate index appreciated by over 15% between the summers of 2013 and 2015, and the impact of the consequent reduction in imported costs on retail prices is still evident beyond the food and energy components. In March, the contribution of other goods prices to CPI inflation, although now at its average in the ten years prior to the financial crisis, remained lower than when I first wrote to you in February 2015. It is also possible that the effects of the earlier appreciation continue to be felt in some of the more import-intensive consumer service sectors. Nevertheless, given the recent recovery in some indicators of imported input prices, as well as the most recent depreciation of sterling, it is possible that the negative impact of the 2013-15 sterling appreciation on retail prices is now past its peak.

Although these factors explain the vast majority of the deviation of inflation from the 2% target in March, subdued domestic cost growth remains an influence. This can be seen in the continued weakness of consumer service-price inflation.[1] Muted domestic cost growth can be seen more directly in the subdued rates of pay growth that have persisted despite the tightening of the labour market over the past few years. The unemployment rate has now fallen back to the level prevailing before the financial crisis. There are a number of possible explanations for the continued weakness of pay growth, as set out in my previous letters and the Bank's *Inflation Report*. The weakness of productivity growth since the recession, shifts in the composition of the workforce and the low level of consumer price inflation are all likely to have played a role. The net result has been that both pay and unit labour cost growth remain below historical norms and, in the judgement of the MPC, below the rates consistent with inflation being at the target.

---

[1] Particularly after accounting for what will very probably turn out to be a temporary boost to the inflation rate of these components partly from the sharp increase in airfares in March related to the proximity of the CPI price collection date to the Easter holidays.

The outlook for CPI inflation

The twelve-month CPI inflation rate of 0.5% in March was a little higher than anticipated at the time of the February *Inflation Report* and my letter to you three months ago. As described above, in Footnote 1, this probably reflects a higher Easter-related spike in airfares than expected. This is likely to prove temporary and the MPC expects that CPI inflation will fall back in the April data, before rising gradually thereafter.

The outlook for inflation over the next three years is set out in detail in today's May *Inflation Report*. The MPC's projections are normally conditioned on asset prices prevailing in the run-up to each *Report*. However, as set out in the box on page 40 of that *Report*, current asset prices are likely to have been affected by market participants' perceptions about the consequences of the forthcoming referendum on the UK's membership of the European Union. In particular, there is evidence that the referendum is having a marked influence on the sterling exchange rate. The evidence in that box suggests that roughly half of the 9% fall in the exchange rate since its November 2015 peak might be accounted for by referendum effects, including uncertainty about the outcome together with concerns that a vote to leave might reduce the openness of the UK economy and its long-run potential supply. Once the uncertainty over the outcome is resolved it is possible that the exchange rate will adjust again, consistent with market participants' view of the outlook at that time.

Following its usual approach, which is to assume government policy is followed, the MPC's May projections are conditioned on an assumed continuation of EU membership. The Committee has therefore taken a judgement not to let that part of the fall in the exchange rate that appears to have been associated with the referendum feed through to its growth or inflation projections.

Conditional on those assumptions, the broad outlook for inflation described by the MPC's projections is in most respects similar to the one I described three months ago. The MPC continues to expect that CPI inflation will pick up over the next year or so as the impact of past reductions in commodity prices fades from the twelve-month calculation and as the effect of the earlier appreciation of sterling on import-intensive goods and services wanes. That recovery in inflation is likely to be supported by the recent increase in oil prices and some additional stimulus from lower market interest rates.

Further ahead, if the path of demand evolves as described in the central forecast – supported by low interest rates and a gradual pick-up in nominal wage growth – then it is likely that the remaining margin of spare capacity in the economy will be used up during 2016, in turn raising domestic costs. In the conditional projections set out in today's *Report* the Committee judges it likely that these factors will be sufficient to return inflation back to 2% by mid-2018.

The most significant risks to this forecast concern the referendum. A vote to leave the EU could have material economic effects – on the exchange rate, on demand and on the economy's supply potential – that could affect the appropriate setting of monetary policy.

4

The recent behaviour of the foreign exchange market suggests that, were the UK to vote to leave the EU, sterling's exchange rate would fall further, perhaps sharply. In isolation, this would boost inflation over the policy horizon.

Demand may also fall, in the face of tighter financial conditions, lower asset prices, and greater uncertainty about the UK's trading relationships. Households could defer consumption, firms delay investment, and global financial conditions could tighten, generating potential spillovers to foreign activity that, in turn, dampen demand for UK exports. All else equal, lower demand would tend to dampen inflation over the policy horizon.

Over time, there may be negative effects on supply, including slower capital accumulation and the need to reallocate resources across the economy in response to changing trading and investment patterns. All else equal, such supply effects would tend to boost inflation over the policy horizon.

Taking these together, it is likely that their combined effect would be to lower growth materially and raise the rate of inflation notably over the MPC's policy horizon. In such circumstances, the MPC would face a trade-off between stabilising inflation on the one hand and stabilising output and employment on the other. The implications for the direction of monetary policy will depend on the relative magnitude of the demand, supply and exchange rate effects.

Beyond the uncertainty over the result and impact of the EU referendum, there remain a number of other uncertainties surrounding the outlook, to which the MPC will also remain alert: the prospects for global growth; the resilience of UK households and corporate spending; the path of productivity growth; and the precise balance between the effects on CPI inflation of the waning drag from external costs and the anticipated recovery in domestic costs. These risks are described in detail in Section 5 of today's May *Inflation Report*.

Over what horizon is it appropriate to return inflation to the target? And what trade-off has been made with regard to inflation and output variability?

The MPC's Remit is clear that the inflation target is symmetric: deviations of inflation below the target are to be treated with the same importance as deviations above it.

The Remit is also clear that the inflation target applies at all times. It recognises, however, that there will be occasions when inflation will deviate from the target as a result of economic shocks and disturbances. In such situations, it would not be feasible to bring inflation back to the target immediately because it takes time for monetary policy to affect the economy. The peak effect of monetary policy on inflation is generally estimated to occur with a lag of between 12 and 24 months. Moreover, attempts to return inflation to the target too quickly could lead to undesirable volatility in output.

The appropriate horizon for returning inflation to the target depends on the trade-off the MPC faces between the speed with which this can be achieved and the consequences of doing so for output and employment. That trade-off depends on the nature of the disturbances that caused inflation to deviate from the target in the first place.

In my previous letters I noted that returning inflation to the target required balancing the persistent drags from sterling's past appreciation and muted world export price growth with increases in domestic cost growth. In the main, and conditional on the UK's continued membership of the EU, the forecasts published in the May *Inflation Report* continue to reflect those effects, with domestic cost growth having evolved broadly in line with the MPC's projections made at the time of the February *Inflation Report*. In that light, fully offsetting the drag on inflation from external factors over the short run would, in the Committee's judgement, involve too rapid an acceleration in domestic costs, one that would risk being unsustainable and involve undesirable volatility in output and employment. Given that trade-off, the MPC will continue to set monetary policy to ensure that growth is sufficient to absorb remaining spare capacity in a manner that returns inflation to the target in around two years and keeps it there in the absence of further shocks.

However, as described above, the referendum on the UK's membership of the European Union could have material implications for the outlook for UK activity and inflation and, in particular, a vote to leave the EU would have the potential to change significantly the trade-off faced by the MPC.

Were inflation to rise above the target and output growth to weaken following a vote to leave the EU, the MPC would need to judge the appropriate horizon over which to return inflation to the target without generating undesirable volatility in output and employment. That horizon would depend on a range of factors, including the likely magnitude and persistence of the pass through to inflation of any exchange rate change, together with the scale of the adjustment necessary to bring demand back in line with supply. In responding to whatever outlook materialises, the MPC would have to make careful judgements about the net effects of these potential influences on the path of demand, supply and inflation in determining the course for monetary policy necessary to deliver the inflation target.

In the event of a vote to remain in the EU, the MPC would reassess the appropriate stance of monetary policy given the constellation of asset prices, the speed with which uncertainty effects dissipate and the underlying momentum in the economy.

The policy action the Committee is taking in response

If the outlook evolves as envisaged in today's *Report*, the MPC will conduct monetary policy so that the margin of spare capacity is absorbed and inflation returns to the 2% target. In line with this outlook, the Committee continues to take significant steps to support the UK economic recovery and so eliminate the remaining slack. Bank Rate has been at a historically low level of 0.5% for more than six years. In addition, the MPC purchased £375 billion of assets financed by the issuance of central bank reserves between 2009 and 2012 and continues to reinvest the cash flows associated with all maturing gilts held in the Asset Purchase Facility (APF) in order to maintain the total stock at that level. As described in the November 2015 *Inflation Report*, the MPC's preference is to use Bank Rate as the active marginal instrument for monetary policy, and expects to maintain the stock of purchased assets at £375 billion until Bank Rate has reached a level from which it can be cut materially. The MPC currently judges that such a level of Bank Rate is around 2%.

6

The MPC has provided its assessment of the likely outlook for policy. In the February 2014 *Inflation Report*, the MPC said that, given the likely persistence of headwinds weighing on the economy, when Bank Rate did begin to rise, it was expected to do so more gradually than in previous cycles. Moreover, the persistence of those headwinds, together with the legacy of the financial crisis, meant that Bank Rate was expected to remain below average historical levels for some time to come.

This assessment has shaped financial market expectations of the future path of UK interest rates as the domestic and global economic expansions have evolved. Expected interest rates are now markedly lower than they were at the start of 2014. That has lowered borrowing costs for many UK households and companies, helping to support demand and inflation. Complementing this, the Bank more broadly continues to provide support to the healthy functioning of credit markets through the Funding for Lending Scheme.

The central projections set out in the *Inflation Report* today are conditioned on a gentle rise in interest rates over the forecast period. Under that central case, the MPC judges it more likely than not that Bank Rate will need to be higher at the end of that period than at present in order to return inflation to target in a sustainable manner.

These projections assume continued membership of the EU. However, the existence of the referendum and the associated uncertainty over its outcome makes macroeconomic and financial market indicators less informative than usual at the current juncture. In light of that, in advance of the referendum, the MPC has indicated that it will react more cautiously to incoming data than would normally be the case. Although some of this uncertainty will dissipate once the referendum result is known, it is possible that some of its effects will persist for some time thereafter.

Whatever the outcome of the referendum and its consequences, the MPC will take whatever action is needed to ensure that inflation expectations remained well anchored and inflation returns to the target over the appropriate horizon.

How does this approach meet the Government's monetary policy objectives?

The MPC's objective is to maintain price stability and, subject to that, to support the economic policy of Her Majesty's Government, including its objectives for growth and employment. Price stability is an essential pre-requisite for economic prosperity. The MPC is acting to return inflation to the target promptly by eliminating the remaining margin of slack in the economy.

229

7

Through co-ordinated action by the MPC, FPC and PRA, the Bank of England is guarding against the build-up of risks and imbalances that could threaten strong, sustainable, balanced growth and therefore making its most effective contribution to the United Kingdom's economic performance.

Yours sincerely

Appendix F: Sample of Letter of Response on Inflation Report from the Chancellor of the Exchequer to the Governor of the Bank of England

HM Treasury, I Horse Guards Road, London, SWIA 2HQ

12 May 2016

Mark Carney
Governor
The Bank of England
Threadneedle Street
London
EC2R 8AH

Dear Mark

CPI INFLATION

Thank you for your letter of 12 May on behalf of the Monetary Policy Committee (MPC) regarding March's CPI inflation figure, written under the terms of the MPC remit.

As you expected at the time of your February letter, inflation has remained below 1% in the past few months. I agree with your assessment that falling prices of food and energy and the past appreciation of sterling explain most of the deviation from target.

You make clear that the MPC continues to expect that inflation will pick up over the next year. Indeed, the MPC judges it more likely than not that Bank rate will need to be higher at the end of the forecast period in order to return inflation to the 2% target in a sustainable manner.

As you mention in your letter, the outcome of the EU referendum represents the most significant uncertainty in the UK economic outlook. It is my view that all the economic evidence available suggests that leaving the EU would do considerable and permanent damage to the UK economy. In April HM Treasury published an analysis of the long term impact of leaving the EU. The central estimate is that after 15 years outside of the EU Britain would be worse off by £4,300 per household per year.

As you point out in your letter, the EU referendum is already having an effect, and that uncertainty is beginning to weigh on economic activity. Your letter highlights the fact that sterling has fallen 9% since its November 2015 peak. Investment decisions are being postponed, consumers are holding back on purchasing decisions, and commercial real estate transactions fell by around 40% in Q1 2016.

The MPC's assessment is that a vote to leave the EU would mean both materially lower growth and notably higher inflation. Your letter acknowledges that "the MPC would face a trade-off between stabilising inflation on the one hand and stabilising output and employment on the other." So one choice would impose costs on families as higher inflation reduced real household incomes; the other choice would impose costs on families with a hit to the economy and to jobs. This is the kind of lose-lose situation that a vote to leave the EU creates. Either way, Britain would be poorer.

In these uncertain times clarity about our macroeconomic framework is vital. I confirm that the Government's commitment to the current regime of flexible inflation targeting, with an operational target of 2% CPI inflation, remains absolute. The target is symmetric: deviations below the target are treated the same way as deviations above the target. Symmetric targets help to ensure that inflation expectations remain anchored and that monetary policy can play its role fully.

As set out in my previous letters, I welcome that the MPC remains vigilant to both upside and downside risks to its forecast and stands ready to act if these risks materialise, to ensure inflation remains likely to return to target in a timely fashion.

I am copying this letter to the Chairman of the Treasury Committee and depositing it immediately in the libraries of both houses and on the Treasury website.

GEORGE OSBORNE

Appendix G: Highlights of Central Bank of Nigeria's Monetary Policy Committee Decisions, 2003-2016

YEAR	MONTH	MINIMUM REDISCOUNT RATE (MRR) %	MONETARY POLICY RATE (MPR) %	CASH RESERVE REQUIREMENT (CRR) %	LIQUIDITY RATIO (LR) %
2003					
	March	-	-	-	-
	April	-	-	-	-
	June	-	-	-	-
	August	15.00	-	-	-
2004					
	February	-	-	-	-
	June	-	-	-	-
	December	-	-	-	-
2005					
	January 24 & 25	13.00	-	-	-
	June 15	13.00	-	10.00	-
	November 1	-	-	-	-
2006					
	February 14	13.00	-	5.00	40.00
	June 8	14.00	-	5.00	-
	August 9	14.00	-	-	-
	November 28	Decision taken to replace MRR with MPR			
2007					
	February 7	-	10.00	3.00	40.00
	June 5	-	8.00	-	-
	August 1	-	8.00	-	-
	October 3	-	9.00	-	-
	December 4	-	9.50	-	-
2008					
	February 5	-	9.50	-	-

YEAR	MONTH	MINIMUM REDISCOUNT RATE (MRR) %	MONETARY POLICY RATE (MPR) %	CASH RESERVE REQUIREMENT (CRR) %	LIQUIDITY RATIO (LR) %
	April 1	-	10.00	-	-
	June 2	-	10.25	4.00	-
	August 5	-	10.25	-	-
	September 18	-	9.75	2.00	30.00
	December 11	-	9.75	-	-
2009					
	January 14	-	-	-	-
	February 9	-	9.75	-	-
	April 8	-	8.00	1.00	25.00
	May 21	-	-	-	-
	November 3	-	6.00	-	-
2010					
	January 4 & 5	-	6.00	-	-
	May 12	-	6.00	-	-
	September 21 & 22	-	6.25	-	-
	November 23	-	6.25	-	-
2011					
	January 25	-	6.50	2.00	30.00
	March 21 & 22	-	-	2.00	30.00
	May 23 & 24	-	8.00	4.00	-
	July 25 & 26	-	8.75	-	-
	September 19	-	9.25	4.00	-
	October 10	-	12.00	8.00	-
	November 21	-	12.00	8.00	-
2012					
	January 30 & 31	-	12.00	8.00	30.00
	March 19 & 20	-	12.00	8.00	30.00
	May 21 & 22	-	12.00	8.00	30.00
	July 23 & 24	-	12.00	12.00	-
	Sept. 17 & 18	-	12.00	12.00	-

YEAR	MONTH	MINIMUM REDISCOUNT RATE (MRR) %	MONETARY POLICY RATE (MPR) %	CASH RESERVE REQUIREMENT (CRR) %	LIQUIDITY RATIO (LR) %
	November 19 & 20	-	12.00	12.00	30.00
2013					
	January. 21	-	12.00	12.00	30.00
	March 18 & 19	-	12.00	12.00	30.00
	May 20 & 21	-	12.00	12.00	30.00
	July 22 & 23	-	12.00	Introduced a CRR on Private Sector Deposits at 12% Introduced a CRR of 50% on Public Sector Deposits	30.00
	September 23 & 24	-	12.00	Retained the CRR on Private Sector Deposits at 12% Retained the CRR Public Sector Deposits at 50%	30.00
	November 18 & 19	-	12.00	Retained the CRR on Private Sector Deposits at 12% Retained the CRR on Public Sector Deposits at 50%	30.00
2014					
	January 20 & 21	-	12.00	Retained the CRR on Private Sector Deposits at 12% Introduced a CRR of 75% on Public Sector Deposits	30.00
	March 24 & 25	-	12.00	Raised the CRR on Private Sector Deposits from 12 to 15% Retained the CRR on Public Sector Deposits at 75%	30.00
	May 19 & 20	-	12.00	Retained the CRR on Private Sector Deposits at 15% Retained the CRR on Public Sector Deposits at 75%	30.00
	July 21 & 22	-	12.00	Retained the CRR on Private Sector Deposits at 15% Retained the CRR on Public Sector Deposits at 75%	30.00
	September 18 & 19	-	12.00	Retained the CRR on Private Sector Deposits at 15% Retained the CRR on Public Sector Deposit at 75%	
	November 24 & 25	-	13.00	Raised the CRR on Private Sector Deposits to 20% Retained the CRR on Public Sector Deposits at 75%	

235

YEAR	MONTH	MINIMUM REDISCOUNT RATE (MRR) %	MONETARY POLICY RATE (MPR) %	CASH RESERVE REQUIREMENT (CRR) %	LIQUIDITY RATIO (LR) %
2015					
	January 19 & 20	-	13.00	Retained the CRR on Private Sector Deposits at 20% Retained the CRR on Public Sector Deposits at 75%	30.00
	March 23 & 24	-	13.00	Retained the CRR on Private Sector Deposits at 20% Retained the CRR on Public Sector Deposits at 75%	30.00
	May 18 & 19	-	13.00	Harmonized the Public & Private Sector CRR at a single rate of 31%	30.00
	July 23 & 24	-	13.00	Retained the CRR at 31	30.00
	September 21 & 23	-	13.00	Reduced the CRR at 25	30.00
	November 23 & 24	-	11.00	Reduced the CRR at 20	30.00
2016					
	January 25 & 26	-	11.00	Retained the CRR at 20	30.00
	March 21 & 22	-	12.00	Raised the CRR to 22.50	30.00
	May 23 & 24	-	12.00	Retained the CRR at 22.50	30.00
	July 25 & 26	-	14.00	Retained the CRR at 22.50	30.00
	September 19 & 20	-	14.00	Retained the CRR at 22.50	30.00

Source: Central Bank of Nigeria, Monetary Policy Committee Reports (Various Issues)

Appendix H: Central Bank of Nigeria's Monetary Policy Committee Decisions, March, 2003 – September, 2016

MEETING DATE	CONSIDERATIONS	DECISIONS
2003		
March, 2003	• No new policy action was introduced during the month.	• Status quo maintained • No new monetary policy action was introduced during the month.
April, 2003	• No new policy action was introduced during the month.	• Status quo maintained • No new monetary policy action was introduced during the month.
June 2003	• No new policy action was introduced during the month.	• While a change in the stance of monetary policy was not considered desirable, the need for greater fiscal prudence was emphasized.
August 2003	• Changed the frequency of MPC Meetings from fortnightly to monthly.	• Reduction of Minimum Rediscount Rate (MRR) by 150 basis points from 16.5 to 15.0 per cent with effect from August 17, 2003.
2004		
February 2004	• The need to douse inflationary expectations and bring the rate down. • Modest improvement in growth performance of the real sector, helped by the strong agricultural performance and enhanced capacity utilization in the manufacturing sector.	• Approval of a selective withdrawal of public sector funds from the banking system, targeting a total of ₦40 billion.
June 2004	• The need to sustain the phased recall of public sector funds with the deposit money banks.	• Withdrawal of public sector deposits amounting to ₦74.5 billion (75.60 per cent of such deposits) from the deposit money banks to the CBN with effect from July 21, 2004.
Dec., 2004	• The challenge posed by financing of the deficit and the sharing of the excess crude oil revenue • The current fiscal operations and money supply are expected to stay within its programme target while inflation is expected to moderate further.	• There was no new monetary policy action introduced at the meeting.

2005		
January 24-25, 2005	• The need to moderate inflation in view of the amount of the proposed budget deficit for 2005, the bulk of which would be financed through savings from 2004 windfall crude oil receipts.	• Reduction of the MRR by 200 basis points, in order to reduce the cost of private sector borrowing for productive investment. • Adoption of two weeks maintenance period for the CRR. • Adoption of an exchange rate band of plus/minus 3.0 percent, to sustain exchange rate stability, anchor expectations and minimize transaction costs.
June 15, 2005	• Until the Pension Funds Administrators are appointed, funds realised from the Pension Fund should not be invested in the Nigerian Treasury Bills instead they should be invested in long-term securities or sterilized. • The revision of the definition of Liquid Assets to include 3-year bonds.	• The withdrawal of ₦60 billion public sector deposit from the banks to the CBN, which should be concluded within a period of 2 months. • The maintenance of the prevailing minimum rediscount rate (MRR) of 13.00 percent. This action would help sustain the prevailing policy measure in encouraging credit to the growth sectors of the economy. • The upward revision of the cash reserve requirement (CRR) by 50 basis points from 9.50 to 10.00 per cent in order to further mop up excess liquidity in the system. The Committee further agreed that, henceforth, the debiting of banks accounts with CBN to meet the stipulated CRR should be effected immediately after the monthly FAAC meetings. This is based on the observation by the Committee that the FAAC related liquidity, is the major source of excess liquidity in the economy. • The revision of the definition of Liquid Assets to include 3-year bonds. • The sustenance of the exchange rate band of +/- 3 percent.
Nov., 1, 2005	• The need to review the rules and procedures guiding the forex market with a view to simplifying and improving upon them. • The need for fiscal authorities to make adequate provisions in the 2006 budget for Treasury Instruments for appropriate liquidity management in 2006.	• Complete the sale of ₦60 billion of CBN instrument, and sell more if need be. • Sale of Treasury Bills which will be sterilized for liquidity management. • Sale of additional foreign exchange to mop up liquidity. • Move all NNPC deposits with commercial banks to the CBN and sterilize much of it with effect from October 31, 2005. All banks that collect revenues on behalf of the NNPC are expected to remit all such funds to the CBN within 48 hours of the collection. Failure to remit such funds will attract a penal

2

238

| | | interest charge of MRR plus 5. Any MD of a bank who misreports NNPC deposits with it or falsifies any returns to the CBN will be suspended for three months in the first instance. |
| | | • To ensure effective monitoring and implementation of liquidity management programme, the MPC set up a Monetary Policy Implementation Committee which shall meet every two days to review developments and take necessary actions. |

2006

February 14, 2006	• The need to maintain single digit (core) inflation.	• The Bank will work towards zero ways and means. However, where it becomes absolutely necessary, ways and means will not be more than 5 percent of last year's revenue; and such lending will attract the prevailing MRR + 1 per cent rate of interest.
		• CBN will continue with regular OMO operations and issuance of new bills, both TBs and CBN bills.
		• MRR will be maintained at 13 percent in line with the anti-inflation stance of the MPC.
		• As a measure of tight monetary stance, M2 will be kept within the range of 15 to 17 percent target.
		• CRR is to be maintained at 5 percent, while the liquidity ratio will be retained at 40 percent.
		• Wholesale-DAS will commence on 20th February, 2006 to foster exchange rate convergence between the DAS and the inter-bank market rates.
June 8, 2006	• Some of the risks exist owing to persistent excess liquidity in the rest of 2006, if current trend remained unchanged	• Raised the MRR from 13.00 percent to 14.00 percent, to take effect from 12th June, 2006;
	• The prolonged disruption in oil production would reduce government revenue from oil, and to meet the planned programme, government resort to high powered money, is expected to be more inflationary.	• Maintained the CRR at 5.00 percent.
		• Resolved to sustain the on-going liberalization of the forex market as well as effectively monitor the market to maintain stability of the naira.
		• The Monetary Policy Implementation Committee (MPIC) would continue to keep daily surveillance on monetary operations.
		• With the deployment of the electronic Financial Analysis Surveillance System (eFASS), the Bank will leverage on that to ensure the proactive implementation of monetary policy.
		• The OMO shall continue to be the major instrument of monetary policy.
		• The Committee, further assured that it would respond to changes in economic prospects as needed

3

239

		to support the attainment of its objectives.
August 9, 2006	• Approved a new framework for monetary policy implementation. The IT and other logistics requirements are to be sorted out between now and October, 2006. Pilot implementation is expected to commence on or before November 1st, 2006.	• Maintained the MRR at 14.00 percent with a proviso to review the MRR should the threat to monetary policy continue. • Sustained the CBN's zero tolerance to lending to government. • Reaffirmed that there is no control on interest rate or pegging of lending rate to the MRR. • Approved operational guidelines on the CBN Discount Window. • Approved guidelines for discount window operations in FGN bonds. • Sustained the on-going liberalization of the forex market.
November 28, 2006	• Gave consideration to the policy setting rules such as the monetary policy response function, the frequency of changes in the MPR, significance of inflation considerations in determining the MPR, the problem of price, credit and operational risks, sensitization of operators and other stakeholders, training, etc.	• Adoption of a new monetary policy framework to be effective from Monday December 11th 2006. • The new monetary policy framework would be launched on Monday December 4, 2006. • The new Monetary Policy framework would introduce a new Monetary Policy Rate (MPR) to replace the Minimum Rediscount Rate (MRR). • The MPR would be the main instrument of the new monetary policy framework and will determine the lower and upper band of the CBN standing facility and is expected to have the capability of acting as the nominal anchor for other rates. • Discontinue outright rediscounting of bills in the CBN to encourage trading among the market operators. • Ensure the full deployment of Information Technology (IT) infrastructure (RTGS, T24, and eFASS) for the effective implementation of the new monetary policy framework. • Convene meeting of the MPC every other month to review developments in the economy.
February 7, 2007	• Rising autonomous private inflows, which is expected to lead to persistent excess liquidity in the system. • Anticipated high election spending. • Falling prices of crude oil.	• The MPC decided to leave the MPR unchanged at 10 percent. • Release the 8.00 percent special Cash Reserve Requirement (CRR) invested on behalf of the banks by the CBN to the Deposit Money Banks (DMBs) on maturity to enable the DMBs utilize the amount of reserve money released for regular operations. • Keep the CRR unchanged at 3.00 percent • Maintain the liquidity ratio at 40.00 percent. Allow the collaterized placements among deposit money

4

		banks to count as liquid assets, for purposes of liquidity ratio computations; and • Exclusion of domiciliary deposit accounts from the definition of broad money (M2) and the computation of banks' CRR.
June 5, 2007	• The rising autonomous private inflows and the risk of over-appreciation of its naira/dollar exchange rates.	• Introduce tenured repo at MPR • Reduce the MPR by 200 basis points from the 10.00 percent to 8.00 percent. • Reduce the width of the interest rate corridor from +/- 300 to+/-250 basis points. • The combined implication of the above is that the deposit facility now stands at 5.50 percent while the lending facility would be 10.50 percent, both down from 7.00 and 13.00 percent, respectively. • Both facilities are expected to be used as a last resort. Consequently the frequent usage of these facilities will attract penalty. • Increase the issuance of primary market instrument to mop up about N100 billon. • That interbank placements shall henceforth form part of the deposits for calculating banks liquidity • The continued use of OMO in liquidity management.
August 1, 2007	• The challenge arising from rising autonomous private inflows and the challenge of further appreciation of the naira/dollar exchange rate. • Potential pressure/risk arising from low inflation including the virement or capital vote to finance recurrent expenditure and the distribution of part of the excess crude account.	• Retain the MPR at 8.00 percent. • Approve increase sale of financial securities to pre-emptively and proactively mitigate the impact of increase fiscal injections on systems liquidity.
October 3, 2007	• To deepen inter-bank trading and encourage banks to free resources to enlarge the credit market.	• The MPC decided to raise the MPR by 100 basis points (i.e. from 8.00 to 9.00 percent). The new MPR rate would also double as the repo rate-the rate at which the CBN would lend to banks. • Continue the sale of foreign exchange for purposes of liquidity management. • Embark on active open market operations. • DMB deposits with the CBN would seize to earn interest.
December 4, 2007	• The anticipated imminent fiscal surge and continuing increase in capital inflows. • The need to drive down core inflation to single digit level and sustain inflation along	• The MPC decided to raise the MPR by 50 basis points (i.e. from 9.00 per cent to 9.50 percent) to signal a tightening of policy stance. • Issue new primary instruments to mop up a

5

241

	its present path.	significant portion of the anticipated excess liquidity in the system. • Continue with the regular open market operations (OMO).

2008		
February 5, 2008	• The need to ensure that inflation in 2008 is within single digit. • The rapid growth of money supply did not translate to higher inflation during the year, partly on account of improved supply conditions. • The credit to government remained negative all through the year.	• Leave MPR unchanged at 9.50 percent. • To continue the use of OMO for liquidity management and appropriate exchange rate policies.
April 1, 2008	• The need to keep inflation under control given the expected huge fiscal injections in the month ahead. • The potential impact on liquidity of the recent distribution of the Naira equivalent of US\$2.008 billion excess crude oil revenue and the second round distribution of same amount scheduled for June 2008.	• Raise the MPR by 50 basis points from 9.50 percent to 10.00 per cent. • Issue treasury bills for liquidity management. • Increase the sale foreign exchange as the need arises.
June 2,2008	• To ensure that price stability and real activity levels are recognized and actions taken to address them. In view of the sharp growth of credit to the private sector by 96 per cent and of M2 by 62 per cent on a year-on-year basis by March 2008. • Also as fiscal expansion is all time high, threats of resurgence of inflation are very high. In addition, there is the threat of imported inflation owing to global rise in prices.	• Strengthen the use of instruments such as open market operations and special sale of foreign exchange. • Raise the MPR by 25 basis points from 10.00 percent to 10.25 percent. • Increase the CRR by 100 basis points from 3.00 per cent to 4.00 percent with effect from June 09, 2008. • Set up a technical committee to work out other intervention securities to further strengthen the effectiveness of liquidity management.
August 5, 2008	• The need to moderate the impact of fiscal operations on liquidity through innovative mechanism involving monetization to ensure that macroeconomic stability is maintained. • Although the expected good harvest of agricultural produce and the implementation of the rice import intervention scheme would help to moderate inflation, the inflation rate may still remain in the double-digit.	• The MPR will remain unchanged at 10.25 percent since the core inflation is expected to remain at a relatively moderate level. • After reviewing developments in the financial market and the misplaced perceptions that interest rate trends are linked to the requirement of a common year-end, the MPC decided that the common year-end for banks would no longer be a requirement and therefore left the decision to the discretion of the banks. • In order to ensure a transparent pricing regime in the money market and thereby foster healthier competition, banks are required to fully disclose to

6

242

		the public their deposit rates as well as their base lending rates and other charges for all the sectors of the economy. Theses should be published on their respective websites and updated daily. The banks are required to report these rates to the CBN to enable the Bank to publish a summary of the rates for each deposit money bank every month.
Sept., 18, 2008	• The financial crisis has slowed down the industrialized economies, reflecting sharp fall in demand, while crude oil prices have been softening in the international oil market. • The headline inflation and food prices have been on the increase, while core inflation has been in single digits.	• Reduce the MPR from 10.25 percent to 9.75 percent. • Reduce CRR from 4.00 percent to 2.00 percent with immediate effect. • Reduce the liquidity ratio from 40.00 percent to 30.00 percent. • Allow repo transactions against eligible securities for 90 days, 180 days and 360 days; and the CBN will now buy and sell securities through the two-way quotes.
Dec., 11, 2008	• The need to ensure a stable foreign exchange market rate regime.	• Leave the MPR unchanged at 9.75 percent. • Reduce banks foreign exchange net open position from 20.00 to 10.00 percent of shareholders' funds with effect from Monday, December 15, 2008. • CBN to participate actively in the daily interbank foreign exchange market by buying and selling through the two-way quotes.
2009		
January 14, 2009	• The need to allow the exchange rate to adjust in response to market conditions. • The need to restore stability in the foreign exchange market given the uncertainties and the speculative pressures in the market.	• CBN is reintroducing the rDAS with effect from Monday, January 19, 2009, and will be conducted on Mondays and Wednesdays, and will revert to wDAS at the appropriate time. • Bids for the purchase of foreign exchange under the rDAS must be cash-backed at the time of the bid. • Funds purchased from CBN at the Auction shall be used for eligible transactions only, subject to stipulated documentation requirements. Such funds shall not be transferrable in the interbank foreign exchange market. • Authorized Dealers shall return to the CBN any utilized funds within five business days after delivery, at the rate of purchase. • Purchases by banks on behalf of their customers will be published in thee dallies fortnightly. • Interest earned on Letters of Credit established and for which settlement has not been effected, shall be repatriated to the CBN for repurchase at the bid rate at the rime the funds were purchased • The foreign exchange Net Open Position (NOP) of

7

243

			banks will be reduced from 10.00 percent to 5.00 percent from Monday, January 19, 2009.
February 9, 2009		• The need to address inflation and exchange rate concerns. • The need to address high interest rate by relaxing monetary conditions. • The need to ensure that credit continues to flow to the rest of the economy.	• MPR will be retained at 9.75 percent • Open market operations will be actively used for achieving effective liquidity management • The CBN is seriously concerned about the rising lending rates and especially the re-pricing of existing facilities by banks as well as the wide spread between deposit and lending rates. The CBN will be meeting with bank chief executive officers to agree on modalities to check excesses, especially in light of the global economic and financial crisis. • To anchor expectations and stabilize the exchange rate, MPC remains committed to managing the exchange rate within a band of +/- 2.00 percent until further notice. • The difference between the CBN buying and selling rates shall not be more than 1.00 percent, while that of the banks and BDCs will not be more than 1.00 percent and 2.00 percent respectively around the CBN rate.
April 08, 2009		• The need for the monetary policy to have the support of appropriate fiscal policy and structured reforms in order to address the global economic and financial crisis.	• Reduce MPR from 9.75 percent to 8.00 percent. • Reduce the Liquidity ratio from 30.00 percent to 25.00 percent with effect from April 14, 2009. • Reduce CRR from 2.00 percent to 1.00 percent with effect from April 14, 2009.
May 21, 2009		• The need to address the problem of excess liquidity in the system without necessarily putting pressure on interest rates. • The need to reduce the wide premium between the official and parallel market rates. • The need to review the series of control measures in the foreign exchange market to ensure that it returns to fully liberalized regime, as well as explore the possibility of introducing futures and swaps in the foreign exchange market.	• To issue short-term instruments to be synchronized with the DMO's issuance of the FGN Bonds to mop-up excess liquidity in the system. • To return to a regime of fully liberalized foreign exchange market over the next three months. As a first set of measures towards the return to Wholesale Dutch Auction System (wDAS), the Committee decide to increase the net foreign exchange open position (NOP) for banks from 1.00 to 2.5 percent with immediate effect, while keeping in view the possibility of raising it further at the end of June 2009. • Banks no longer mandatorily required to sell to the CBN, after 5 days funds sourced from non-rDAS and non-oil export proceeds and may use such funds from interbank transactions. • Removal of the requirement that banks transact foreign exchange at 1.00 percent around the CBN rate. The CBN will now participate in the interbank foreign exchange market at prevailing rate.

8

244

		• Effective June 1, 2009, rDAS will be twice weekly. • Approval-in-Principle (AIP) has been granted to 50 non-bank Class 'A' BDCs. The list of the BDCs will be published from Saturday, May 23, 2009. As from next week (beginning from May 25, 2009), about US$60 million will be sold to BDCs per week. The BDCs are expected to sell at retail rate of not more than 2.00 percent above the CBN selling rate. • Government Agencies and Oil Companies will have discretion to sell foreign exchange at the interbank foreign exchange market or to the CBN with effect from May 25, 2009.
November 3, 2009	• While inflation has decelerated, the need to recognize that seasonal factors and the planned deregulation of the prices of petroleum products pose a major risk to inflation in the near to medium-term. • The existing paradox of the co-existence of system-wide liquidity shortages, as reflected in the data on monetary and credit aggregates and abundant liquidity with some banks as evidenced from the data on standing facilities.	• MPR will remain unchanged at 6.00 percent, but asymmetric corridor of interest around the MPR is introduced. The rate on standing lending facility will remain at 200 basis points above the MPR, while the rate on the standing deposit facility will be 400 basis points below the MPR • Quantitative easing to bridge the gap currently estimates at about N500 billion between the levels of the current monetary aggregates and the benchmark levels for 2009. The modalities for QE include investments in bonds to be issued by AMCON, however subject to approval by NASS. Other modalities include the redemption of promissory notes issued by the FMF as well as by the CBN in connection with the retirement of debt and liabilities arising from purchase and assumption of failed banks. • Purchase of loans by banks under AMCON will be based on terms aimed at strengthening the balance sheets with a focus on asset quality, improving liquidity and capital adequacy as well as on reducing debt overhang relating to the stock market in order to stimulate activity in the capital market. • With effect from November 16, 2009, the temporary ban placed by the CBN on the use of Bankers Acceptances (BAs) and Commercial papers (CPs) will be lifted. • In view of the fact that the audit of banks been concluded and adequate provisions have been made for non-performing loans to stimulate credit growth and strengthen banks' balance sheets, the 1.00 percent general provision on performing loans contained in the existing prudential guidelines is hereby waived for the year 2009, as a countercyclical measure.

9

2010		
January 4-5, 2010	• The need to increase financing for infrastructure development to support economic growth. • The need to maintain the growth trajectory of the economy, to ensure that lending rates are not placed under further upward pressure, and to provide sufficient liquidity during the resolution process of the banking system.	• Leave the Monetary Policy Rate (MPR) unchanged at 6.00 per cent with the asymmetric corridor of interest rates remaining at 200 basis points above the MPR and 400 basis points below the MPR. • Extend CBN's guarantee on all interbank transactions up till December 31, 2010. However, the CBN has the discretion to terminate the guarantee on a case-by-case basis as part of the ongoing reform process. • Approve the Monetary Programme for 2010/2011 and the Monetary, Credit, Foreign Trade and Exchange Guidelines for Fiscal years 2010/2011.
May 12, 2010	• Ensuring that the growing risk of fiscal deficit accumulated in the wake of the abating global financial and economic crises does not endanger the stability of financial markets. • Monitoring imbalances in capital flows across industrial and emerging markets resulting in different rates of recovery. This is to ensure that inflows of capital into the country are sustainable, and thus, avoid formation of asset bubbles. • The continuing global credit crunch despite unprecedented measure taken by central banks to inject liquidity in troubled financial institutions/markets. Thus underscores the need for focus on both supply side (monetary) and demand side (fiscal factors) in unlocking the credit markets.	• Leave MPR unchanged at 6.00 percent. • Retain the asymmetric corridor of interest rates at 200 basis points above the MPR and 500 basis points below the MPR for Standing Lending Facility and Standing Deposit Facility respectively. • Extend the CBN guarantee for all interbank transactions and foreign credit lines as well as pension funds placements with banks from December 31, 2010 to June 30, 2011. This is to provide ample time for the conclusion of the banking sector resolution and publication of audited accounts for the period up to December 2010. It is expected that by June 2011 all creditors and investors will have sufficient information to take an independent view of the risk of individual counterparties.
Sept., 21, 2010	• The need to tame the inflationary pressure in the economy given the government spending in an election year. • The liquidity implications of the purchase of non-performing loans (NPLs) by AMCON.	• The resumption of active Open Market Operations for the purpose of targeted liquidity management. • An increase in MPR by 25 basis points from 6.00 percent to 6.25 percent • Adjustment of asymmetric corridor to 200 basis points above and 300 basis points below MPR for Standing Lending Facility and Standing Deposit, respectively. This effectively increases interest payable on standing deposits with the CBN by 225 basis points forthwith.
Nov., 23, 2010	• The need to reduce elevated inflation levels. • Rising government expenditure and borrowings with the possible crowding out effects on the private sector. • The need to moderate demand pressure in	• Retain the MPR at 6.25 percent. • To adjust the corridor to +/- 200 basis points, implying Standing Lending Facility (SLF) rate at 8.25 percent, and Standing Deposit Facility (SDF) rate at 4.25 percent.

10

	the foreign exchange market leading to reduction in external reserves.	• Maintaining the policy stance of a stable exchange rate. • Continue to monitor inflationary trends with a view to taking appropriate steps as and when necessary.

2011

January 25, 2011	• The risk of inflation is on the upward side, as a result of the liquidity injections from the likely increase in government spending as AMCON purchase and rising global energy and food prices and the expected pass-through to the domestic economy. • The existing subsidy regime on petroleum products which is not sustainable in view of government's current finances.	• Raise the MPR by 25 points from 6.25 percent to 6.50 percent with immediate effect. • Maintain the symmetric corridor of +/- 200 basis points. • Raise the CRR by 100 basis points from 1.00 percent to 2.00 percent with effect from February 1, 2011. • With effect from March 1, 2011, raise the Liquidity Ration by 500 basis points from 25.00 percent to 30.00 percent.
March 21-22, 2011	• The heightened risk of inflation. • The rising international food and energy prices. • The impact of import costs on domestic prices. • The challenges that fiscal stance posed to the external value of the Naira and the likely front-loading or public expenditure in the election period.	• Retain the Symmetric Corridor of +/- 200 basis points. • Retain the current CRR of 2.00 percent and the liquidity ratio of 30.00 percent. • Extend the CBN guarantee on interbank transactions and guarantee of foreign credit lines by three months from June 30, 2011 to September 30, 2011.
May 24, 2011	• The importance of continuing structural reforms and infrastructural development to enhance domestic production to reduce the import bill and its pass-through effects on inflation. • The inflationary impact of the likely deregulation of petroleum product prices.	• Further tightening of monetary policy. • Increase CRR from 2.00 percent to 4.00 percent with effect from June 8, 2011 to align with the next reserve averaging maintenance period. • Increase MPR by 50 basis point from 7.50 percent to 8.00 percent. • Maintain the symmetric corridor of +/- 200 basis points around the MPR.
July 26, 2011	• The need to address the impact of huge injections of liquidity in the system to correct the negative real interest rate situation in the market. • The need to attract foreign capital inflows to build up reserves to protect the economy against possible external shocks.	• To tightened monetary policy. • To raise MPR by 75 basis points from 8.00 percent to 8.75 percent. • To maintain the corridor at +/- 200 basis points around the MPR.
Sept., 19, 2011	• Continuing expansionary fiscal stance and high component of recurrent expenditure. • Liquidity surge expected from AMCON intervention, following conclusion of bank recapitalization. • Sharp rise in the month-on-month inflation	• Tightening of monetary policy. • Increase MPR by 50 basis points from 8.75 to 9.25 percent. • Maintain the current symmetric corridor of +/- 200 basis points around the MPR. • Retain the current CRR of 4.00 percent.

11

	rate, despite falling headline inflation rate on year-on-year. • Need to have positive real interest rates. • Resisting demand pressures in the foreign exchange market driven by significant liquidity injections in the economy.	
October 10, 2011	• The declining oil prices, declining foreign reserves, increased demand for foreign exchange, fiscal dominance and capital flow reversals.	• Raise MPR by 275 basis points from 9.25 percent to 12.00 percent. • Maintain the current symmetric corridor of +/- 200 basis points around the MPR. • The CRR is increased from 4.00 percent to 8.00 percent from the maintenance period beginning October 11, 2011. • The net open position (NOP) is reduced from 5.00 percent to 1.00 percent of shareholders' funds with immediate effect and with full compliance by Friday, October 14, 2011. • It was further agreed that reserve averaging method of computation be suspended in favour of daily maintenance until further notice.
Nov., 21, 2011	• Continuing demand pressures in the foreign exchange market. • The slow rate or reserve accretion as indicators that liquidity conditions may still need further tightening. • High lending rates and their impact on real sector.	• Retain MPR at 12.00 percent and symmetric band at +/- 200 basis points • Retain the CRR at 8.00 percent. • To adjust the mid-point of target official exchange rate from N150/US$ to N155/US$ and maintain the band of +/-3.00 percent. This means that the naira should float roughly within a range of N150/US$-N160/US$, unless extraordinary shocks necessitate a change in stance. • To encourage the CBN to continue to seek convergence wDAS and interbank rates to reduce arbitrage opportunities, avoid speculative attacks, and the emergence of a multiple-exchange rate environment.
2012		
January 31, 2012	• The need to sustain the high output growth that the country has seen in the recent years, partly because of the slowdown in the advanced and other emerging economies and partly because of the need to generate employment in the economy. • The need to maintain price stability in a manner conducive to the achievement of employment-generating growth. • Inflationary trend is expected to rise in the	• Retain MPR at 12.00 percent with interest rate corridor +/- 200 basis points. • Retain CRR at 8.00 percent. • Retain minimum liquidity ratio at 30.00 percent. Retain the Mid-point of exchange rate of N151US$ with a band of +/- 3.00 percent.

12

248

	first two quarters in 2012, and then moderate steadily towards the single digit zone by late 2013.	
March 19-20, 2012	• The slowdown in monetary aggregates and fiscal spending and the crowding out effects of high interest rates. • The rising level of domestic debt and its sustainability • The need to continue supporting the naira and build up external reserves, the necessity for attracting and retaining foreign investments, and the need for consistency and stability in the macroeconomic environment	• Retain MPR at 12.00 percent with interest rate corridor of +/- 200 basis points; • Retain CRR at 8.00 percent. • Retain minimum liquidity Ratio of 30.00 percent. • The Committee also resolved to watch closely developments with respect to the fiscal stance and to respond appropriately if, and when, the need arises.
May 21-22, 2012	• Slowdown in global economic activities, particularly in the US, Europe and China. • Slowdown in domestic output, especially, sharp decline in agricultural output and oil and gas sectors. • Possible softening of crude oil prices in international markets with potential fiscal revenue loses and the likely pressure on the foreign exchange market and exchange rate. • The inflationary threat that has re-surfaced in the first quarter of 2012, after having moderated in the fourth quarter of 2011. • Imminent increase in electricity tariff, which may lead to inflationary pressures. • High interest rates in the face of declining GDP output. • Security concern in the country • Slow pace of structural reforms induced by failure to improve power supply, establish and implement reliable PPP framework that can attract funding for infrastructure and delay in passing the PIB.	• Retain MPR at 12.00 percent with interest rate corridor of +/- 200 basis points. • Retain CRR at 8.00 per cent. • Retain minimum liquidity Ratio of 30.00 per cent.
July 23-24, 2012	• Stemming the inflationary pressures arising from both domestic and external sources. • Sustaining a stable exchange rate for the naira. • Creating a buffer for the external reserves • Mitigating the impact of the continued slowdown in global economic activities, particularly, in the US, Europe and China on the Nigerian economy.	• Retain the Monetary Policy Rate (MPR) at 12.00 per cent with symmetric corridor of +/-200 basis points. • Increase the Cash Reserve Requirement (CRR) from 8.00 percent to 12.00 percent with effect from July 25th. • Reduce the Net foreign exchange Open Position (NOP) to 1.0 per cent from 3.00 percent with immediate effect.
September 18, 2012	• The need to protect the domestic economy and buildup external reserves given the rise	• Retain the MPR at 12.00 percent with +/- 200 basis points corridor.

13

249

	in crude oil prices and uncertainties surrounding the global economy. • Potential large inflow of "hot money" resulting from further monetary easing in the US and Europe and improves yield on fixed income instruments. • Persisting high core inflation.	• Retain CRR at 12.00 percent. • Retain the Net Open Position at 1.00 percent.
November 19-20, 2012	• The need to moderate headline and food inflation which are trending upwards, while core inflation rate is declining. • The declining GDP growth due to external factors: uncertainties surrounding the resolution of the fiscal cliff in the US and possible negative impact on oil price developments.	• Retain the MPR at 12.00 percent with a corridor of +/- 200 basis points around the midpoint; • Retain the CRR at 12.00 percent. • Liquidity Ratio at 30.00 percent.

2013

January 21, 2013	• Slowdown in global economy due to uncertainty and contraction in the Euro area and Japan. • Significant fall in demand for oil, leading to a fall in oil prices and government revenue. • The declining GDP growth trajectory and headline inflation.	• Retain the MPR at 12.00 percent with a corridor of +/- 200 basis points. • Retain the CRR at 12.00 percent. • Liquidity Ratio at 30.00 percent.
March 18-19, 2013	• The need to stem upward trend in headline and food inflation and pressure on exchange. • The need to stimulate growth in the real sector, given the slowdown in overall GDP and agricultural GDP growth, inability of the SMEs to borrow at the current lending rates and crowding out. • The Quantitative Easing in US and the EU, which has resulted in increased inflows to the emerging market and the need to insulate the economy from risks associated with external shocks and capital flow reversals.	• Retain the MPR at 12.00 percent with a corridor of +/- 200 basis points. • Retain the CRR at 12.00 percent. • Liquidity Ratio at 30.00 percent. • Retain the Net Open Position at 1.00 percent.
May 20-21, 2013	• High lending rates in the economy declining core inflation, stable exchange rates and relative reserve accretion.	• Retain the MPR at 12.00 percent with a corridor of +/-200 basis points. • Retain the Cash Reserve Requirement at 12.00

14

	• Retaining current monetary policy stance to sustain the macroeconomic gains of tight monetary policy and to continue to rein-in inflationary expectations.	percent. • Liquidity Ratio at 30.00 percent. • Net Open Position at 1.00 percent.
July 23, 2013	• The build-up of excess liquidity and sluggish growth in private sector credit. • The risk posed to government revenue through oil theft, new discovery of shale oil, other competing oil exporters and possible rise in fiscal deficit and loose fiscal stance in 2013 compared to 2012.	• Retain MPR at 12.00 percent with symmetric corridor of +/- 2 percent. • Retain the Cash Reserve Ratio (CRR) at 12.00 percent. • New: Introduce 50.00 percent CRR on public sector deposits (FGN, States, LGAs and all MDAs). Private sector deposits will still attract 12.00 percent CRR.
September 23-24, 2013	• The reduction in risks of currency instability due to US FED postponement of its decision on tapering assets purchase, improved outlook for financial stability in Europe after German elections. • The monetary stance maintained by the US Federal Reserve is positive for international oil prices and portfolio flows.	• Retain the MPR at 12.00 percent with symmetric corridor of +/-2 percent. • Retain CRR at 12.00 percent on private sector deposits. • Retain 50.00 percent CRR on public sector deposits (FGN, States, LGAs and all MDAs).
November 18-19, 2013	• The prevailing monetary policy stance had a positive impact on stabilizing the exchange rate and attracting portfolio investment, thus, driving the strong recovery of asset prices on the Nigerian Stock Exchange. • The global monetary conditions were likely to remain loose going into Q1, 2014, however, it is expected that 2014 will be the year for QEs-tapering in the US and interest rates rises in Europe, both of which will lead to some pressures on the exchange rate and stock prices, due to the impact of capital flows, while election spending in Nigeria, in the same year will bring pressure to bear from the fiscal side. • The redemption of AMCON bonds of N1 trillion in December 2013, by exchanging them for FGN Treasury Bills on its books will drastically reduce the contingent liability on the FGN by N1 trillion, thus, impacting positively on the economy and the credit rating of the FGN and the banking industry. • To mitigate the huge loss of government debt due to poor cash flow management.	• Retain the MPR at 12.00 percent with symmetric corridor of +/-2 percent. • Retain CRR at 12.00 percent on private sector deposits. • Retain 50.00 percent CRR on public sector deposits (FGN, States, LGAs and all MDAs). • Liquidity ratio at 30 percent.

2014

January	• Depletion of fiscal buffers (External reserve	• Retain MPR at 12.00 percent +/- 200 basis points and

15

251

20-21, 2014	and ECA). • Falling Portfolio and FDI inflows. • Widening gap between the Official and the BDC exchange rate. • Creeping increase in core inflation.	Liquidity Ratio at 30.00 percent. • Increase Public Sector to 75.00 percent from 50.00 percent. • Retain Private sector CRR at 12.00 percent. • The CBN to take immediate steps to redress the supply-demand imbalance in the BDC segment, while maintaining its focus on anti-money laundering activities.
March 24-25, 2014	• Recent resurgence of core inflation, in spite of the downward trend in headline inflation (Core Index and Farm Produce items). • Increase pressure in the foreign exchange market arising from key developments in the US over the Federal Reserve's unwinding of its assets purchase programme. • Sudden surge in domiciliary account balance, which may offset the gains from imposing 75.00 percent CRR on public sector funds.	• Retain MPR at 12.00 percent +/- 200 basis points and Liquidity Ratio at 30.00 percent. • Retain Public Sector to 75.00 percent. • Increase Private Sector CRR to 15.00 percent (300 basis points), from 12.00 percent.
May 19-20, 2014	• The upward trend in core inflation, which rose from 7.2 percent in February, 2014, to 7.5 percent in April, 2014, could be a major factor in the upward trend in prices. • Increased yields and interest rates in the US and low level of economic activity in the emerging, markets, could have impact on foreign exchange inflows and the stability of the naira exchange rate. • The high domestic liquidity could exert sustained pressure on both the exchange rate and consumer prices, as well as accentuate the already high demand for foreign exchange which could further deplete the country's external reserves, in an effort to defend the Naira.	• Retain MPR at 12.00 percent with a corridor of +/- 200 basis points around the midpoint and liquidity Ratio at 30.00 percent. • Retain Public Sector CRR at 75.00 percent • Retain Private Sector CRR at 15.00 percent.
July 21-22, 2014	• The anticipation of inflationary pressure that is expected to come from a likely aggregate spending in the run up to the 2015 general election. • The necessity for sustaining a stable naira exchange rate, given the implications of the US Fed's QE tapering for inflows and external reserves.	• Retain MPR at 12.00 percent with a corridor of +/- 200 basis points around the midpoint and liquidity Ratio at 30.00 percent. • Retain Public Sector CRR at 75.00 percent • Retain Private Sector CRR at 15.00 percent.
September 18-19, 2014	• The high banking system liquidity and it potential effects on inflation and exchange rates as the sector is said to be in possession	• Retain MPR at 12.00 percent with a corridor of +/- 200 basis points around the midpoint. • Public Sector Cash Reserve Requirement (CRR) at

16

252

	of excess reserves averaging over ₦300 billion. • The need to sustain a stable exchange rate and foreign reserve, given the fact that there could be the possibility of capital reversal as the Fed's Quantitative Easing in the US ends in October, amidst declining oil output and weakening oil prices. • The upward trend in headline inflation likely to evolve from the domestic security challenges and aggregate spending in the run for the 2015 general election.	75.00 percent. • Private Sector Cash Reserve Requirement at CRR at 15 percent.
Nov., 24-25, 2014	• The declining external reserves, which arose from the continued slide in oil prices and capital flow reversal, given the end of QE by the US Federal Reserves on October 29, 2014, as well a, the demand side aided by excess liquidity in the banking system and speculative activities. • The high banking system liquidity which translated to an increase credit expansion to the economy, but also led to an upward pressure in the Foreign Exchange Market and Standard Deposit Facility window of the bank. • The upward trend in headline inflation likely to evolve from falling oil prices accompanied by external reserves depletion and food supply shocks arising from increasing insurgency activities in some parts of the country, as well as aggregate spending in the run up to the 2015 general elections.	• Increase the MPR by 100bps from 12.00 to 13.00 percent. • Increase the CRR on private sector deposits by 500 bps from 15.00 percent to 20.00 percent with immediate effect. • Move the midpoint of the official window of the foreign exchange market from N155/US$ to N 168/US$. • Widen the band around the midpoint by 200 bps from +/- 3 percent to +/- 5 percent. • Retain Public sector CRR at its current level of 75.00 percent. • Maintain Asymmetric Corridor of +/- 200 basis point around the MPR.
	2015	
January 19-20, 2015	• Sustained decline in oil GDP, and its impact on reserve accretion. • The recurring excess liquidity in the banking system. • The gradual normalization of monetary policy by the US Federal Reserve, which could lead to capital outflows, especially from portfolio investments and increase pressure on currencies in emerging and developing countries including Nigeria.	• MPR at 13.00 percent with a corridor of +/- 200 basis points around the midpoint, and Liquidity ratio(LR) at 30.00 percent • Public Sector Cash Reserve Requirement (CRR) at 75.00 percent. • Private Sector Cash Reserve Requirement (CRR) at 20.00 percent.
March 23-24, 2015	• The need to reduce the wide divergence between the Interbank and the BDC	• MPR at 13.00 percent with a corridor of +/- 200 basis points around the midpoint, and Liquidity Ratio (LR)

17

253

	exchange rates, and currency substitution and partial dollarization in the economy. • The gradual increase in headline inflation would be moderated by the prevailing tight monetary policy stance.	at 30.00 percent. • Public Sector Cash Reserve Requirement (CRR) at 75.00 percent. • Private Sector Cash Reserve Requirement (CRR) at 20.00 percent
July 23-24, 2015	• The opportunity for further policy changes remains largely constrained in the absence of supporting fiscal measures to stimulate output growth and stabilize the exchange rate.	• Retain MPR at 13.00 percent with a corridor of +/- 200 basis points around the midpoint. • Retain the CRR at 31.00 percent.
September 21-22, 2015	• The overall macroeconomic environment remained fragile, as growth has been dampened by declining private and public expenditures. • The implementation of the TSA and elongation of the tenure of state government loans, as well as loans to the oil and gas sectors could heighten liquidity conditions in banks and impair their financial intermediation role, thus affecting economic growth. • It is expected that pressure on food prices would be moderated by anticipated improved food harvests in the coming months, while business confidence would continue to improve, as the Government continues to unfold its economic plans.	• Retain the MPR at 13.00 percent. • Retain the symmetric corridor of +/- 200 basis points around the midpoint. • Reduce the CRR from 31.00 to 25.00 percent. • Retain the Liquidity Ratio at 30.00 percent.
November 23-24, 2015	• The sustained improvement on supply of power and refined petroleum products, progress with counter-insurgency in the North-East and the inauguration of the Federal Executive Council and assumption of office of the Ministers are expected to provide additional incentive for growth in the economy. • Concerned that the previous liquidity injections embarked upon through lowering of the Cash Reserve Ratio (CRR) in the last MPC has not translated to increased lending to key sectors.	• Reduce the MPR from 13.00 percent to 11.00 percent. • Change the symmetric corridor of 200 basis points around the MPR to an asymmetric corridor of +200 basis points and -700 basis points around the MPR. • Reduce the CRR from 25.00 to 20.00 percent. • Retain Liquidity Ratio at 30 percent.
2016		
January 25-26, 2016	• The need to strengthen the framework for foreign exchange management, with a view to ensuring a more effective and liquid foreign exchange market.	• Retain MPR at 11.00 percent; • Retain the Asymmetric corridor at + 200 basis points and -700 basis points. • Retain the CRR at 20.00 percent.

18

	• The need to allow a reasonable time to see the impact of the last MPC's decisions on the economy. • The need for more coordination between the monetary and fiscal policies, as a prerequisite for resolving the nation's economic problems.	• Retain Liquidity Ratio at 30.00 percent.
March 21-23, 2016	• The need to moderate the inflationary pressure stemming from excess liquidity in the banking system, which was contributing to the current pressure in the foreign exchange market with a strong pass-through to consumer prices. • The need to increase the policy rate, so as to encourage foreign and domestic investments, as the current headline inflation at 11.18 percent rate vis-à-vis , the existing policy rate at 11.00 percent has given rise to negative in real interest rates.	• MPR is raised by 100 basis points from 11 percent to 12.00 percent. • The Asymmetric Corridor is narrowed from + 200 basis points and -700 basis points to +200 and -500 basis points. • The CRR is raised by 250 basis points from 20 percent to 22.50 percent. • Retain Liquidity Ratio at 30.00 percent.
May 23-24, 2016	• The need to increase the supply of foreign exchange in the market. • Expectation of moderation of inflationary pressures by deregulation of the downstream sector. • Expectation that effective implementation of the capital expenditure portion of Budget would stimulate growth.	• Retain MPR at 12.00 percent. • Retain the Asymmetric Corridor at +200 and -500 basis points. • Retain the CRR at 22.50 percent. • Retain the Liquidity ratio at 30 percent. • Introduce greater flexibility in the inter-bank foreign exchange market structure and to retain a small window for critical sectors transaction.
July 25-26, 2016	• The need to fast-track the implementation of the 2016 Budget. • The current inflationary pressure was largely structural and tightening would worsen prospect of growth recovery. • The high inflationary trend has culminated into negative real interest rates in the economy resulting in discouraging of savings and foreign investors from investing new capital.	• Increase the MPR by 200 basis point from **12.00** to 14 percent. • Retain the Asymmetric Corridor at +200 and -500 basis point. • Retain the CRR at 22.50 percent. • Retain the Liquidity ratio at 30.00 percent.
September 19-20,2016	• The need for the FGN to have a robust fiscal policy to complement monetary policy. • The need to prioritize the use of monetary policy instruments in dealing with stability issues around key prices (consumer prices and exchange rate) as prerequisites for growth. • To reverse the negative growth trend,	• Retain MPR at 14.00 percent. • Retain the Asymmetric Corridor at +200 and -500 basis point. • Retain the CRR at 22.50 percent. • Retain the Liquidity Ratio at 30.00 percent.

19

255

	reducing interest rate to spur credit growth might be counter-productive, as it provides opportunities for lending to traders who deploy same liquidity in putting pressure on the foreign exchange market, thus pushing up the exchange rate. • Lowering interest rates would also provide opportunity to the public sector to borrow to boost consumption and investment spending, and with increased consumer demand for goods without corresponding efforts to boost industrial output would further exacerbate the already heightened inflationary condition.	

Source: Central Bank of Nigeria, Monetary Policy Committee Reports (Various Issues)

Appendix I: Central Bank of Nigeria, Funding Interventions, 2000-September, 2015

Case	Facility	Purpose	Set Up Year	Seed Fund (N' billion)	Interest Rate (%)	Tenor	Amount Disbursed/ Credit Risk Guarantee Cover Issued (N' billion)	Amount Repaid (N' billion)	Remark
1.	Power & Aviation Intervention Fund (PAIF)	To fast-track development of electric supply projects and aviation sector in order to improve credit to airlines. PAIF was designed as part of quantitative easing measures to address the paucity of long-term & acute power shortage in the country	2010	300	7	15	249.614	58.639	N249.614 billion disbursed iro 55 projects - 39 power projects (N128.852 billion) and 16 airline projects (N120.762 billion). A total of N58.639 billion repaid iro 51 projects up to September 2015 – 36 power projects (N26.797 billion), 15 airline projects (N31.841 billion)
2.	Real Sector Support Facility (RSSF)	To support large enterprises for start-ups & expansion financing needs of N500 million up to a maximum of N10 billion. Aimed at closing the short term & high interest gap for SMEs/Manufacturing & Start-ups. Real sector targets are manufacturing, agric value chain & selected service sub sectors	2015	300	9	15	3.5		Only one (1) project, amounting to N3.5 billion has been disbursed from inception to September 2015
3.	Nigeria Electricity Market Stabilization Facility (NEMSF)	Put the Nigerian Electricity Supply Industry on a route to economic viability and sustaining by facilitating the settlement of legacy gas debts and payment of outstanding obligations due market participants, service providers & gas suppliers during the interim rules	2015	213	10	10	64.755		N213 billion seed fund in a Refinancer-NESI Stabilization Strategy Ltd. Total sum of N64.755 billion disbursed to 18 participants - 5 Discos (N41.055 billion), 7 Gencos (N18.457 billion) and 6 Gascos

		period								(N5.241billion) from inception in 2015
4.	Commercial Agriculture Credit Scheme (CACS) Fund	To finance commercial agric enterprises. States could borrow up to N1 billion for on-lending to farmers' cooperative societies & other agric devt. Initiatives	2009	200	9	Exit date 2025	310.845	138.343	N310.845 billion disbursed iro 396 projects from inception in 2009. Total sum of N138.343 billion iro 134 fully repaid & 153 steady repayments up to September 2015
5.	SME/Manufacturing Refinancing & Restructuring Fund (SME/RRF)	To refinance/restructure banks' existing loan portfolios to SME/Manufacturing Sector	2010	200	7	15	368.525	122.724	N368.525 billion disbursed iro 603 projects from inception in 2010. Total sum of N122.724 billion iro 602 projects repaid up to September 2015
6.	Micro, Small & Medium Enterprises Development Fund (MSMEDF)	To channel low interest funds to MSME sub-sector though PFIs	2013	220	9	5	51.834		N51.834 billion wholesale amount disbursed under the MSMEDF commercial component to Participating Financial Institutions (PFIs) since inception in 2013
7.	Agricultural Credit Guarantee Scheme Fund(ACGSF)	To provide 75% guarantee cover on bank loans extended for agricultural purposes in Nigeria	2001	3	Different bank rates		92.815	63.322	Established in 1978 with N100 million, but reviewed in 2001 and increased share & paid-up capital to N3 billion. N92.815 billion Guarantee Covers iro 978,756 loans issued from inception, while N63.322 billion iro 738,100 loans repaid up to September 2015

8.	Small & Medium Enterpris es Credit Guarante e Scheme (SMECGS)	To promote access to credit for SMEs by providing guarantee for banks' credits, esp. in manufacturing, agric. Value chain & educational institutions	2010	235	Prime lending rate of the participatin g bank	7	4.219	2.439	N4.219 billion Guarantee covers iro 87 projects from inception in 2010, while N2.439 billion iro 40 projects fully repaid loans up to September 2015
9.	Nigeria Incentive -based Risk Sharing System for Agricultur al Lending (NIRSAL)	To provide credit risk guarantees associated with the agribusiness value chain. NIRSAL does not place capital or credit lines with banks or other institutions for onward lending to borrowers. It helps farmers with affordable financial products, reduce the risk of financial institutions that grant them loans, build capacities of banks to lend to the agricultural sector.	2010	75			21.673		N21.673 billion iro 247 Credit Risk Guarantee (CRG) covers issued from inception in 2010
10.	Interest Draw Back Program me (IDP)	To reduce the burden of interest paid on loans under the Agricultural Credit Guarantee Scheme. Interest rate rebate program to assist farmers borrowing under the ACGS to reduce effective borrowing rate	2004	2			2.510		N2.510 billion iro 276,199 claims settled since inception in 2004
11.	Agricultur al Credit Support Scheme (ACSS)	To enable Nigerian farmers exploit the untapped potentials in the agric. Sector	2006	50	8				Interest rate will be 14%, but 6% rebate upon timely repayment, thus bringing the interest rate to 8% indicated
12.	Entrepre neurship Develop ment Centres (EDCs)	The Project was set up to unleash the entrepreneurial spirit of youths to own/set up their own businesses, create employment and reduce poverty							Cumulatively from inception, 19,625 participants were trained out of a total target of 15,000, 13,549 jobs

Source: Central Bank of Nigeria, Annual Report and Statement of Accounts (Various Issues)

INDEX

Sovereign debt crisis, 142, 146, 148,
149, 173
Special Purpose Entity, 150, 151
Stagnation, 37
Stimulus packages, 162, 172
Structural Adjustment Programme,
187
Subordinated currency, 103
Sunkel, Osvaldo, 37, 204
Supreme Court, 122
Surplus labour, 20
Surplus liquidity, 178
Sweden, 92, 106, 107
Switzerland, 88

T

Targeted Longer Term Refinancing
Operations, 136
Tax shock, 92
Taylor Rule, 91
Thailand, 100, 101, 200
Traore, Karim, ii
Treaty of Maastritcht, 131

U

Udoji Salary Awards, 13
Unit Trust of India, 180
United Kingdom, ii, 36, 88, 92, 95,
107, 110, 111, 197, 199, 200, 203
United States, vi, 74, 79, 80, 82, 85,
88, 98, 101, 102, 105, 107, 115,
122, 123, 125, 127, 128, 146, 158,
162, 170, 199

V

Very Long-term Refinancing
Operations, 142

W

Washington, D.C, 117, 118, 197,
200
West African Economic and
Monetary Union, 107

www.ingramcontent.com/pod-product-compliance
Lightning Source LLC
Chambersburg PA
CBHW061148220326
41599CB00025B/4399